Group Play Interventions for Children

Group Play Interventions for Children

STRATEGIES FOR TEACHING PROSOCIAL SKILLS

Linda A. Reddy

AMERICAN PSYCHOLOGICAL ASSOCIATION

WASHINGTON, DC

Published by
American Psychological Association
750 First Street, NE
Washington, DC 20002
www.apa.org

To order
APA Order Department
P.O. Box 92984
Washington, DC 20090-2984
Tel: (800) 374-2721; Direct: (202) 336-5510
Fax: (202) 336-5502; TDD/TTY: (202) 336-6123
Online: www.apa.org/pubs/books
E-mail: order@apa.org

In the U.K., Europe, Africa, and the Middle East, copies may be ordered from
American Psychological Association
3 Henrietta Street
Covent Garden, London
WC2E 8LU England

Typeset in Trump Medieval by Circle Graphics, Columbia, MD

Printer: United Book Press, Inc., Baltimore, MD
Cover Designer: Berg Design, Albany, NY

The opinions and statements published are the responsibility of the authors, and such opinions and statements do not necessarily represent the policies of the American Psychological Association.

Library of Congress Cataloging-in-Publication Data
Reddy, Linda A.
  Group play interventions for children : strategies for teaching prosocial skills / Linda A. Reddy.—1st ed.
      p. cm.
  Includes bibliographical references and index.
  ISBN-13: 978-1-4338-1055-8 (alk. paper)
  ISBN-10: 1-4338-1055-7 (alk. paper)
  1. Group play therapy. 2. Social skills in children. I. Title.
  RJ505.P6R426 2011 2012
  618.92'891653—dc23
                                    2011030070
British Library Cataloguing-in-Publication Data
A CIP record is available from the British Library.

Printed in the United States of America
First Edition

DOI: 10.1037/13093-000

To my girls—Ashley, Cailyn, and Donna—and
in loving memory of my mother, Gerri M. Reddy,
and my friend, Dr. Priscilla Spencer.

CONTENTS

ACKNOWLEDGMENTS

This volume is the shared product of the energies and creativity of many people—colleagues, doctoral students, teachers, parents, and children. First and foremost, I would like to thank Dr. Priscilla Spencer for introducing me to research on developmentally appropriate games. Her collaboration and friendship were instrumental in the early development of the Child ADHD Multimodal Program (CAMP) and some of the group play interventions in this book. I also thank Dr. Craig Springer for his creativity in some of the game designs. Special thanks goes to the hundreds of children, parents, teachers, and elementary schools that have provided me with "laboratories" to create and implement ("try out") numerous group play skill sequences and group play interventions. I would like to thank my graduate students who cofacilitated numerous children's training groups with me over the years. Deep appreciation goes to my family for their love, support, and patience over the years during the development of many aspects of this book.

Group Play
Interventions
for Children

INTRODUCTION

■——■

For decades, scholars and clinicians have recognized play as a universal behavior shared by all children (Janssen & Janssen, 1996; Lowenfeld, 1939). It is estimated that by the age of 6, children are likely to have engaged in more than 15,000 hr of play (Schaefer, 1993). Play has strong therapeutic value and is considered to be the language of children, with toys and games serving as their words. "For children to play their experiences and feelings out is the most natural dynamic and self-healing process in which children can engage" (Landreth, 2002, p. 14). Researchers have established numerous benefits of play, including the fostering of healthy cognitive development (Bornstein & O'Reilly, 1993; Piaget, 1962), language development (Lyytinen, Poikkeus, & Laakso, 1997; McCune, 1995; Tamis-LeMonda & Bornstein, 1994), social competence (Howes & Matheson, 1992; Parten, 1932), and physical development (Pellegrini & Smith, 1998). Research on play therapy has shown positive outcomes in the areas of self-concept, locus of control, behavioral change, anxiety, and cognitive ability (Ray, Bratton, Rhine, & Jones, 2001).

Not only does play therapy promote healthy development, it also prevents or alleviates emotional and behavioral difficulties among children and adolescents (Landreth, Sweeney, Ray, Homeyer, & Glover, 2005). Interventions using play have emerged as developmentally appropriate, flexible, and effective for children and adolescents (Reddy, 2010; Reddy, Files-Hall, & Schaefer, 2005a). This is particularly important in light of the findings of two presidential commissions (President's New Freedom Commission on Mental Health, 2003; U.S. Department of Health and Human Services, 2000), which strongly recommend an increase in the identification of children's mental health issues and access to developmentally appropriate treatments as part of the transformation of the mental health system. Play interventions are one tool that can be used to meet this need.

For more than 6 decades, play therapy has been recognized as the oldest and most popular form of child therapy in clinical practice (Association for Play Therapy, 2001; Parten, 1932). The Association for Play Therapy (2001) defined *play therapy* as "the systematic use of a theoretical model to establish an interpersonal process wherein trained play therapists use the therapeutic powers of play to help clients prevent or resolve psychosocial difficulties and achieve optimal growth and development" (p. 20). Play sessions help children develop self-understanding, self-acceptance, personal power, self-control, and self-discipline that contribute to attaining academic, social, and personal goals (Landreth, 2002). In schools, counselors routinely use play therapy as a preventative intervention for children and to address a variety of developmental needs in children from various backgrounds. Additionally, play-based assessments and intervention approaches are routinely taught in master's and doctoral level training programs across the country.

In an era of cost-containment and emphasis on outcomes, the need to support the effectiveness of an intervention is increasingly important for practitioners, third-party payers, and consumers. As a result of managed behavioral health care, professionals are pressured to use established, theoretically based, cost-effective, and flexible interventions (Reddy, 2010; Reddy & Savin, 2000). Group play intervention is one tool that can effectively improve the social and behavioral outcomes for children. Additionally, group play interventions are effective in promoting positive social, emotional, and behavioral functioning in children, as well as in preventing the onset of more severe and costly disorders.

Prosocial skill (i.e., social skills) difficulties in children are among the most highly referred concerns of parents and teachers (Christophersen & Mortweet, 2003; Gresham, 2000). The goal of this volume is to offer professionals (e.g., school counselors, nurses, teachers, social workers, occupational therapists, school psychologists, psychologists) a user-friendly book on group play intervention that targets the most common prosocial skills for children.

In this book, group play interventions are

- well-defined and well-designed,
- guided by developmental theory and developmentally appropriate,
- based on empirically supported principles,
- theoretically driven,
- skill intensive, and
- easy to adopt and implement in schools or clinics.

The usefulness and effectiveness of group play interventions are reinforced through the modeling, role playing, and coaching of complementary group play skill sequences (see Part II of this volume) and implementation of group play interventions (see Part III). Group play skill sequences are step-by-step cognitive and behavioral instructions for performing a specific prosocial skill (e.g., introducing oneself to others, inviting others to play). Group play skill sequences teach, reinforce, and refine children's prosocial skills through structured instruction, modeling, role play, coaching, and feedback. Group play skill sequences are essential *prerequisite skills* for children to successfully participate in group play interventions.

This book offers practitioners the first generation of group play interventions for prosocial skill development in elementary age children. Many of the group play skill sequences (Part II) and group play interventions (Part III) were developed from clinical practice, developmental theory, concepts and principles, and research on children's social, emotional and behavior functioning. It is my hope that the volume fosters future intervention development and research in this area.

This book was designed to provide practitioners with the ingredients to assemble a developmentally appropriate, highly engaging, and skill-intensive group play intervention program. To this end, the book is organized in four parts. Each part provides an overview, research results, and essential steps for conceptualizing and implementing groups for elementary school children.

Part I includes five chapters that outline the "nuts and bolts" for child group play intervention. Each chapter builds on previous chapters, providing a step-by-step approach for conceptualizing group play intervention. Chapter 1 includes an introduction that examines the historical significance of play and play therapy, evidence for group work, and group play interventions for children. Chapter 2 focuses on how to include children with common childhood mental disorders and conditions (special needs) in group play intervention. Chapter 3 describes important pregroup considerations for creating and establishing group play intervention for children. Chapter 4 outlines several positive instructional and behavioral management strategies for group play intervention. Strategies are provided in a step-by-step fashion to assist practitioners in offering a potent, enjoyable, and behaviorally productive training experience for children. Chapter 5 discusses the vital role of caregiver involvement in children's group play intervention. Methods for promoting caregiver involvement are outlined. Additionally, techniques to help caregivers improve and sustain children's skills acquired during group training to other important settings are discussed.

Part II includes 43 group play skill sequences practitioners can select to teach children prerequisite prosocial skills for successfully participating in group play interventions. Group play skill sequences are a step-by-step behavioral approach to teach children prosocial skills through modeling, feedback, and role playing with adults and peers. Group play skill sequences are designed to prepare (prime) children *before* they participate in group play interventions.

Part III includes 67 group play interventions conceptualized into eight teaching modules. The eight teaching modules are (a) making and maintaining friends; (b) identifying emotions and appropriately expressing emotions; (c) following directions and impulse control; (d) sharing, joining a group, and group cooperation; (e) anger management; (f) anxiety and stress management; (g) developing appropriate personal space; and (h) effective planning and time management. Each group play intervention includes a description of the targeted domain area, skills taught, required materials and resources, and detailed step-by-step instructions on the implementation and group facilitation process.

Part IV includes closing comments and future directions. This book is intended to serve as a springboard for future intervention development and research. Illustrative group play intervention sessions are offered, as is a list of recommended Internet resources with information on play therapy. Also, free downloadable forms are available online (http://pubs.apa.org/books/supp/reddy). These include web resources, as well as an example of a group screening tool for prospective participants in group play therapy, a sample form from the Group Complaint Book, and a form for collecting child feedback on group therapy.

I
FOUNDATIONS

Chapter 1. Grounding Group Play Interventions for Children in Research

Group play interventions offer a dynamic approach for developing and refining fundamental life skills (i.e., social skills) for children. Children learn from each other, encourage each other, support each other, solve problems together, and share joys and disappointments. In the context of group play, children learn about their similarities, differences, and unique qualities through creative expression. Group play interventions provide opportunities for children to maximize their self-control and interpersonal skills for living. Thus, group play interventions can create a "teaching social laboratory" for children, a place to test their social behavior, practice new behaviors, and define and redefine themselves among friends. The group serves as a practice arena in which children can experiment with old and new behaviors, identify feelings and behaviors in themselves and others, and learn how their behaviors affect others and the environment.

In recent years, clinicians and researchers have sought to identify the specific forces inherent in play interventions that make them a therapeutic agent for change. Communicating, teaching, abreacting, and rapport building are among the major therapeutic powers (factors) that make play interventions unique (Drewes, 2009; Reddy, Files-Hall, & Schaefer, 2005). *Communicative power* encompasses the notion that children naturally express their conscious and unconscious thoughts and feelings better through play than by words alone. *Teaching power* is the idea that children attend to and learn better when play is used to instruct. *Abreaction power* is the concept that children can relive past stressful events and release the associated negative emotions in the safe environment of the play world. *Rapport-building power* illustrates that children tend to like therapists who are playful and fun loving (Schaefer, 1993). These four therapeutic factors or powers provide a safe context in which children can express themselves spontaneously in play with peers. Additionally, play therapy allows children to experience situations that are not allowed in reality, such as mastery and control over people and events (Sweeney & Homeyer, 1999). For a comprehensive listing of the 20 therapeutic factors of play, see Drewes and Schaefer (2009).

A number of well-known schools of play therapy (e.g., client-centered, cognitive–behavioral, family, psychodynamic) emphasize one or more of the curative powers of play. The prescriptive–eclectic school of play therapy advocates that play therapists become skilled in numerous therapeutic powers and differentially apply them to meet the individual needs of children (Kaduson, Cangelosi, & Schaefer, 1997). Filial therapy, originally developed by Guerney (1964), trains parents in child-centered play therapy techniques. This enables parents to become therapeutic agents in their children's lives by conducting play sessions at home. Landreth and his colleagues (e.g., Smith & Landreth, 2003, 2004) conducted numerous investigations on the efficacy of filial therapy with children. For example, filial therapy (individual and group) has been found to be efficacious with mothers of children in a shelter facility (Smith & Landreth, 2003); with teachers of deaf and hard of hearing preschool children (Smith & Landreth, 2004); with teachers, grandparents, and peer helpers (Baggerly & Parker, 2005); and with parents (Bratton & Landreth, 1995; Costas & Landreth, 1999).

Despite play therapy's strong theoretical history, some have questioned its clinical utility and efficacy (e.g., Lebo, 1953; Reade, Hunter, & McMillan, 1999). The main criticism of play therapy has been that the field, in general, lacks rigorous research designs and data analytic methods (Bratton, Ray, Rhine, & Jones, 2005; Phillips, 1985). Research in this area is often based on anecdotal reports or case study designs, with limitations seen in psychotherapy outcome literature, such as small sample size, no control and/or treatment alternative groups, and limited or no generalizability of findings to natural settings (LeBlanc & Ritchie, 1999). Over the past 2 decades, well-designed, controlled play intervention studies have emerged. Three meta-analytic studies examined the effectiveness of play therapy with children (Bratton et al., 2005; LeBlanc & Ritchie, 1999; Ray et al., 2001). LeBlanc and Ritchie's (1999) meta-analysis included 42 experimental studies, dated from 1947 to 1997. The reviewed studies came from multiple sources, including journals, dissertations, and unpublished studies. The studies selected included control or comparison group designs with sufficient data and statistical information. The average age of the children in the studies was 7.9 years old; no child was older than 12 years. Play therapy yielded an overall positive effect size of .66, reflecting a moderate treatment effect.

The authors also investigated the specific characteristics of play therapy related to outcome success. Two significant factors were parental involvement in the children's therapy and the duration of therapy. Studies that included parents as cotherapists resulted in an effect size of .83 (i.e., large positive treatment outcome), compared with an effect size of .56 (i.e., moderate positive treatment outcome) for studies that did not include parents. Also, treatment regimens of eight sessions or more were found to sustain treatment outcomes. Several factors unrelated to outcome were noted, such as the type of presenting problem, the treatment context (group vs. individual), and the age and gender of the participants.

Ray et al. (2001) conducted a meta-analysis that included 94 experimental studies dated from 1940 to 2000. The studies included journal articles, dissertations, and/or unpublished research using a control or comparison group design and pre–post measures. The child participants ranged in age from 3 to 16 years old, with a mean age of 7.1. Results revealed that play therapy yielded an overall effect size of .80 (i.e., a large positive treatment outcome).

Characteristics of play therapy associated with outcomes were explored, such as the examination of different theoretical models. Studies were coded as follows: (a) 74 studies were humanistic–nondirective play therapy, (b) 12 studies were behavioral–directive play therapy, and (c) eight were not coded due to lack of information. The humanistic–nondirective category demonstrated a slightly larger effect size (.93) than the behavioral–

directive category (.73); however, the authors cautioned that this difference was likely due to the disproportionate number of studies in the two categories. A comparison of the effect of general play therapy with that of filial play therapy found that the latter exhibited a greater effect (1.06) than the former (.73). Similar to LeBlanc and Ritchie's (1999) findings, routine parental involvement in treatment was a significant predictor of outcome ($p = .008$). The treatment context (i.e., individual or group format), the population (clinical vs. analog), and the age or gender of the participants were not related to outcomes.

Bratton et al. (2005) conducted a meta-analysis that included 93 controlled outcome studies (journal articles, dissertations, and/or unpublished studies, which used a control or comparison group design and pre–post measures) published from 1953 to 2000. The child participants ranged in age from 3 to 16 years old (mean age of 7). Similar to the 2001 meta-analysis, the 2005 meta-analysis revealed that play therapy yielded an overall effect size of .80, with the humanistic–nondirective model producing an overall larger effect size of .92.

Collectively, the three meta-analytic studies revealed that play therapy interventions have moderate to large positive effects (i.e., .66–.80) on outcomes. Play interventions were found to be effective for children across treatment modalities (group and individual), age groups (3–16 years), gender, referred versus nonreferred populations, and treatment orientations (humanistic–nondirective and behavioral–directive). Thus, these reviews provide support for the clinical utility and efficacy of play therapy.

RESEARCH SUPPORT FOR CHILD GROUP THERAPY

Research on group therapy has evolved from general theoretical issues to an emphasis on specific client population concerns (Fuhriman & Burlingame, 1994; Reddy et al., 2004). This shift in focus, coupled with an increased awareness of the importance of children's mental health, has sparked interest in the clinical utility and efficacy of psychosocial group interventions with children (Duchnowski & Friedman, 1990; Hall & Reddy, 2005).

Numerous literature reviews have assessed the effectiveness of child and adolescent group therapies (e.g., Abramowitz, 1976; Beeferman & Orvaschel, 1994; Gazda & Larsen, 1968; Hoag & Burlingame, 1997). For example, psychosocial groups have been shown to be effective in treating children and adolescents of divorce (e.g., Alpert-Gillis, Pedro-Carroll, & Cowen, 1989; Crosbie-Burnett & Newcomer, 1990; Pedro-Carroll, 2005), anxiety (e.g., Koszycki, Benger, Shlik, & Bradwejn, 2007; Mortberg, Karlsson, Fyring, & Sundin, 2006), social skills (e.g., Berner, Fee, & Turner, 2001; Greco & Morris, 2001), depression (e.g., Arean et al., 2005; Clarke, Rohde, Lewinsohn, Hops, & Seeley, 1999; Fine, Forth, Gilbert, & Haley, 1991; Fine, Gilbert, Schmidt, Haley, Maxwell, & Forth, 1989), suicide (e.g., Shulman & Margalit, 1985; Wood, Trainor, Rothwell, Moore, & Harrington, 2001), sexually acting out behavior (e.g., Butler & Fontenelle, 1995), impulsivity (e.g., Baer & Nietzel, 1991; Barkley, 1990), social isolation (e.g., Edelson & Rose, 1981; LaGreca & Santogrossi, 1980), substance abuse (Stinchfield, Owen, & Winters, 1994), sexual abuse (e.g., Deblinger, Stauffer, & Steer, 2001; McGain & McKinzey, 1995; Reeker, Ensing, & Elliott, 1997), and learning disabilities (e.g., Amerikaner & Summerlin, 1982; Campbell & Bowman, 1993).

The majority of the programs described are short term (i.e., eight to 10 sessions), nonexperimental in nature (i.e., no placebo control group), cognitive–behaviorally oriented, highly structured (scripted), and implemented in controlled research clinics (e.g.,

Dagley, Gazda, Eppinger, & Stewart, 1994; Reddy et al., 2004). In addition, the majority of children included in these studies were predominately Caucasian males between the ages of 9 to 12. Therefore, programs with group play interventions that can be transported and flexibly delivered in a variety of school and community settings (e.g., clinics, private practice) are urgently needed.

Value of Group Play

Group therapy has been recognized as a vital treatment modality for children and adults for decades (e.g., Moreno, 1932; Ruitenbeek, 1969; Yalom, 2005). It is based on the premise that individuals are social beings who embrace therapy because of its interpersonal focus (Foulkes & Anthony, 1957). Early contributors to the theory and practice of group therapy recognized the interactive and dynamic processes of groups, which undoubtedly set group therapy apart from individual therapy (Moreno, 1932). Cody Marsh (1931), a pioneer of milieu therapy, expressed this distinction by stating, "By the crowd they have been broken, by the crowd they shall be healed" (p. 329).

Group play is a fundamental process in which children naturally communicate with their peers. Its value to children and therapeutic processes is vital (Sweeney & Homeyer, 1999). Landreth (2002) suggested, "Children express themselves more fully and directly through self-initiated spontaneous play than they do verbally because they are more comfortable when playing with other children" (p. 14). Play is an effective way for caregivers to communicate their thoughts and feelings to children while also promoting positive parent–child interactions. Children can be taught social skills through planned as well as unplanned (spontaneous) play by engaging in shared play interactions. The use of group play helps pinpoint possible behavioral difficulties, allows children to see the impact of their behavior on other children, and can facilitate conflict resolution among children without the assistance of an outside source (adult or peer; Christner, Stewart, & Freeman, 2007).

Scholars have identified a number of factors that can facilitate the development of social skills in the context of group play. Group play allows children to see the impact of their behavior on other children (Christner et al., 2007). For example, Timler, Olswang, and Coggins (2005) asserted that "effective participation in cooperative play requires children to be responsive to their peers by answering peers' questions, acknowledging peers' comments, asking for information when needed, and commenting about ongoing activities" (p. 172). Sweeney (1997) summarized several advantages of therapeutic play groups. Group play (a) promotes spontaneity in children, which in turn may encourage their participation in play and their willingness to take risks during play; (b) allows children's emotions to be dealt with at two levels—the interpersonal issues among individual group members and interpersonal issues between the group facilitator and group members; (c) fosters learning in children by their observation of different ways to express emotions and behaviors and different ways to cope and solve problems; (d) offers many opportunities for growth and exploration through play; (e) serves as a microcosm of society and provides significant opportunities for children to set limits and reality test with others; (f) may reduce children's tendencies to engage in repetitious play or retreat into fantasy play and helps children refocus on the here and now; and (g) provides children with the opportunity to practice social behaviors, master new social behaviors, give and receive help from others, and comfortably experiment with different ways of expressing emotions and behavior.

Using Group Play Interventions: Developmentally Appropriate Games

The group play interventions described in this book use *developmentally appropriate games* (DAGs). DAGs are gross motor activities that are competency-based, enjoyable to children, and can significantly increase motivation and skill development. DAGs are based on four principles:

1. Each child has the opportunity to choose and participate at his or her ability level.
2. Additional opportunities to play and practice skills increase as the DAG proceeds.
3. Elimination of a group member is not possible. As a result, children become more active members of the group and exhibit greater cooperation, cohesion, and problem solving.
4. Children with varying abilities can interact positively with one another (e.g., Reddy, 2010; Reddy, Spencer, Hall, & Rubel, 2001; Reddy, Springer, et al., 2005).

Research has shown that interventions taught and reinforced in the home, school, and community are the most effective and sustainable (Barkley, 1998; Reddy, 2010; Reddy, Springer, et al., 2005). Group DAGs are highly effective ways to engage children's interest and motivation while simultaneously teaching them important skills for the home, school, and playground. Group games provide children with opportunities to interact naturally with peers and adults and to learn appropriate behaviors and skills in the context in which they will be used. DAGs and activities also enhance children's socialization through group contact, increase self-confidence through group acceptance, and provide recreational and leisure activities (Reddy, 2010; Reed, Black, & Eastman, 1978). Treating children in a natural play group context increases the likelihood of maintaining and generalizing treatment gains over time (Hoag & Burlingame, 1997).

Group DAGs enhance children's feelings of creativity, accomplishment, autonomy, and positive regard for themselves and others while also teaching them important life skills for work and play (e.g., Reddy, 2010; Reddy et al., 2001; Torbert & Schneider, 1993). Children who participate in group DAGs share an affiliation in which they can encourage each other's growth through positive social interactions. DAGs also provide cognitive, social, and physical challenges that encourage children to persist and try alternative solutions (Bunker, 1991; Reddy, 2010; Reddy et al., 2001).

Research has shown that DAGs improve the participation, cooperation, social skills, self-esteem, and visual motor skills of regular education, emotionally disturbed, and perceptually impaired children more than traditional school-based games (Ferland, 1997; Reddy, 2010; Reddy, Springer, et al., 2005). For example, Bay-Hinitz and Wilson (2005) examined the effectiveness of a cooperative games intervention with 70 preschool children ranging in age from 4 to 5 years old. This empirically supported intervention for aggressive preschool children used teacher-directed cooperative board games and other cooperative activities to reduce aggressive behavior. It required minimal training and could be used by parents, mentors, and paraprofessionals. Results revealed that children who participated in the cooperative games intervention exhibited more participation and prosocial behaviors than did those in traditional competitive games. Orlick (1988) reported similar findings.

Garaigordobil and Echebarria (1995) examined the effects of a cooperative game program on the social behavior and self-concept of 178 mainstreamed children (ages 6–7). The researchers implemented 22 play sessions, including games that were designed to enhance children's cooperation, sharing, symbolic play, and feelings of self-worth.

Significant improvements in classroom behavior (e.g., leadership skills, cheerfulness, sensitivity–respect to others, aggression, apathy, anxiety) were found.

Schneider (1989) compared the effects of DAGs versus free play (i.e., 15–20 minutes per session) on the self-esteem of 36 kindergarten students across 17 sessions. Teacher and child self-report ratings of self-esteem improved more among students who participated in DAGs than among those in free play.

Shen (2002) investigated the effectiveness of short-term, child-centered, group play therapy in elementary school settings with children in Taiwan who had experienced an earthquake 3 years prior to the study. Thirty children ranging in age from 8 to 12 years old were assigned to an experimental group (15 children) or control group (15 children). Children in the experimental group scored significantly lower on anxiety and suicide risk than children in the control group after group play therapy.

The efficacy of play interventions with children diagnosed as emotionally disturbed was also investigated by Hand (1996). Two groups of children ages 10 to 12 were systematically observed during recess. One group participated in traditional games in which success was defined as the defeat or elimination of others, but the other group participated in DAGs three times per week for 16 weeks. Greater reductions in verbal and physical aggression and the use of time-out were found among children in the DAG group.

Reed et al. (1978) investigated the effectiveness of a parent–child group training program for perceptually disabled children who ranged in age from 6 to 12 years old. Children in the group had few friends, seldom participated in peer group activities, and were verbally and physically aggressive. The program consisted of 1-hour sessions held twice a week for 16 weeks. Games that enhanced social skills and perceptual motor abilities (e.g., visual motor skills, visual acuity, and body awareness) were implemented. Parent ratings revealed improved peer interactions at home and school, including greater group participation and rule following and fewer behavior problems.

Reddy and associates (Reddy, 2010; Reddy et al., 2001; Reddy, Springer, et al., 2005; Springer & Reddy, 2010) conducted several investigations examining the efficacy of DAGs in a children's group training program as part of a Child Attention-Deficit/Hyperactivity Disorder (ADHD) Multimodal Program (CAMP). CAMP is an empirically supported intervention that treats the social and behavioral needs of young children diagnosed with ADHD (ages 4–8). Grounded in social learning theory and behavioral principles, this is a developmentally skill-based program for children used DAGs to increase social skills, self-control, and anger–stress management within a 10-week, structured group format. Parents received concurrent group training that focused on behavioral management techniques in the home, school, and community. One unique feature was that behavioral consultation services were offered to each child's parents and teachers in the home and school. Outcome evaluations of CAMP revealed statistically significant and clinically meaningful improvements in parents' functioning and children's behavior in the home and school at program completion and follow-up.

Pedro-Carroll and Jones (2005) developed and examined the efficacy of the Children of Divorce Intervention Program (CODIP), a school-based prevention program that targeted the needs of children of divorce. CODIP was implemented by specially trained and supervised mental health professionals and paraprofessionals. Developmentally sensitive, play-based activities within a group context were used to help children address the stressful changes that divorce often brings. There was strong evidence for CODIP's effectiveness in reducing the stress of divorce on children and improving their social, emotional, and school adjustment in the short and long term.

Another innovative model is the Denver model, a well-researched, school-based daily play intervention program (Rogers, 2005). The Denver model is grounded in developmental theory and emphasizes the importance of symbolic, interpersonal, and cognitive aspects of play in the development of children with autism. This model was shown to be effective in facilitating the development and growth of young children with autism spectrum disorders. Child participants exhibited significant improvements in symbolic play and affective, reciprocal exchanges during play with their parents.

CONCLUSION

Group DAGs and group play interventions afford children opportunities to learn new skills by participating in structured peer group activities that are behaviorally and cognitively challenging as well as therapeutically rich. DAGs are flexible, require minimum equipment, and can be easily modified to meet specific individual, group, or classroom needs.

Chapter 2 presents ways to effectively tailor group play interventions for children with special needs.

Chapter 2. Group Play Interventions for Children With Special Needs

Children with special needs constitute the largest percentage of youngsters referred to child study teams and mental health clinics in the United States (Reddy & De Thomas, 2006). These children represent a broad spectrum of learning, social–emotional, behavioral, and medical disorders and conditions. A common trait found among this population is difficulties making and maintaining friendships. School personnel, practitioners, and pediatricians often encourage parents to enroll children with special needs in social skills groups to afford them positive peer group experiences that lead to enhanced social skills and successful peer play opportunities.

Group play interventions provide *all* children with the opportunity to interact naturally with peers and adults and to learn appropriate behaviors and skills in the context in which they play and learn. Children with special needs can benefit from group play interventions that are flexible, skill intensive, and novel. Well-designed group play interventions create a positive learning environment in which children can develop new social skills and refine existing ones with adult facilitators (Reddy, 2010; Sweeney & Homeyer, 1999). Group play interventions offer children with special needs the freedom to move, express themselves, and take risks in a structured, safe, and social environment. In groups, these youngsters can interact with other children with similar social and behavior concerns and begin to feel less isolated or anxious about their own behaviors. Group play interventions allow children the opportunity to recognize the impact of their behavior on other children and to learn from positive peer interactions and peer and adult role models (Christner et al., 2007). As Timler et al. (2005) stated, "effective participation in cooperative play requires children to be responsive to their peers by answering peers' questions, acknowledging peers' comments, asking for information when needed, and commenting about ongoing activities" (p. 172). Group play interventions help children develop self-control, self-acceptance, and discipline, which can assist with academic, social, and personal growth (Landreth, 2002; Reddy, 2010).

Group play interventions promote healthy development and may help to prevent or alleviate emotional and behavioral difficulties among children with special needs and their typically developing peers (Landreth, Sweeney, Ray, Homeyer, & Glover, 2005).

Additionally, group play interventions give practitioners the opportunity to observe and monitor behavioral strengths and difficulties in this population. After strengths and weaknesses are identified, group interventions can be designed to build new skills, reinforce existing skills, and use strengths to compensate for weaknesses.

This chapter describes children with special needs who are commonly referred for group training in schools and communities. Common symptom dimensions that may be observed across childhood disorders and conditions are discussed. Additionally, considerations for conceptualizing group play interventions for children with special needs are offered.

CHILDREN WITH SPECIAL NEEDS

School personnel, pediatricians, and other professionals refer a broad range of children with special needs for group training experiences. Commonly referred children may include children with attention-deficit/hyperactivity disorder (ADHD), learning disabilities, language-based disorders, sensory processing disorder, and pervasive developmental disorders such as Asperger's disorder and autism.

Attention-Deficit/Hyperactivity Disorder

ADHD, a neurocognitive (not behavioral) disorder, is seen in approximately 2% to 5% of all school-age children (Reddy & Hale, 2007), representing one to two children in every classroom (DuPaul & Stoner, 2003; Reddy & De Thomas, 2006). ADHD can be broadly defined as a family of related chronic neurobiological disorders that interfere with children's ability to regulate activity level (hyperactivity), inhibit behavior (impulsivity), and attend to tasks (inattention) in developmentally appropriate ways (National Institute of Mental Health, 2000; National Resource Center on ADHD, 2003). Many scholars assert that impairments in executive functioning (i.e., attention, planning, organizing, motor control, and goal-directed behavior) serve as core symptoms in this population (see Barkley, 1997; Reddy, Weissman, & Hale, in press, for a detailed discussion). ADHD includes three subtypes: (a) inattentive type, generally characterized by inattention and distractibility; (b) hyperactive/impulsive type, generally characterized by high levels of activity and the inability to inhibit behaviors; and (c) combined type. The combined type is the most common and involves significant symptoms in inattention, impulsivity, and hyperactivity.

Children with the inattentive type often appear distracted (daydreaming, "out of it") or socially withdrawn. Children with the hyperactive/impulsive or the combined type may struggle with school performance as well as with peer and adult social interactions because of their high level of motor activity and distractibility to external stimuli. These youngsters may be observed impulsively answering questions, talking out of turn, and taking shortcuts when performing tasks, which may result in incomplete and inconsistent in-class assignments and homework. Their impulsive and intrusive nature may at times initiate peer conflict, and their inability to self-monitor during peer activities may inadvertently reinforce peer relation issues, particularly in group contexts. On the other hand, hyperactive/impulsive or combined type children may bring vigor, energy, and creativity to a group. The enthusiasm and excitement they display when performing games or tasks may encourage other children with social or communication difficulties to participate more readily. Similarly, children with inattentive type may present as quiet, calm, and creative and may serve as excellent role models for other children in a group.

Children with ADHD often have high rates of comorbidity with other disorders, such as oppositional defiant disorder, anxiety, depression, and learning disabilities, which can complicate the group training process (Reddy & De Thomas, 2006; Reddy, Weissman, & Hale, in press; Rief, 2005). The heterogeneous nature of ADHD, coupled with its high comorbidity rates, can present a challenge during the assessment and treatment process (Reddy & Hale, 2007).

Learning Disabilities

It is estimated that 2.9 million children receive services for a learning disability in the United States, or approximately 6% of the total public school enrollment (e.g., U.S. Department of Education, National Center for Education Statistics, 2003; U.S. Department of Education, Office of Special Education and Rehabilitative Services, 2003). *Learning disabilities* refer to a group of disorders that affect a broad range of academic and functional skills, including the ability to speak, listen, read, write, spell, reason, and organize information. Although learning disabilities are commonly viewed as disorders that primarily manifest in poor academic performance, research has increasingly shown that children with learning disabilities also struggle with social relationships and at times experience peer isolation and rejection (e.g., Frederickson & Furnham, 2004; Storch, Masia-Warner, & Brassard, 2003; Yu, Zhang, & Yan, 2005). Social difficulties among children with learning disabilities generally manifest, in part, from the interplay between lowered self-concepts associated with poor school performance, as well as neurocognitive impairments in perceiving and navigating their social world. Thus, it is not surprising that children with learning disabilities are frequently referred to social skills groups because they have limited or unsuccessful peer relations.

Common learning disabilities include reading (e.g., decoding, speed, fluency, comprehension), written expression (e.g., spelling, penmanship, writing speed, fluency), and mathematics (e.g., understanding of basic concepts, reasoning, problem solving), or a combination of two or more areas. Reading disabilities are the most prevalent of all learning disabilities, representing 2.5% to 7.5% of school-age children (Kronenberger & Meyer, 2001). The process of reading has many associative social components that are important for children's peer and adult relationships. Children who have delays in reading are typically reluctant or avoid participating in learning and social activities in school. Research has found that children with reading difficulties may experience future academic failure, poor peer and adult relationships, juvenile delinquency, school dropout, and suicide (e.g., Daniel et al., 2006; Shelley-Tremblay, O'Brien, & Langhinrichsen-Rohling, 2007).

Written expression and mathematics learning disabilities can influence the quality of peer relationships, play, and sports activities (Wiener & Schneider, 2002). Proficiency in written language requires complex neurocognitive skills and processes such as visually or auditorily collecting and encoding information, organizing information (sequencing, mental representations), and reproducing what has been processed (Gartin, 2009). The ability to express themselves in writing or drawing lets children share information about themselves and what they learn at school or elsewhere with peers and adults. A written expression learning disability (dysgraphia) often causes spelling errors, handwriting problems, and writing fluency issues (Mayes, Calhoun, & Crowell, 2000). Children with this learning deficit may be less likely to relate to peers through this medium (i.e., writing and drawing). Similarly, math is a universal language. Basic and advanced concepts in mathematics (e.g., addition, subtraction, fractions) and mathematical reasoning (semantic memory of facts, visuospatial relationships of numbers) are important skills embedded in daily social and school-related events (e.g., sports, lunch, gifts, book fairs). Children with limited or poor mathematical concepts and reasoning skills may feel less inclined to participate in social contexts in which basic or more advanced math skills are required.

Youngsters with learning disabilities often exhibit a number of deficits that are also associated with ADHD, particularly the inattentive and combined types. For example, both reading disabilities and ADHD are associated with deficits in naming speed (i.e., the amount of time it takes to name various stimuli such as colors, letters, numbers, and objects), motor planning skills (i.e., ability to execute planned movements), and time perception (i.e., awareness of the time of day or time passed since a specific event; Tannock & Brown, 2000). Practitioners may accommodate children with deficits in naming speed by structuring the timetable for a group activity (e.g., 2 minutes) with ample time for all to participate comfortably in the game. Children with deficits in the area of time awareness and perception may frustrate other group members because they are not in sync with other children's timetables. This problem may be alleviated or offset using highly structured group sessions that incorporate frequent time cues (i.e., verbal and nonverbal prompts).

Considerable attention has been devoted to *nonverbal learning disability* (NLD), sometimes referred to as *right hemisphere learning disability* (Hale & Rubenstein, 2006). Children with NLD often exhibit deficits in visual, spatial, motor skills, and implicit language (e.g., Hale & Fiorello, 2004; Reddy & Hale, 2007; Rourke, 1994). They commonly have difficulties perceiving social cues, attending to visual stimuli, and shifting mental set. Poor social judgment, poor procedural skills, and poor semantic memory, in general, also characterize these children (Ingalls & Goldstein, 1999). They also lack awareness of self and environment (Hale & Fiorello, 2004), which can lead to an inability to develop meaningful social relationships (Johnson, 1988). However, children with NLD also possess a number of strengths, including advanced language and reading skills, the ability to memorize and retain auditory information, and a solid knowledge base (Pierce, 2010). These children are often assets in a collaborative learning environment. However, their social abilities are stunted by their poor processing of nonverbal information (i.e., facial expressions, body language). This is highly debilitating in social situations in which children with NLD struggle to interpret nonverbal cues and social norms, thereby increasing their vulnerability to peer rejection.

Language-Based Disorders

Language-based disorders, such as speech delay, articulation, receptive language, and auditory processing issues, often result in social and behavior difficulties for children. Targeted speech and language services are critical for improving speech and language skills. Moreover, other ancillary services, such as group and individual therapies, can help alleviate social and emotional issues that accompany difficulties in expressing oneself and understanding others.

Language-based disorders can be broadly conceptualized into three areas: expressive language, mixed receptive–expressive language, and auditory processing. Each can uniquely impair social interactions with adults and peers. *Expressive language disorder* is a condition characterized by a child's difficulty or inability to clearly pronounce letters, words, and sentences (American Psychiatric Association, 2000; Whitehurst et al., 1988). This communication disorder is characterized by a limited vocabulary and understanding of grammar, resulting in an immature or delayed level of language development and difficulty with memory related to speech (American Psychiatric Association, 2000).

Mixed receptive–expressive language disorder affects both the receptive and expressive areas of communication. Children with this disorder may receive relatively low cognitive (IQ) scores in the areas of information, vocabulary, and reading comprehension. These youngsters may also have difficulty understanding word problems, instructions, and spatial concepts and may display general difficulties with comprehension and verbal expression of language.

Auditory processing disorder (APD), formerly known as *central auditory processing disorder*, is defined as a difficulty in the efficiency and effectiveness in the manner in which the central nervous system uses auditory information (Paul, 2008). It is an "inability to discriminate auditory patterns, localize sound, and understand speech with competing or degraded stimuli" (Katz & Tillery, 2004, p. 191). It is estimated that rates of APD among school-age children range from 5% to 10% (Riccio, Hynd, Cohen, Hall, & Molt, 1994; Tannock & Brown, 2000). Children with APD exhibit symptoms of inattention, listening problems, distractibility, and difficulty following oral instructions (e.g., Chermak, Tucker, & Seikel, 2002; Katz & Tillery, 2004; Tannock & Brown, 2000). As a result of these complex deficits, children exhibit problems in language, academics, and social skills (Chermak, Somers, & Seikel, 1998).

Children with language-based disorders generally exhibit difficulties with peer interactions. These youngsters tend to lack the confidence to approach a child or a group of children, and they struggle to sustain play interactions more than their typically developing peers. Group play interventions can offer children who grapple with verbal self-expression and feel misunderstood because of their speech and language impairments the opportunity to successfully interact, share, and communicate with other children through play.

Sensory Processing Disorder

Sensory processing disorder, also referred to as *sensory integration dysfunction*, has been defined as "the inability to use information received through the senses in order to function smoothly in daily life" (Kranowitz, 2005, p. 9). Sensory processing disorder is not one specific disorder but an umbrella term that encompasses a variety of sensory integration issues. Children with sensory integration issues have difficulty organizing sensory messages or stimuli from the brain such as visual stimuli, touch, smell, taste, sound, and movement. These children can become negatively stimulated by sensory information (e.g., cry or avoid moderate to loud noise) or positively stimulated by sensory information (e.g., seek out moderate to loud noise), which may derail their ability to manage their behavior in a meaningful, consistent way. These youngsters may also have difficulty using sensory information to plan and carry out actions (i.e., goal-directed behavior). As a result, they can have impaired social interactions, motor planning skills, and difficulties focusing and attending to learning and social opportunities, resembling characteristics seen with ADHD.

It is important to view sensory processing functioning on a continuum rather than from a disordered versus nondisordered perspective. Children may have sensory integration needs that fluctuate during learning and social situations. Fluctuations in sensory processing may at times disrupt children's development of skills and consistent functioning, particularly in groups. In group contexts, sensory integration issues may become particularly evident, and accommodations in directions (e.g., use of one- to two-step directions) may be needed for them to successfully participate in group play activities.

Pervasive Developmental Disorders

Pervasive developmental disorders (PDDs), heterogeneous in nature, affect a small portion (i.e., .6%–1%) of the child population (Simonoff et al., 2008). Children with PDDs often exhibit impairments in attention, learning, executive functioning, and social communication, which may lead to academic and behavioral impairments (e.g., Liss et al., 2001; Simonoff et al., 2008).

Two of the most common PDDs referred to group training programs are Asperger's disorder and autism. Over the past 2 decades, Asperger's disorder has received much attention from researchers and practitioners. It is estimated that from 1 in 1,000 to 1 in 385 children have Asperger's disorder (Prior, 2003). Children with Asperger's disorder experience a consistent pattern of social, behavioral, attentional, and motor difficulties (Buettel, 2006; Klin, Volkmar, & Sparrow, 2000). These youngsters are likely to have difficulties with understanding and monitoring social cues and verbal and nonverbal behaviors; relating to people, objects, and events; and adjusting to changes in routine or familiar surroundings (National Institute of Neurological Disorders and Stroke, 2009). Additionally, they often exhibit repetitive body movements or persistent social behavioral problems that can impede relationship development.

Interventions for children with Asperger's disorder are somewhat limited and commonly focus on classroom problems, such as noncompliance and disruptive disorders (Klin et al., 2000; Sansosti & Powell-Smith, 2006). These children often manifest a host of social emotional difficulties (anxiety, depression, obsessive–compulsive behaviors), due in part to chronic negative peer relations (Klin et al., 2000). Specially tailored treatments such as individual and parent cognitive–behavioral therapies and group play interventions can provide these youngsters with nurturing and intensive skill training experiences (Rao, Beidel, & Murray, 2008).

Autism, the most severe of the PDDs, is characterized by substantial deficits in communication and social functioning, as well as repetitive and stereotyped behaviors. Specifically, autism is identifiable by deficits in imitation, gesturing, observational learning, joint attention, symbolic play, and understanding the expression of emotion (Soucy, 1997). The disorder also tends to involve other important associated features, such as mental retardation, seizures, a greater proportion of males, and high comorbidity with other disorders (Volker & Lopata, 2008). The rate of mental retardation in children with autism is approximately 70% (Fombonne, 2005). In contrast, children with Asperger's disorder or other PDDs have considerably lower rates of impaired intellectual functioning (Volker & Lopata, 2008).

The association between autism and seizure disorders is well established. It is estimated that 8% to 42% of children with autism have epilepsy. There are also a number of genetically based disorders associated with autism. The two most frequently found are fragile X syndrome and tuberous sclerosis, which account for about 10% of all autism cases (Fombonne, 2005).

The considerable deficits in social interactions and communication experienced by many children with autism can impede positive peer interactions and make it challenging to integrate or include them in traditional social skills training groups (Mastrangelo,

2009). Language, social, emotional, and cognitive difficulties are typically identified early in development and constitute important areas that are essential to success in the home, school, and community (Dawson, Osterling, Meltzoff, & Kuhl, 2000; Wimpory, Hobson, Williams, & Nash, 2000). Children with autism generally spend less time interacting socially and have lower quality play interactions with peers than typically developing counterparts (McConnell, 2002). These children often engage in solitary play, at times appear to be in their own world, and are seen engaging in repetitive patterns of behavior (e.g., rocking or rolling the wheels of a car), which causes them to be further ostracized by their peers (Manstrangelo, 2009). Children with autism require a broad array of specialized supports and novel targeted interventions that successfully engage and promote their interests, strengths, and skills. Group play interventions may serve as one therapeutic tool within a multimodal treatment package for these youth.

In summary, children with special needs exhibit a host of behavioral problems and strengths that require careful consideration in group play interventions. Group play interventions can provide children with special needs the opportunity to discover and focus on what they *can* do in a safe learning environment, rather than what they *cannot* do.

COMMON SYMPTOM DIMENSIONS

Children with special needs may exhibit overlapping symptom dimensions that can be particularly useful for practitioners to use in conceptualizing group play interventions. For example, some common symptom dimensions include impairment in attention, hyperactivity, impulsivity, executive functioning, and language processing. Both individually and collectively, these dimensions can result in challenging social interactions with peers, siblings, and adults (Reddy & Hale, 2007). These symptom dimensions are expressed differently based on each child's unique strengths and challenges and the social demands of the environment (e.g., home, school, classroom, lesson, sports team). Screening potential group members for common symptoms may help to identify children for interventions that complement group members' needs, conceptualize group goals, and select group play skill sequences (see Part II of this volume) and group play interventions (see Part III) for optimal learning (an example of a downloadable screener is available at http://pubs.apa.org/books/supp/reddy). With this in mind, group play interventions can be tailored to accommodate or possibly remediate overlapping symptom dimensions for children with special needs so that their group experience is most enjoyable and effective.

Inattention is found in children with a wide range of childhood disorders (Hale, Fiorello, & Brown, 2005; Reddy & DeThomas, 2006). For example, ADHD encompasses a complex mixture of deficits that include inattention, hyperactivity, impulsivity, planning, organization, and self-evaluation skills (Reddy & Hale, 2007). Children with learning disabilities, language-based disorders, APD, and sensory processing disorders often have attentional issues that may make it difficult to accurately diagnose these disorders. Likewise, as many as 65% of children with Asperger's disorder or autism have clinically significant attention and executive function problems that lead to academic and behavioral impairments (Holtman, Bolte, & Poustka, 2005; Liss et al., 2001).

Hyperactivity and impulsivity are common symptoms shared by children with ADHD, language-based disorders, sensory processing disorders, Asperger's disorder, and autism. For example, hyperactivity and impulsivity are the hallmark characteristics of children with ADHD (Reddy & Hale, 2007) and can lead to academic underachievement and behavioral problems. Additionally, children with Asperger's disorder and autism can exhibit clinical levels of hyperactivity and impulsivity as well as low levels of activity and lack of responsiveness.

Many children exhibit impaired executive functioning, which is the inability to plan, organize, monitor, evaluate, and execute behavior toward a goal (Hale & Fiorello, 2004). Although deficits in executive functioning are most associated with children diagnosed with ADHD, these impairments are often identified in children with PDDs, Asperger's disorder, learning disabilities, and language-based disorders (Reddy & Hale, 2007). Executive functioning problems may lead to academic, social, and behavioral difficulties (Liss et al., 2001; Reddy, Weissman, & Hale, in press).

Many children with special needs experience difficulties communicating verbally and nonverbally (expressive language) and/or comprehending what others say to them (receptive language). For example, children with APD tend to have problems discriminating speech and as a result frequently need to have comments, conversations, or directions repeated (Chermak, Tucker, & Seikel, 2002; Meister, von Wedel, & Walger, 2004). Children with NLDs often exhibit deficits in implicit language (Hale & Fiorello, 2004; Rourke, 1994). Also, children with Asperger's and autism can exhibit considerable deficits in displaying appropriate verbal and nonverbal behaviors, depending on the degree of the disability (Hale & Fiorello, 2004).

The four symptom dimensions described serve as examples of common areas to consider when selecting children for training groups and conceptualizing and implementing play group experiences. Group play interventions that include children with special needs who have varied levels of abilities can play an important role in providing children with the support and skill development for successful peer activities.

CONSIDERATIONS FOR GROUP TRAINING

Practitioners should consider several child- and practitioner-focused factors when conceptualizing group play interventions for special needs populations. Child-focused factors to consider include (a) individual strengths (e.g., leadership, humor, help-seeking behavior) and areas of sensitivity (e.g., anxiety, auditory and visual overstimulation), (b) varied complex and challenging behavioral patterns, (c) diffuse neurologic deficits (e.g., cognitive and executive functioning, learning disabilities, seizure disorders), (d) sensory integration issues (e.g., visual, auditory, tactile, smell, and taste domains), (e) expressive or receptive language skills, and (f) medical issues (e.g., vision, hearing, sleep difficulties, asthma, chronic ear and sinus difficulties, blood-related diseases). Practitioner-focused factors to consider may include (a) knowledge of development, language, speech, and sensory disorders (with an emphasis on typical and atypical development); (b) knowledge of neurocognitive processes and pathways for childhood mental disorders; (c) use of positive instructional strategies (e.g., giving two-step directions, summarizing major concepts, asking a child to elaborate on an answer, reviewing key steps to complete a task); (d) use of positive behavioral management strategies (e.g., token economy system, praise, modeling, corrective feedback, time out for positive self-control); (e) use of multimethod teaching, including didactic and differential instruction, visual aids, nonverbal gestures and prompts, structured role plays, and coaching; (f) team building for enhancing staff cohesion, motivation and morale, and skill implementation; and (g) outcome assessment methods (including child, staff, parent, or teacher input) for progress monitoring and establishing postgroup success (e.g., Reddy, 2010; Reddy et al., 2004). For a detailed discussion of other pregroup considerations, see Chapter 3.

CONCLUSION

Group play interventions offer unique and potent therapeutic opportunities for a broad range of children with special needs. Their effectiveness for special needs populations is predicated in part on the careful screening and selection of children for the group. As discussed in Chapter 3, the pregroup screening and group conceptualization processes are critically important to ensure that the children are appropriate for group play interventions, rather than another form of treatment (e.g., individual or family therapies, vocational training, medication, occupational therapies). Children with special needs should be carefully grouped with peers with similar or complementary needs so that they can successfully connect with other children and learn from the experience. Prior to screening and selecting group members, practitioners are encouraged to consider the goals of training, overlapping symptom dimensions among group members, and the range of group play skill sequences (see Part II) and group play interventions (see Part III) for targeted children.

CHAPTER 3. CREATING AND ESTABLISHING GROUPS FOR PLAY INTERVENTIONS

Successful group play interventions are predicated on the thoughtful decision making of numerous pregroup factors and conditions. These pregroup considerations set the stage for highly effective group training that fosters optimal learning, enjoyment, and behavioral management for children with and without special needs.

SCREENING AND SELECTION OF CHILD GROUP MEMBERS

The screening and selection of group members are important when forming play intervention groups. It is recommended that practitioners use a flexible semistructured screening interview when interviewing parents and children for play groups (see an example screener at http://pubs.apa.org/books/supp/reddy). The screening process should take approximately 45 minutes and should include questions that promote a dialogue between the practitioner and the child's parents. It is best to conduct the parent interview in person, rather than on the telephone. This promotes comfort and familiarity for the parent and child and allows for observations of important child and parent verbal and nonverbal interactions. To reduce the possibility of stigma, it is best to refer to the program as a "play group" or "friendship group" rather than a social skills group when introducing and describing the program to prospective parents and children. It is also important to ask about children's behavioral concerns, interests (likes), and strengths that they can bring to the group process. Incorporating a 15-minute semistructured play session with an individual child can be helpful for the selection process. A brief child and practitioner play session (e.g., 10–15 minutes) can provide valuable information on how well the child separates from the parent, interacts with another adult, and manages structure and redirection. A brief consultation (in person or by telephone) with the child's teacher can also add valuable information for the screening and selection process.

The right balance of social, cognitive, and behavioral strengths and challenges among group members is essential for group success (Beyer, 1997; Siepher & Kanadaras, 1985). Prior to screening children and their parents for groups, practitioners may wish to adopt a flexible list of inclusion and exclusion criteria for selecting group members.

The list should be carefully created in conjunction with group goals and curriculum. Examples may include establishing an age range for the group (e.g., ages 7–9), the number of boys and girls to include, children with low to moderate levels of impulsivity, limited or no history of peer aggression (hitting or biting peers), adequate language processing skills (expressive or receptive), and mild to moderate levels of anxiety.

Ideally, children should be at relatively similar developmental stages and levels of ability to participate in the group and follow the group session content and format. The practitioner can also achieve this balance by combining children who are experiencing moderate to high levels of social, cognitive, or behavioral difficulty with those who are experiencing low levels. For example, a child who displays good self-control (i.e., control of his or her hands, feet, and mouth) can serve as a role model for a child who has limited or poor self-control skills. On the other hand, a child who is somewhat impulsive, highly verbal, and enthusiastic about participating may serve as a good role model for a child who is inhibited and anxious.

In general, it is advised that group members be approximately 1 to 2 years apart in age. Running play groups with children with an age difference of more than 3 years can result in significant cognitive, social, and developmental differences among members. However, it is equally important to consider the individual child's social developmental stage in relation to his or her chronological age when selecting and grouping members.

SELECTING ADULT GROUP FACILITATORS

The adults invited to facilitate the group are critically important to the group process and should be chosen carefully. Adults who are often asked to facilitate group play interventions include teachers, teacher aides (paraprofessionals), social workers, psychologists, parents, grandparents, child care workers, and undergraduate and graduate students. It is important to recognize that group play interventions require a set of interpersonal, intrapersonal, instructional, and behavioral management skills that may be unique to other intervention models. For example, adult facilitators need to be comfortable modeling group play techniques and implementing play intervention skills in a childlike manner to actively engage and teach the children. It is critical that adults present with a positive affect (smile often, be a cheerleader), verbally praise children and other adults, and use an enthusiastic, energetic voice (like a game show host) during all training sessions.

When properly modeled, enthusiasm about the group play skill sequences (see Part II) and group play interventions (see Part III) is contagious and bolsters child engagement and learning. Group play interventions require adults to present with a relaxed, positive disposition (i.e., playful, fun loving) especially during times of conflict between child–adult and child–child interactions. Through modeling, adults should demonstrate that it is okay to make mistakes ("Even adults make mistakes") and display positive coping strategies when mistakes or disappointment occur. Practitioners should adopt a shared leadership role so that there is not one perceived leader (i.e., a teacher in charge). This helps reduce a sense of hierarchy and increases group cohesion. Adults should have good child handling skills, so that they are able to balance being in charge of the group and reinforcing group goals and rules while playing with the children. Furthermore, adults must be able to work with each other and with children spontaneously and seamlessly, without being caught in roles and power struggles. Group play can be stressful at times, and it is advised that adults adopt a *tap out* technique, a verbal or nonverbal signal to alert other members when one adult needs a break from the activity.

Group play interventions can be successfully implemented in a variety of settings, including schools (e.g., homeroom, gym class), mental health clinics, and private practices. However, the type of setting in which group training is offered may create opportunities as well as challenges for practitioners and group members. For example, group play interventions implemented in a school setting have the advantage of training children (classmates) in a natural context in which group members have daily exposure to the training environment, other group members, and adults facilitating the group. Group members are frequently drawn from a local peer pool, such as a classroom, set of classrooms, or a grade level. Group facilitators tend to be school personnel, including teachers, social workers, and school psychologists, who are familiar with the setting (training room) and the potential group members.

Groups that run during the regular school schedule are convenient for practitioners and children alike. The convenience of this setting can make group training an easily accessible intervention opportunity and often results in favorable attendance rates. Additionally, groups implemented in schools afford children the opportunity to formally (in a classroom or group) and informally (between class periods, lunch, recess) interact and practice skills learned from peers and adult facilitators on a daily or weekly basis. School-based groups can also give practitioners timely access to information about group members' daily and weekly social behaviors. Behavioral issues of children with special needs often wax and wane, at times considerably, depending on the social and academic demands in the classroom or school environment. Information on behavioral incidents and changes in behavior patterns may be helpful in selecting group play interventions and planning future sessions. Additionally, for some children school-based play interventions may serve as a potent venue for skill development and transfer to other important contexts in their lives, such as home, community or neighborhood, and lunch and recess periods.

School-based groups do involve some limits on privacy and confidentiality. For example, who is and is not attending groups may become common knowledge. This information may lead to positive or negative peer perceptions of group members. Additionally, school operating hours (e.g., 8 a.m. to 3 p.m.) may impede the possibility of parent involvement or parent training as an adjunct to child group play interventions.

Group play intervention programs that are offered in community mental health clinics or private practice settings present prospective parents and children with unique opportunities as well as challenges. For example, in clinic and private practice settings children are typically recruited from the larger community—from different schools, towns, and counties. Also, children at risk for or with special needs are commonly referred by a variety of sources, including parents, teachers, pediatricians, and other professionals (e.g., school and clinical psychologists, pediatric neurologists).

In contrast to schools, clinics and private practices can provide a greater sense of privacy and confidentiality to prospective parents and children because of location and the strict confidentiality laws (i.e., requirement of written parental consent) practitioners must abide by when exchanging information. Moreover, the hours (after school, evenings) and days (weekends) of operation of some clinics and private practices afford more flexibility for scheduling group interventions and may increase the possibility of parent involvement. Recruitment from the larger community also provides parents and children increased opportunities to work with families they might not otherwise meet. As a result their social support network is extended, and they gain valuable information from others about community resources. In contrast to the school setting, current information on individual behavior incidents and shifts in behavioral patterns in school might be more difficult for practitioners to obtain in clinics and private practices. In these settings, practitioners often rely on parents' anecdotal reports of school functioning, which can limit the utility of such information for making timely adjustments for play intervention sessions.

Attention to the physical setting, the arrangement of the environment, and the materials within the environment are crucial to achieving a successful group play intervention experience in school or community settings. Although opinions differ on appropriate dimensions and layout, it is generally recommended that the area (training space) be well-lit and ventilated, pleasantly decorated, and safe, with limited amounts of furniture and safety electric outlet plugs. Other training setting elements to consider are

- access to bathrooms, tissues, and hand sanitation liquids;
- a partially or fully carpeted room;
- age-appropriate art supplies, such as crayons, markers, scissors, paper, paints, clay or Play-Doh, and glue;
- aggression-releasing toys (e.g., inflatable punching bag, dolls);
- spacious arrangement of furniture such as tables and chairs; and
- toys that allow for self-expression (e.g., musical instruments, dress-up clothes, building materials).

GROUP FORMAT

Practitioners are encouraged to carefully consider the format of their group play interventions prior to screening group members and starting groups. Three general guiding questions to consider are: (a) Will the group be structured or unstructured? (b) Will the group be closed or open? and (c) Will the group be time limited or ongoing?

It is generally advised that children with special needs benefit most from highly predictable and structured group intervention experiences (Beyer, 1997; Reddy, 2010; Siepher & Kanadaras, 1985). For example, research has found that children with ADHD and Asperger's disorder are often inattentive and distractible and frequently require verbal and nonverbal reminders and visual cues to redirect their attention and stay on-task in group contexts (see Chapter 4 for details). When intervention routines are consistent and explicitly reviewed, modeled, and reinforced by practitioners, children's engagement, interest, and skill acquisition are best realized (Livanis, Solomon, & Ingram, 2008). Developing a routine and written group schedule can instill a greater sense of organization, predictability, and comfort for children in group interventions. However, it is important to note that *structured group* does not imply rigid, inflexible group routines. Some flexibility (i.e., give and take) is always needed, particularly in groups in which children with and without special needs are included and when behaviors change during the course of training.

Practitioners may consider whether to offer a closed or open (ongoing) group. A *closed* group typically includes a specific set of children who start and end the group together. The advantage of a closed group is that the same children and practitioners participate throughout its duration, which enhances group cohesion, peer and adult relationships, a sense of comfort and trust, and the ability to implement a sequential group session plan. An *open* group includes new group members as the group progresses. The advantage of open groups is that the context allows participants the opportunity to meet a variety of other children and further develop and refine social skills for welcoming and transitioning new members. This type of group, however, may be more challenging for children who have difficulties with transitions and who exhibit social anxiety with peers or groups.

Finally, practitioners may consider whether to offer a time-limited (e.g., six or eight sessions) or ongoing group (e.g., number of sessions to be determined by staff, parents, or group members). *Time-limited* groups can offer practitioners a set framework for establishing group goals and planning each session prior to screening group members and starting groups. A group that includes six play intervention sessions may focus on beginning social communication skills, such as introducing self to others, sharing about oneself, introducing others, and joining in a conversation; however, a group that includes 12 training sessions may focus on these skills as well as the identification of emotions in oneself and others and appropriate expression of basic emotions (e.g., happy, sad, angry, scared). Time-limited group training may offer a greater sense of intensity and novelty that may motivate children who work best with short-term goals and intensive experiences.

Ongoing groups, in general, may offer greater opportunities to develop group member affiliation and ownership when group intervention sessions are planned collaboratively with practitioners and children. Additionally, ongoing groups can run naturally during the course of the academic school year, and each season of the school year (fall, winter, spring) may be an occasion to incorporate different sets of play skills and training. For example, fall sessions may focus on meeting and getting to know new friends and teachers, winter sessions on developing and maintaining friendships, and spring sessions on fostering leadership and self-control skills.

The length of time of each group intervention session is an important consideration that may affect group or individual success. For example, it is generally advised to run group play sessions for 20 to 40 minutes with children under 8 years and 40 to 60 minutes for children 8 to 12 years of age (Reddy, 2010; Reddy, Springer, et al., 2005; Sweeney & Homeyer, 1999). Although group play intervention sessions are by nature highly engaging, their length must be carefully considered in relation to both the children's ability to sustain efforts in training and their prior peer group experiences. For example, children who are impulsive and inattentive in general will have more difficulties sustaining attention and efforts during longer group play experiences. Also, children with special needs frequently have limited and, at times, poor peer group experiences during play dates, especially long play dates. Thus, it is recommended that group sessions be short in duration and, if appropriate, only gradually lengthened when children have been consistently successful in short, limited group play experiences.

GROUP SIZE

The size of the group can vary (e.g., four children, 12 children, an entire classroom), depending on the group's goals and setting. A general rule for group size is the younger the children, the smaller the group. For example, three to six children under 8 years of age and six to eight children over 8 years old are recommended (Reddy, 2010; Sweeney & Homeyer, 1999). These numbers are suggestions and may be reduced or increased based on the group members' needs, ability levels, and amount of staff support required to appropriately run the group. For example, a group that contains several children with neurocognitive disorders (e.g., learning disabilities, ADHD) may require a highly structured and supportive environment that includes a low staff-to-child ratio (one adult to every three children in a small group). However, a group that includes nondisabled youngsters and one or two children with special needs may run well with one or two adult facilitators in a larger group context (i.e., classroom).

GROUP AGENDA

After the type of group has been established, a group agenda should be formed. This agenda will structure the group but should remain flexible enough that minor alterations can be made. It should structure the overall focus of group interventions so each session is clear, routine, predictable, and thus easy for the children to follow (see the example of group play intervention sessions in Part IV). The agenda must be established before the intervention begins because it is important to have an outline that describes how each session will be run. Although many aspects of group interventions should remain open to collaboration, children should not generate their own group agenda. However, group facilitators may choose to involve children in this process by addressing the agenda within the context of a group discussion.

At the beginning of each session, the group agenda should be enthusiastically described to the children, offering a structure (road map) for how each session will flow. A poster outlining the group agenda can be beneficial. A group agenda may include (a) welcoming the group members to the play group, (b) encouraging members to say their names, (c) reviewing group goals and linking them to the positive reward system, (d) reviewing group rules and how to use the bathroom and time-out passes, and (e) enthusiastically telling the group about the fun games for that session (e.g., headline of the news to come). In general, reviewing the group agenda should take about 5 minutes. Examples of group play intervention sessions are provided in Part IV of this volume.

GROUP GOALS

Practitioners should establish group goals before the first group session and link them to a positive reward system that is implemented during all sessions. The same goals should be used for all sessions and should complement the overall objectives of the group play interventions. Group goals should be written in a positive manner (focus on what to do, rather than what not to do), in language that children easily understand (i.e., brief, concrete, behaviorally specific). One suggestion is that no more than three group goals be used. It is critical that group goals are explicit (concrete), monitored and reinforced during each group session, and not aspirational in nature (e.g., "be a good citizen or person," "be respectful to others"). Group goals that have been effectively used with elementary-age children include (a) follow directions, (b) use my words to express my thoughts and feelings, and (c) keep my hands to myself (Reddy, 2010; Reddy, Springer, et al., 2005).

For groups that include children with disabilities (e.g., ADHD, learning disabilities, communication impairments), group goals can be modified and further defined to enhance children's understanding and ability to successfully accomplish the goals. For example, the group goals could be modified to these: (a) follow directions with one (or two) reminders; (b) use appropriate words and gestures with others (defined as showing a kind, nonaggressive look and voice when talking with peers or adults; no back talk, impolite hand gestures, or negative comments); and (c) keep my hands, feet, and mouth to myself (defined as using a calm indoor voice when telling others thoughts and feelings, keeping my hands and feet to myself, asking permission before touching other people and their objects). Additionally, pictures that show a child engaging in each group goal may be useful for younger children and children with special needs (e.g., mixed expressive and receptive language disorders).

GROUP RULES

Group rules are different from group goals. Group rules are established with group member feedback in the first two sessions and are the ground rules (guidelines) for instilling group member ownership and a sense of safety. Children should be encouraged to share their ideas on group rules and offer specific examples. Writing ideas and suggestions on a blackboard or easel for the group to review can enhance recall, instill group cohesion, and foster cooperation toward the established rules. Guidelines for establishing rules include the following:

- Rules should be limited to five or six to enhance child and adult recall and the ability to monitor them.
- Rules should be phrased in positive, proactive language that emphasizes *to do* behaviors rather than *not to do* behaviors. Examples include "raise your hand before speaking" and "stay seated," rather than "do not talk out" or "do not leave your seat or space."
- Rules should be phrased in brief and behaviorally specific terms. Examples include "keep your eyes on teacher or me," "wait your turn," "raise your hand," and so forth. Rules that are not concrete and behaviorally specific are often difficult for children to comply with and for adults to track. Examples of rules not to use may include "listen," "pay attention," "behave," "wait," and "be nice."
- As with group goals, group rules should be reviewed at the start of each group session and monitored and reinforced throughout the group training. Children should be called on to read the group rules, encouraged to provide brief examples of or explain each, and praised for their understanding and compliance.
- It is advisable to briefly praise children for following specific group rules. For example, "Ashley [pause], good job raising your hand before speaking!" Children who violate group rules should receive verbal correction or reprimands (see Chapter 4 for behavioral management strategies).

Following are some additional helpful tips to consider when formulating group rules:

- Adults should not call on a child who shouts out answers or does not have his or her hand raised.
- When a child shouts out an answer, tell the group (not the child) you will only call on children who have their hands raised and are quiet.
- Children who shout out answers should *not* be given eye contact, because eye contact for inappropriate behavior may reinforce the behavior.
- If the noise level increases in the group, tell the children that the group will take a brief break (examples of group breaks may include (a) closing eyes and not talking for approximately 15 seconds, (b) engaging in a quiet group stretch exercise, or (c) shutting the lights off for 15 seconds).

- If the lights need to be turned off, ask a child who is following directions and rules well to do this. This allows the child to have a positive leadership role, a motor break, and reinforces appropriate behavior for the group.
- It is advisable to refrain from using a group clap to indicate that the noise level is too high or a new learning activity is about to be introduced, as this may over-stimulate some children.

CHILD PREPARATION

Children often feel anxious when entering new social situations and may be reluctant to join the group. Because group training involves meeting new adults and peers, establishing group membership for themselves, and adjusting to training, children are likely to become stressed or anxious. Therefore, it is important that practitioners develop a plan for the initial reception (welcome) of the group. Activities aimed at reducing anxiety and helping children feel safe may set a comfortable tone for the remainder of group sessions. For example, it may be helpful to discuss a simple *separation process plan* with parents (or other adults) before the first group session. In this plan, parents should be told to establish a clear and potent reward for their child's compliance in joining the group. This reward should immediately follow the group session. In addition, parents should be advised not to linger in waiting rooms or at the group door and not to oversoothe their children. If the group session is to take place in a school, the adult facilitator can pair an anxious child with a nonanxious child with whom he or she is familiar, using the buddy system as a stress-reduction technique. In addition, an anxious child can be offered the role of assistant or helper. Helpers should be rotated frequently to offer all children equal opportunity to assume this role.

ADULT FACILITATOR PREPARATION

A final critical pregroup consideration is the careful preparation (training) of adult facilitators in the use of positive instructional and behavioral management strategies. It is paramount that practitioners take time to review instructional and behavioral management strategies, as well as model, practice, and coach the implementation of these strategies prior to the start of the group and during the group process (see Chapter 4 for specific strategies).

CONCLUSION

In summary, a number of pregroup considerations have been offered to practitioners for conceptualizing, selecting, and implementing group play skill sequences (Part II) and group play interventions (Part III). In Chapter 4, we see how the use of positive instructional and behavioral management strategies further establishes and fosters the learning environment for group play interventions.

Chapter 4. Group Instructional and Behavioral Management Strategies

—

Research has linked teachers' use of positive instructional and classroom behavior management strategies to academic and behavioral success among school-age children (e.g., Leflot, van Lier, Onghena, & Colpin, 2010; Reddy & Newman, 2009; Sugai & Horner, 2002). For example, Leflot et al. (2010) found that teacher behavior management (e.g., reduced use of negative remarks, increased rate of praise statements) predicted improved students' on-task behavior and talking out behavior, which in turn mediated the impact of a universal classroom prevention intervention on the development of disruptive behaviors (hyperactive and oppositional behavior). These findings are significant, as high rates of school-age children exhibit disruptive behaviors in peer groups and schools (Reddy & Newman, 2009; Reddy, Newman, DeThomas, & Chun, 2009; Visser & Lesesne, 2005).

Instructional and behavioral management strategies are important related approaches for promoting children's learning, engagement, and skill transfer (Reddy, 2010). Instructional and behavioral management strategies should be used together to foster an enjoyable learning environment for play interventions. Thus, positive instructional and behavioral management strategies are key ingredients for teaching and reinforcing group play skill sequences (see Part II of this volume) and group play interventions (Part III). Considerations and step-by-step guides are offered to practitioners that promote engagement (enjoyment) and learning of critical social skills and self-control strategies for children.

POSITIVE INSTRUCTIONAL STRATEGIES

Positive instructional strategies can be used to promote children's learning, engagement, and skill generalizability (transfer) to other important settings. The basic premise of this book is that children learn positive social behaviors when adults actively teach, model, reinforce, and coach children in group play contexts. Instructional strategies are important for teaching and reinforcing group play skill sequences (Part II) and group play interventions (Part III). As discussed, group play skill sequences play an important role in preparing (priming) children to participate effectively and enjoyably in group play interventions. Four main strategies that promote children's learning of group play skills include *formal instruction* (verbal and written description or review of skills or steps to perform the activity), *modeling* of skill sets (imitation and practice), *role play* (application of skill sets in common peer, school, and home situations), and *performance feedback* (coaching and encouragement).

Group play skill sequences teach children specific prosocial skills through a series of behavioral steps (Reddy, 2010; Reddy & Goldstein, 2001). First, play skills are introduced and taught through formal instruction in which adults (concretely and enthusiastically) review each behavioral step of the skill. The behavioral steps for each skill should be presented in simple, written language on an easel or blackboard in front of the group. An adult or child reads each behavioral step out loud (verbal description), followed by explanation or discussion. Second, skills are further explained and reinforced through modeling (adult and child demonstration of skill or behavior), and third, through role playing (guided mock play group situations in which to apply skill or behavior). Modeling and role playing can be conducted by group members or done using puppets, dolls, or story characters.

It is recommended that skill sequences be taught through a three-phase role play (modeling) approach (Reddy, 2010; Reddy, Springer, et al., 2005). This approach has been found to be effective in skill development and transfer for children with ADHD. First, the group play skill sequence is role played (modeled) by two adults. Second, the play skill is role played (modeled) by an adult and child; third, the play skill is role played (modeled) by two children, with adult coaching and encouragement. It is recommended that role plays be conducted in three common social contexts: (a) peer group, (b) home, and (c) school (see Part II for detailed examples).

It is advisable that adults and children set a positive, playful atmosphere before each role play by saying together (using arm gestures), "READY, SET, ACTION!" The three-phrase role play approach allows for the gradual reduction of adult participation–assistance (scaffolding) in children's application of skills. During role plays, children should be encouraged to politely evaluate whether the role player (adult or child) demonstrated each skill step correctly. They then have the opportunity to practice and observe these behavioral steps through behavior rehearsal (modeling or role playing learned skill or behavior), after which adults can offer *performance feedback* (praise or corrective feedback regarding rehearsed skill or behavior). In performance feedback (coaching) the goal is behavioral change based on the child's new and prior knowledge of social behaviors, ability to convert knowledge into social behavior, and ability to accurately evaluate his or her skill performance.

GROUP BEHAVIOR MANAGEMENT STRATEGIES

Perhaps the most challenging aspect of group work with children is identifying effective ways to anticipate and manage problem behaviors that emerge during play. Thus, in group play social and behavioral issues that naturally occur can serve as opportunities for learning, self-awareness, and skill development. Several evidence-based group behavioral management strategies are recommended to foster a positive learning and safe play environment for groups. These include positive reinforcement, corrective feedback, verbal and nonverbal prompts, effective commands, implementing a positive motivational system, and methods of teaching self-control.

Positive Reinforcement

A number of social reinforcements can be used to enhance children's prosocial behaviors. Too often, adults (e.g., group facilitators, parents, teachers, coaches) will attend and respond more to children exhibiting negative, rather than positive, behaviors. This tendency occurs, in part, because negative behaviors often disrupt adults and the flow of activities. As a result, positive behaviors are frequently overlooked or taken for granted by adults. In group training, attending and reinforcing children's prosocial behaviors are critically important for social skill development. Both verbal and nonverbal praise are strongly encouraged throughout all group sessions. For verbal praise, adults should issue specific, positive behavioral feedback (labeled praise) that highlights what the children are doing correctly. For example, "Jerome, thank you for helping Jeff clean up," and "Linda, I appreciate you raising your hand quietly." Specific, positive behavioral praise communicates positive adult attention, specifies what the child is doing correctly, and encourages the child to continue to use appropriate behavior. In contrast, unlabeled praise ("good work," "way to go"), although positive, fails to adequately communicate what the child is doing correctly. Additionally, the use of nonverbal praise is a valuable technique for group play training. For example, nods, thumbs-up, positive eye contact, smiles, affectionate pats (arm, shoulder, back), and sitting near the child are all powerful ways to recognize children's efforts in groups. Nonverbal praise also has the added benefit of offering public and private recognition to children.

Five general guidelines for providing positive reinforcement are offered. First, adults should provide each child with individual praise and positive attention (smile, eye contact) during each group session. Second, verbal praise should be varied. Praise such as "Good . . . " can become monotonous and less powerful when used often. Third, make sure to deliver both verbal and nonverbal praise with a warm, positive facial expression (e.g., smiles, nods, soft eyes). Fourth, practitioners may initially feel that they are overpraising when providing social reinforcement for each child. This is normal, and the contingent use of a social reinforcement routine will feel more natural with time. Finally, after each group session it is important to tell teachers and parents what each child did well and ask them to acknowledge (praise) each child for her or his efforts.

Corrective Feedback

Negative behaviors naturally occur during group play. Corrective feedback (or reprimands) is an important teaching (coaching) tool for children's group training. This technique is used to point out in specific behavioral terms what children are doing wrong and how they should behave differently. After corrective feedback is provided, children should be given the opportunity to perform the correct behavior with adult supervision and encouragement. Following feedback, children should receive specific praise for performing the appropriate behavior. As corrective feedback or reprimands are intended to express specific disapproval of children's behavior, practitioners should use *I* statements to describe how the behavior adversely affects others in the group and suggest an alternative behavior that is acceptable. For example, "Ashley [pause], I do not like it when you do not share the paper with John and Jeff. I want you to give some paper to John and Jeff now," or "Jim [pause], I do not like it when you shout out in group. Please raise your hand when you want to talk now." Additionally, corrective feedback can be issued privately with an individual child or group.

To give corrective feedback, follow these steps:

1. Point out the specific behavior that the child performed incorrectly;
2. use *I* statements to describe how the behavior impacted others;
3. ask the child to perform the specific appropriate behavior; and
4. praise the child for performing the specific appropriate behavior.

Ratio of Positive Reinforcement to Corrective Feedback

Both positive reinforcement and corrective feedback are useful teaching tools for group interventions. Practitioners should provide positive reinforcement to children for appropriate behavior more often (i.e., approximately 5:1 ratio) than corrective feedback for inappropriate behavior. The ratio of 5:1 is a general rule that should be monitored and modified as needed.

Verbal and Nonverbal Prompts

Verbal and nonverbal prompts are effective ways to enhance learning engagement and appropriate behavior in groups. Verbal and nonverbal prompts can be used to remind children of group goals, rules, or appropriate behavior in general. Examples of verbal prompts may include "eyes on me," "right now it is your turn," "freeze your arms and legs," "I need your listening ears on," and "remember to use your indoor voice."

Nonverbal prompts offer children signals that can be given either privately (addressing a particular child) or communally (addressing the group). Examples of private nonverbal prompts include a light touch (i.e., the adult gently places a finger or hand on the child's shoulder and presses lightly), desk tap (the adult gently taps the child's desk to redirect attention), adult eye contact, and the use of proximity to the child (i.e., the adult moves within 3 to 5 feet of the child). Group nonverbal prompts include hand signals that calm or quiet the group, such as "serpent hands" (adult clasps forefingers to thumb, to motion a mouth closing; children mimic the gesture), placing a finger to the mouth, and the peace sign (adult raises two fingers in the air; children mimic the gesture). Group prompts can also be created with the children. For example, children may suggest that the group raise a finger up or put a hand on head to communicate that it is time to be "quiet, please."

Giving Effective Commands

The strategy *giving effective commands* (directions) is an effective method for increasing compliance and reducing behavior problems in groups. Adults often unintentionally provide vague directions or directions with multiple steps, which makes it difficult for all children to follow directions successfully. Directions that are vague and include multiple (more than two) steps are exceedingly difficult for children with neurocognitive impairments such as ADHD, learning disabilities, and receptive and expressive language disorders to follow. This strategy provides adults with a systematic approach to offer clear (concrete) behavioral directions so that children (with and without disabilities) can be successful in the group process.

To give effective commands, follow these steps:

1. State the child's name and then pause (2–3 seconds).
2. Gently remove potential distractions if possible (e.g., turn the child away from a peer interaction).

3. With a positive, playful tone of voice and facial expression, encourage the child to look at you (e.g., "[Child's name], I need to see your eyes now"). Directions should be stated in specific (concrete) behavioral terms. Words such as *listen, respect others,* and *behave* are not behaviorally specific.

4. Give the child a one- or two-step direction, and end the statement with the word *now*. Examples include "Ashley [pause], please put away the toy and come to me *now*"; "Chris [pause], please return the bathroom pass and join the group *now*." Directions should not be framed as asking the children favors. For example, "Could you please help me?" is a favor, but "Please help me pass out paper now" is a direction.

5. Provide specific praise to the child after he or she follows the direction. Examples include, "Ashley [pause], great job for putting away the toy and coming to me!"; "Chris [pause], great job returning the bathroom pass and joining the group!"; "John [pause], I really like the way you cleaned up the crayons!"

6. In the event the child does not follow initial directions, wait 15 seconds before repeating them. The 15-second pause is critical for enhancing compliance and reducing frustration for both adult and child. Rapidly repeated directions can result in anger and noncompliance. Also, keep in mind that some children require more time to process language in general and verbal directions specifically.

7. After repeating the directions, do *not* walk away from the child. It is important to stay in the child's "zone" (i.e., 3–5 feet) and monitor her or his implementation of the direction. It is important to give verbal directions and praise in close proximity to the child, not from across the room. A distance of approximately 3 to 5 feet between adult and child is recommended.

Finally, keep in mind that no child follows all directions. Choose directions that are critical for children to follow, and be sure to monitor the children through each step of the direction.

Positive Motivational System

A schedule of reinforcement, such as a *positive motivation system* (e.g., token economy system) can be a highly effective method to reward and monitor positive behaviors within and between group sessions. A positive motivation system is most potent when it is displayed on a group chart (e.g., names of children are listed in rows and group sessions are listed as columns) for all the children to see. It is important that practitioners make the system a central component of the group experience by reviewing the group goals in relation to the motivational system (i.e., point to the group chart) at the beginning and end of each group session. Children are given rewards for following each of the established group goals. As one example, at the end of each group play session, children will be given rewards for following the three group goals of (a) follow directions, (b) use my words to express my thoughts and feelings, and (c) keep my hands and feet to myself. One token, which can be in the form of a small sticker or point, is given for each of the three goals attained during the session. With adult encouragement and assistance, each child should then be asked to briefly assess whether she or he attained the goal during the session. Next, a sticker or point for each goal the child attained is recorded next to the child's name on the group chart. This discussion is best held in front of the entire group, as the group should be encouraged to clap for each child after the group goals are reviewed. The group clap encourages cooperation and social approval. Children should be encouraged to work on goals they had difficulty accomplishing (e.g., "Chris [pause], you had difficulty following directions today, but I know you will do better at following directions during the next group").

Two additional methods for reinforcing positive behaviors are sticker books and mystery motivators (rewards). After the children are given stickers for their efforts toward group goals, they can be given the opportunity to select stickers that correspond to the number of goals attained and place them in their personal sticker books. The sticker books can be taken home by the children when the group ends. Mystery (surprise) rewards can be offered in a treasure chest or prize bag (e.g., the children blindly reach into the bag and select a prize) at the end of each group session or after a specific number of stickers (points) are earned.

Positive Self-Control Techniques: Time Out (Break Time)

Self-control skills are critical for group play. Children can learn a host of prosocial behaviors through watching others (modeling), coaching, talking about the importance of these behaviors, and engaging in role plays. However, when peer conflict arises and children become angry or distressed, their ability to remember and use the social skills taught through these methods can quickly diminish. Thus, it is important that both social skills and self-control skills and techniques are actively taught in group contexts in which peer conflicts naturally occur.

An effective positive self-control technique is the use of a three-level *time-out (break time) method* (Reddy, 2010; Reddy, Spencer, Hall, & Rubel, 2001; Reddy, Springer, et al., 2005). In this approach, the primary goal is to prompt children's positive self-control skills through a step-by-step self-regulation process that includes adult corrective feedback, coaching, and contingent praise. Traditionally, time out is widely known and used as a punishment or negative consequence given to children for inappropriate behavior. This method focuses on the use of time as a form of punishment, in which the child is placed in a time out for approximately 60 seconds for each year of his or her life (e.g., a 6-year-old is placed in time out for 6 minutes). Although this traditional method of time out links child misbehavior to a negative consequence (i.e., time away from a reinforcement), it does not teach children how to identify the emergence of negative emotions and behaviors, monitor their negative emotions and behaviors, and regain their self-control during social situations.

It is recommended that a three-level time-out method be used for self-control training in group play interactions. The term *time out* can be substituted with *break time* if needed to reduce the potential for negative stigma or sensitivity for children. Practitioners should be alert to this sensitivity, especially in children with a history of behavioral issues or those with special needs, as it is common that these children have been frequently punished with time outs by caregivers and others. Level one time out is designated by a specific chair placed on the far side of the group room, which distances the child from being directly involved in the group's activity. Level two time out is a chair located directly outside of the group room, which further distances the child from the group activity and decreases the level of visual and auditory stimulation for the child. Level three time out is a chair in a separate room, which completely eliminates the visual and auditory stimulation of the group activity. It is suggested that a child be accompanied by an adult when level two or three time out is implemented. In addition, children in level two or three should successively approach group reentry by spending a brief period of time (e.g., 45–60 seconds) in the previous level time-out chair. This reentry method is highly recommended to gradually prepare the child to rejoin the group and not be overwhelmed (from visual or auditory stimulation) by the group play activities.

For this method, time out can be initiated by an adult or child. An adult can verbally recommend that a child needs a time out (see the section Giving Effective Commands) or establish with the group a private signal (e.g., a gentle tap on shoulder) to redirect the children into time out. During time out, there should be no talking, and the child or adult in time out should be left alone. A time-out pass can be used to allow an adult or child to nonverbally communicate to others in the group that he or she needs to take a break from the group activities.

Here are some additional time-out guidelines:

- The technique of time out should be positively (with an enthusiastic tone of voice) presented by adults as a positive self-control technique at the beginning of each group session. The children should be told that taking breaks is important for everyone, including adults. The three levels should be briefly described. The children should be told specifically that time out is not used to punish them but to help them get themselves back in control. The children should be told that this method (it can be described as a privilege) can be used by adults, too.
- Adults should specifically model the use of time out during the first two group sessions and then periodically use the method during the remaining sessions. If modeled correctly (i.e., the adult takes the time-out pass, briefly tells the group that he or she needs to take a break, sits on level one chair), this should evoke smiles and giggles from the children. Through adult modeling, children can learn that time out is a positive, acceptable, and effective way to regain control of their hands, feet, and mouth (Reddy, Springer, et al., 2005).
- Positive reinforcement, such as verbal praise (behaviorally specific), should be given when children self-initiate time out or comply when adults recommend the use of time out.
- Time out can be terminated when an adult observes that a child has regained self-control. The amount of time that the child takes in time out is not important. Instead, the goal is to regain positive self-control (i.e., control of the child's arms, legs, and mouth). Keep in mind that a child may regain self-control of his or her body in as little as 60 seconds or less.
- Any discussion of the reasons for time outs should be kept to a minimum and only conducted after the time out is over, in private, or between play group activities. If a discussion is needed, it is important that adults do not overdiscuss or process events leading up to the time out.

Positive Self-Control Technique: The Group Complaint Book

The Group Complaint Book may be used during group play to defuse negative emotions and behaviors and positively redirect children who are displaying mild to moderate levels of distress from peer interactions to a calming (e.g., writing, drawing) activity. This technique allows children to document what upset them, when it occurred, who it involved, what they did afterward, and draw a picture of how they feel about the situation. This step-by-step process allows children to document feelings, thoughts, and behavior without disrupting the group process.

An adult should review and sign the Group Complaint Book approximately 10 minutes before the group ends to briefly address the child's reported concerns. The adult's review and signature of the child report communicates to the group and the child the appropriate use of the book and acknowledges children's feelings about interactions. An example Group Complaint Book is displayed at http://pubs.apa.org/books/supp/reddy. The book should be clearly labeled, stored in a three-ring binder, and easily accessible for children to use. Each entry should include two pages, with the first page listing the date of the incident, the reporting child's name, and brief information about the incident. The second page should be left blank to allow the child to draw how she or he feels.

CONCLUSION

This chapter summarized evidence-based instructional and behavioral management strategies for group play interventions. Collectively, these strategies provide practitioners an integrative approach for fostering a highly enjoyable and engaging learning environment for children.

Chapter 5. Caregivers in Promoting Group Skill Generalization

This chapter discusses the importance of caregiver[1] involvement in sustaining and generalizing gains obtained in children's group play interventions. Child–parent interactions play a critical role in teaching, refining, and reinforcing prosocial skills in children. Possible roles and approaches for involving caregivers in children's group play intervention sessions are presented. Additionally, techniques caregivers can use to sustain and transfer skills learned in group play interventions are outlined.

Caregivers who are knowledgeable and participate in their children's treatment process can significantly enhance the prosocial skills children acquire in group training. Caregivers can play an important role in transferring skills acquired during group training experience to other important settings (e.g., home, school, neighborhood) in children's lives. The more involved caregivers are in their children's treatment, and the more educated they are about effective behavioral strategies to sustain treatment gains, the better equipped they will be to recognize and track their children's progress (Mendlowitz et al., 1999).

Caregiver involvement in children's group treatment offers valuable opportunities for caregivers to learn more about their children and their children's group experience, as well as providing professionals with an understanding of their children's needs and strengths for training (Reddy, Weissman, & Hale, in press; Siebes et al., 2007). Caregivers can also help practitioners anticipate and identify obstacles that may arise in their children's group treatment and generate solutions for obtaining goals (Siebes et al., 2007).

Caregivers who are involved in their children's treatment have been shown to produce an array of positive child mental health outcomes (e.g., wellness, self-control, social

[1]*Caregiver* refers to a biological parent, adoptive parent, foster parent, legal guardian, or other family member, such as a grandparent, aunt, or uncle.

affiliation) in the home, school, and community (e.g., Barrett, 2000; Cheney & Barringer, 1995; Comer, Haynes, Joyner, & Ben-Avie, 1996). For example, parents or guardians who display high levels of parental involvement (i.e., attendance at family therapy, weekly parent visits, telephone calls) were associated with low readmission rates to child residential treatment facilities compared with youth with low levels of parental involvement. Additionally, those with high levels of parental involvement in treatment exhibited greater improvements in family functioning and social and behavioral impairments at discharge (Lakin, Brambila, & Sigda, 2004). Parental involvement has been found to predict children's social–emotional functioning as measured by the Child Behavior Checklist (Achenbach, 2001; Noser & Bickman, 2000). Waugh and Kjos (1992) reported that high levels of parental involvement were related to improvements in school and home functioning, as well as reduced hospitalizations, psychopathology, and behavioral problems for adolescents with behavioral and emotional problems. In a study focused on an intensive half-day, school-based therapeutic setting, caregiver involvement (i.e., attendance at therapeutic home visits and therapeutic meetings, completion of rating scales, communicating with the therapeutic team) was associated with improved children's problem solving, increased ability of caregivers to provide social and emotional support to the family, and overall child adaptive functioning at discharge (Richards, Bowers, Lazicki, Krall, & Jacobs, 2008).

Although research suggests that it is beneficial to involve caregivers, it is important to note common obstacles that may arise when practitioners seek to engage caregivers in children's group treatment process. For example, caregivers may have time scheduling constraints that inhibit their ability to fully participate in their children's treatment. It is important that practitioners keep this in mind and use flexible and perhaps creative ways of communicating with and involving caregivers (see the information in a later section of this chapter, Roles and Approaches for Caregiver Involvement). Also, caregivers' knowledge and expectations of their children's group process (e.g., father and mother have different expectations or goals for the group) may impede involvement. In addition, involvement may inadvertently be hindered by a lack of knowledge about how and when caregivers are to participate in and support their children's group experience (Suveg et al., 2006).

Practitioners can overcome some of these obstacles by modeling effective use of praise, discouraging caregivers from the use of negative critical statements (Kendall et al., 1992), addressing discrepancies among caregivers early in treatment, and providing structure by outlining the children's group schedule before treatment begins (Suveg et al., 2006).

Along with caregiver involvement, caregiver and child interactions provide an essential foundation for children's development, caregiver–child attachment, acquisition of prosocial skills, and future relationships.

CAREGIVER AND CHILD INTERACTIONS

It has been known for some time that the quality of child and caregiver relationships and interactions is crucial to children's psychological, cognitive, and physical development (Bettmann, 2006; Bowlby, 1980). Caregivers' level of availability, ability, and willingness to provide care and protection for their children influence the children's sense of safety, value, self-worth (competence vs. incompetence), level of attachment (secure or insecure), and quality of future child and adult relationships (Bowlby, 1980; Greig et al., 2008). Children with caregivers who are neglectful, inattentive, withdrawn, and possibly abusive tend to exhibit feelings of worthlessness and incompetence and may exhibit inappropriate behaviors with peers or adults.

Elementary-age children spend a considerable amount of time with their caregivers and often view their caregivers as the most important models in their lives. Therefore, they are highly influenced by their caregivers' values and behaviors. If caregivers are viewed as important prosocial models, they can have a powerful, positive effect on their children's lives, especially during early development (Edwards, 2002). As a result, children are more motivated to maintain positive interactions and appropriately manage their emotional and behavioral expressions in social situations (Edwards, 2002).

Strong, positive caregiver and child relationships and interactions support the development of mastery in children (Edwards, 2002). Caregivers can serve an influential role in reinforcing children's striving for mastery and learning because they are available to facilitate their development in unique ways (Edwards, 2002). For example, caregivers can promote mastery by teaching specific skills and behaviors through modeling, instruction, and interpretation (Bornstein, 1989) and engaging them in meaningful conversations (Hart & Risley, 1995). Through various experiences children learn that caregivers respond to and meet their needs and provide security and trust. As a result, these meaningful experiences set the stage for children to view and use caregivers as teachers and mentors for support while mastering new skills (Edwards, 2002). In addition, through continuous child–parent interactions (learning moments), children begin to learn specific cognitive, linguistic, and social–emotional skills and develop confidence (i.e., efficacy) in their ability to learn additional skills (Bandura, 1993). Thus, it is important that practitioners emphasize the impact of caregivers' verbal and nonverbal behaviors on their children's skill development and well-being.

Practitioners who forge positive collaborative relationships with caregivers will ultimately increase caregivers' motivation and involvement in their children's learning and behavioral and social–emotional functioning (Kutash, Duchnowski, Sumi, Rudo, & Harris, 2002). As a result, these caregivers may make a greater investment of time and energy in their children's group treatment process and possibly in parent–child interactions (Mendlowitz et al., 1999). Practitioners can capitalize on caregivers' motivation by teaching caregivers various ways to model important social, emotional, and self-control skills that are beneficial for children's friendship development (Ginsburg & Schlossberg, 2002; Reddy, Weissman, & Hale, in press). Examples of such strategies are offered later in this chapter in the Caregiver Techniques to Promote Group Play Intervention Skill Maintenance and Generalization section. Possible roles and approaches for caregiver involvement in children's group treatment are outlined in the following discussion.

ROLES AND APPROACHES FOR CAREGIVER INVOLVEMENT

Caregivers can assume different roles when working with practitioners regarding their children's education or treatment. For example, caregivers can be consultants or collaborators (Kendall, Chu, Pimentel & Choudhury, 2000). As *consultants*, caregivers can provide practitioners with valuable information regarding the nature of their children's difficulties as well as strengths. Facilitating communication with caregivers helps practitioners obtain information about a child's level of motivation and a family's overall attitude toward treatment. For instance, caregivers can provide practitioners with examples of what their children enjoy doing for fun or would enjoy receiving as a possible motivator for positive behavior exhibited in group. Caregivers can also be *collaborators*, a role in which they help carry out important treatment components. For example, practitioners can work with caregivers on modeling positive attitudes toward treatment and can coach them on how to prepare children for starting and ending group treatment. Working with caregivers as collaborators may help with follow-through on out-of-session (between sessions) tasks that are crucial for children's success in treatment (Reddy, Weissman, & Hale, in press; Springer & Reddy, 2010).

Other effective ways caregivers can be involved in their children's group process include (a) parent group training programs, (b) bibliotherapy, (c) parent support groups, (d) distribution of informational material, (e) web-based resources and supports (also see Part IV), and (f) telephone communication. Each approach is described in the following discussions.

Parent Group Training Programs

Parent group training programs provide caregivers with education, support, and training on child behavioral management strategies that promote confidence and effective parenting skills (e.g., Andrews, Swank, Foorman, & Fletcher, 1995; Brestan & Eyberg, 1998; Cousins & Weiss, 1993; Eyberg, 2003; McMahon & Forehand 2003; Webster-Stratton, 2000). The goal of parent training is to guide parents into becoming active and positive cotherapists in their children's treatment (Briesmeister & Schaefer, 1998). As cotherapists, caregivers apply what they have learned in parent training to real-life scenarios with their children in the home and community. Caregivers fulfill this role by providing feedback and reinforcing positive behavioral strategies displayed by their children outside of treatment.

Parent training programs have been shown to reduce children's disruptive behaviors exhibited in the home (Sanders, Markie-Dadds, Tully, & Boron, 2000; Springer & Reddy, 2010) and improve family member interactions (e.g., Brotman et al., 2005; Humphreys, Forehand, McMahon, & Roberts, 1978; Kazdin & Wassell, 2000). In a meta-analytic review of parent training program effectiveness, components that reduced children's externalizing behaviors included "increasing positive parent–child interactions and emotional communication skills, teaching parents to use time-out and the importance of parenting consistency, and requiring parents to practice new skills with their children during parent training sessions" (Kaminski, Valle, Filene, & Boyle, 2008, p. 567).

Parents who completed parent training programs reported reduced stress levels, increased self-perceptions of parenting competencies and efficacy, and positive changes in children's behavior at home and/or school (e.g., Anastopoulos, Shelton, DuPaul, & Geuvremont, 1993; Anastopoulos, Smith, & Wein, 1998; Fischer, 1990; Reddy, Springer, et al., 2005; Springer & Reddy, 2010). Parents also report higher levels of consumer satisfaction with practitioner-assisted parent training programs versus self-directed programs (Sanders et al., 2000).

The decision to offer a parent training group to develop caregivers' skills and sustain gains from group play intervention sessions should be carefully considered because of the amount of time and resources needed. First, consider whether the goals of the parent group will complement the skills taught in the children's group training. Parent group training goals that increase parents' use of behavioral techniques for positive self-control (e.g., reward system, three-level time-out, use of effective commands) can complement the children's group goals of improved social skills. Second, decide what type of between-session homework would promote both parent skills and child group outcomes. For example, parents can be given homework on the same group play skill sequences taught in the children's group session to do at home with their children.

Common goals outlined in parent training group manuals include (a) increase parents' knowledge and awareness of their children's strengths and weaknesses; (b) teach and systematically maintain the use of behavioral techniques in the home, school, and public places; (c) improve parent–child interactions by teaching parents effective methods for managing anger and stress; and (d) learn tools to manage their children's behavior (Reddy, Files-Hall, & Schaefer, 2005). Some additional aspects included in parent training programs are group discussions, role plays, and homework. Parents also may receive informational booklets that contain outlines of each training session, lists of resources, and contact information for fellow group members and group facilitators. An example of a parent and child group training program that includes play group interventions is described in Reddy (2010) and Reddy, Files-Hall, and Schaefer (2005).

Bibliotherapy

Bibliotherapy is an alternative to traditional therapy in that therapeutic services are delivered via printed materials (manualized programs). Typically, this approach has been used for the management of adult anxiety, eating disorders, and depressive disorders (e.g., Loeb, Wilson, Gilbert, & Labouvie, 2000; McKendree-Smith, Floyd, & Scogin, 2003; Newman, Erickson, Preworski, & Dzus, 2003) with outcomes that are comparable to standard therapist-conducted treatments (Mains & Scogin, 2003).

Because bibliotherapy relies heavily on clients' independent motivation to learn (i.e., to read), ability to read, and willingness to make meaningful changes in daily routines, caregivers may be especially motivated to use materials that produce immediate positive changes in their children's behavior (Rapee, Abbott, & Lyneham, 2006). Bibliotherapy approaches may be appealing because of their inherent flexibility, as caregivers are able to progress on their own schedule through the materials. This approach may be particularly appealing to highly motivated caregivers who learn through reading or those with hectic professional and personal schedules. Bibliotherapy is also beneficial because caregivers (a) have knowledge of their children across important areas of functioning, including social, behavioral, and academic–cognitive; (b) may have some degree of distance from their children's difficulties; and (c) are more broadly present and available in their children's lives than are practitioners (Rapee et al., 2006).

One example of a caregiver bibliotherapy approach is the Positive Parenting Program (Connell, Sanders, & Markie-Dadds, 1997). The Positive Parenting Program uses a structured 10-week workbook that teaches strategies for day-to-day parent–child interactions. The workbook is supplemented with regular telephone sessions. Parents reported that they were able to establish rapport and develop a therapeutic alliance with their mental health practitioner via telephone contact despite the loss of visual cues. Additionally, the rate of targeted children's behavioral problems was reduced by 67%.

As is true with any treatment approach, bibliotherapy may not work for all caregivers. Several factors may impede the success of bibliotherapy programs. These include caregivers' limited time to use the program; caregivers' low acceptability of treatment; caregivers' inability to read, understand, or implement treatment strategies; caregivers' low sense of efficacy to implement the program or strategies; and caregivers' negative expectations of the treatment approach (Rapee, Abbott, & Lyneham, 2005).

Bibliotherapy methods do not replace traditional models of treatment, but they do offer a potent and flexible mode of treatment delivery to caregivers and practitioners alike. Another flexible way of engaging parents in their children's group process is through the development of a parent support group.

Parent Support Groups

The format of parent support groups offers a flexible environment in which caregivers can comfortably express their concerns (tell their own stories), receive support from others, support others, and obtain valuable information and resources (Slowik, Willson, Loh, & Noronha, 2004). Parent support groups, like parent training programs, can build a caregiver's sense of efficacy ("can do" attitude) and decrease the social isolation and stigma often associated with caregivers who have children with social skills difficulties. Support groups tend to have a less formal atmosphere than traditional parent training groups, which encourages more spontaneous and flexible interactions into which practitioners can infuse anecdotal experiences and humor.

Practitioners should consider some formalities before developing a parent support group. It is important to determine the maximum and minimum number of caregivers to enroll. This number will depend heavily on how many children are enrolled in the children's group; however, the optimal number of caregivers is typically eight to 10. A small- to moderate-size support group preserves a comfortable atmosphere in which everyone has an opportunity to participate. Practitioners should also consider the location where they will hold the support groups. For example, support groups can be held in a home, classroom, school, community center, private practice office, or clinic. The location of the support group can create a specific atmosphere. For example, a support group offered at caregivers' homes might offer a more intimate atmosphere than a group held in a private practice office or a classroom. It is wise to choose a location that is most convenient for parents. If the majority of the group members work, evening or weekend times may be the best. Similar to parent group training, support groups that run concurrently with children's groups may be more time-efficient, aid in day care arrangements and costs, and enhance overall participation (attendance). Unlike traditional parent training programs, support groups should allow greater flexibility for unplanned discussions in which caregivers can share concerns and socialize.

Typically, practitioners provide parents with an outline of the support group goals prior to starting groups. Common goals and objectives for parent support groups include (a) reducing parental isolation, building self-esteem, and supporting positive parenting; (b) exposing caregivers to other families; (c) improving communication and problem-solving skills; (d) promoting leadership and shared leadership within the group; (e) linking caregivers to resources in the community and within the group; and (f) helping caregivers become more competent and confident in their parenting role (Falconer, Haskett, McDaniels, Dirkes, & Siegel, 2008; Gay, 2003).

Practitioners may consider providing refreshments as an incentive for parents to come and socialize with other parents. Some parent support group facilitators also provide parents with resource books that contain lists of nearby resources, phone numbers and e-mail addresses of group members, and a notebook in which parents can take notes during each session.

Distribution of Informational Materials

Another way to promote caregiver involvement is through the distribution of informational flyers and materials. These may take the form of simple fact sheets with brief "tips and tricks" to solve common problems (e.g., sleeping, eating, temper tantrums) and more extensive information that describes specific childhood mental disorders or treatment options (e.g., medication, therapies, speech–language and/or occupation therapies).

Providing caregivers with informational materials can significantly increase their knowledge and modify preconceived notions and beliefs about their children's difficulties (Brent, Poling, McKain, & Baugher, 1993). A higher level of knowledge about specific symptoms, conditions, and mental health disorders has been shown to improve caregiver attitudes toward treatment acceptance and adherence (e.g., Bennett, Power, Rostain, & Carr, 1996; Corkum, Rimer, & Schachar, 1999; Rostain, Power, & Atkins, 1993).

Although all forms of material are helpful in educating and involving caregivers in their children's group process, it is critical that practitioners do not overwhelm caregivers with too much written information. One way to avoid this is by using paperless, web-based resources and supports.

Web-Based Resources and Supports

Web-based resources and supports offer practitioners another option to facilitate caregiver involvement in their children's group process. Web-based support can include websites, e-mail, blogs, and Internet support forums. Providing caregivers with specific websites offers them immediate access to practical information, online support groups, and resources. For families that have computers, websites are an easy and convenient way (with 24-hour access) to look up valuable information at times that are most suitable to them. This approach provides options that are cost-effective and easily accessible for both practitioners and caregivers but in no way replaces the value of face-to-face contact (Lyneham & Rapee, 2006).

E-mail can be used to foster communication between caregivers and practitioners as well as among caregivers whose children are participating in groups. Practitioners may also decide to use e-mail to disseminate information to caregivers outside of the school and clinic. E-mail correspondence is particularly useful for caregivers with busy work and family schedules.

Despite the advantages of using web-based resources and supports, practitioners must keep in mind important ethical and professional considerations. Prior to starting children's groups, practitioners are encouraged to develop guidelines for e-mail use with caregivers. Guidelines for e-mail correspondence should be made clear and explicit to all caregivers. These guidelines may include topics and concerns to be discussed and communicated over e-mail, practitioners' availability to respond to e-mail, and e-mail expectations.

A crucial guideline to discuss with caregivers prior to e-mail use is that e-mail should *not* be used to communicate emergencies. Caregivers should notify 911 in the event of an emergency and not rely on web-based communications in any emergency situation.

The notion of immediate access to others can create the misunderstanding that all messages will be responded to immediately, so it is important that practitioners inform caregivers that they are not accessible via e-mail 24 hours a day. One way practitioners can avoid an overreliance on e-mail is to decide how frequently they plan on responding to caregivers' e-mails. For example, practitioners can inform caregivers that they will only respond to emails twice weekly.

Caregivers' use of e-mail should be kept at a minimum to protect privacy. As a rule, confidential information and concerns should not be sent via e-mail. For example, practitioners should inform caregivers that e-mail correspondence is not private and that anyone can access their messages. Beneficial and safe ways to communicate via e-mail may include setting up or canceling appointments, informing one another of upcoming vacations, and sharing websites and articles of common interest.

Language in e-mails can be misunderstood or misconstrued, so practitioners should be careful that communication is clear and concise, so that e-mails are not confusing or misleading. At times, e-mails may come across as impersonal, but caregivers and practitioners alike should be aware that this medium should be used for simple communication and not for elaborate, complicated discourse.

Communication over the Internet does not replace face-to-face contact, but it does provide individuals with resources that are quick, easy to use, and generally hassle-free. Another form of contact that may be simpler and easier for caregivers to use to communicate with practitioners is telephone communication.

Telephone Communication

Telephone communication or consultation is a cost-effective way for practitioners to develop relationships and collaborate with caregivers. Telephone consultation can be a convenient way for practitioners to reach families who might otherwise be unable to access mental health services on a regular basis (Nixon, Sweeney, Erickson, & Touyz, 2003). Telephone communication can take the form of quick informational updates on group topics, group scheduling, or a more extensive discussion of what the children were taught in a particular group session. For example, telephone contact reminders may aid in treatment adherence, reduce attrition, prevent relapse, and be helpful when obtaining follow-up status on children's progress (Nixon et al., 2003).

CAREGIVER TECHNIQUES TO PROMOTE GROUP PLAY INTERVENTION SKILL MAINTENANCE AND GENERALIZATION

Three techniques are presented next for promoting and sustaining skills learned from group play interventions. These techniques are (a) caregivers' use of positive attention to manage children's behavior, (b) use of time out (break time) to promote positive self-control in the home, and (c) managing children's behavior in public.

Use of Positive Attention to Manage Children's Behavior

One technique that is useful in managing children's behavior while also improving caregiver–child relationships is caregivers' use of *positive attention* (i.e., structured *special time*). This technique is a daily, 10- to 15-minute, child-focused activity implemented by a caregiver in the home. This technique should be implemented daily (at least one time per day in the home) at a time convenient for the caregiver. It is strongly recommended that only 10 to 15 minutes be used to ensure that the caregiver can realistically fit the technique (special time) into the family's daily schedule. During child-focused time, the caregiver positively attends to or participates in a home activity (i.e., video game, house, board game) of their child's choosing for the set time period.

The purpose of this technique (special time) is for the caregiver to focus positively on the child's behavior during a child-directed activity in the home for a set (limited) period of time. It is important that the caregiver and child discuss special time together and review the rules of special time before beginning the activity. Rules may include (a) 10 to 15 minutes of an age-appropriate game or activity the child chooses in the house, (b) special time occurs during a time the caregiver finds most convenient, (c) the child, not the caregiver, chooses and directs the activity, and (d) special time may end early if the child misbehaves after two warnings are given. One tip is that the child and caregiver should set a timer together to increase awareness and reinforce compliance with the technique and time restriction. As mentioned, this technique should be used in the home so that the caregiver can easily end the activity at the designated time or end the activity early in the event the child's misbehavior persists after the two warnings.

This technique (special time) should not be implemented when caregivers are upset, stressed, need to use the bathroom, or are about to run an errand. It is advised that the caregiver relax and casually watch the child play. Caregivers can show their interest by describing out loud what their child is doing (e.g., "I like the way you are playing with the cat." or "Nice drawing!"). Caregivers' use of action-oriented words and excitement is useful for reinforcing to the child that they are attending to and enjoying the child and her or his activity. During this activity, caregivers should avoid asking questions and giving commands but should make use of praise, approval, and positive feedback. The use of nonverbal gestures is another positive way for caregivers to reinforce their child's positive behaviors. For example, using hugs, pats on the shoulder, smiles, winks, and nods are all ways to communicate positive attention. Thus, the use of praise and positive feedback should be behaviorally specific and accurate. It is important that caregivers not go overboard, because using too much praise may dilute its powerful effect or annoy the child.

Caregivers should be encouraged to view misbehavior during special time as an opportunity to teach the child prosocial skills. The following steps are recommended when misbehavior occurs during the 10 to 15 minutes of special time:

- The first time the misbehavior occurs, the caregiver should tell the child what he or she specifically is doing wrong during the play, remove eye contact with the child, and turn their body slightly away from the activity and child for about 30 seconds. The caregiver should have no facial expression and should not talk to the child. If the child's misbehavior stops, the caregiver should resume eye contact with the child and offer positive attention (verbal and nonverbal) to the child and play activity.
- If the misbehavior occurs again, the caregiver should calmly tell the child what she or he specifically is doing wrong during the play, remove eye contact, and turn their body slightly away from the activity and child for about 45 seconds. Again, after the misbehavior stops, the caregiver should positively attend (e.g., eye contact, smiles) to the child.
- If the misbehavior occurs a third time, the caregiver should tell the child what he or she specifically is doing wrong during the play and that special time is over for today. The child should be informed that he or she has an opportunity for special time the next day. The caregiver should leave the activity and engage in an adult activity. The child should be redirected to a positive activity. No further discussion should occur between the child and caregiver.
- Caregivers should always show approval immediately (do not wait!). Also, parents should be specific about what they like about what the child is doing (focus on the positive behaviors) and should never give a backhanded compliment (e.g., "Nice job not kicking anybody").

Time Out (Break Time) to Promote Self-Control at Home

Time out is traditionally used to punish (negatively reinforce) children for misbehaving. This time-tested method links negative child behavior to a negative consequence (i.e., remove child from activity or privilege). In contrast to the traditional method of time out, the technique proposed here—time out or break time—is designed and implemented to promote adults' and children's self-control skills. Time out is a positive self-control technique that caregivers can use in the home. Children should be instructed that taking a time out is not a punishment but a positive way to calm down. The goal of time out is to reduce the amount of stimulation (i.e., visual and auditory) children are receiving from their environment and to allow them to regain control. Time out can be child- or adult-initiated and should be modeled by adults in the home.

The amount of time in time out (break time) is not the focus of this technique; rather, the emphasis is on regaining one's self-control. For example, one child or adult may only need 60 seconds to regain control, yet another child or adult may need 5 minutes. Additionally, this technique should be used in situations in which the child or adult is experiencing mild to moderate levels of distress, not just in situations of high levels of distress (e.g., full tantrums, explosive anger). It is strongly recommended that caregivers catch their children early when they are exhibiting distress. Encouraging children to take a break early on promotes children's awareness of their feelings, behaviors, and self-regulation skills. One way to teach children or adults about how to catch themselves early in the behavior process is to show a picture of a thermometer or draw a horizontal line with the bottom labeled 0 (*no bad feelings*), the middle labeled 5 (*some bad feelings*), and the top labeled 10 (*a lot of bad feelings*). Additional numbers and labels can be added to illustrate and emphasize this point. Discuss with the children the idea that at times they may have no bad feelings (e.g., represented by a 0 rating; feeling happy and calm), while at other times they may experience bad feelings (e.g., represented by a 4 or 5 rating; feeling nervous, jumpy, or irritated). Also, discuss when they may feel really upset (e.g., represented by a 10 rating; feeling mad, yelling or screaming). Emphasize that it is good to take time outs or breaks when they are at a 4 or 5 rating to prevent getting to 10. Following is a description of how to implement time out (break time) in the home.

IDENTIFY A SPECIFIC LOCATION FOR TIME OUT

The time-out area should have clear boundaries and be away from distractions (e.g., television, computers); a place such as the living or dining room is advised—somewhere that is viewed as neutral by all family members and is accessible to everyone. Caregivers should not use the stairs, a child's bedroom, or a bathroom for time out. The time-out area should have a comfortable chair positioned where the caregiver can observe the child.

IDENTIFY A TIME-OUT PASS FOR THE ENTIRE FAMILY

The time-out pass can be a small pillow, a small stuffed animal, or a homemade sign (break pass) that is not owned by anyone in the family. It is important that the pass is identified and acknowledged by everyone in the family and left near the time-out chair. When a person is taking a time out, he or she should pick up the pass. The time-out pass indicates (nonverbally) to others not in time out that the person in time out needs a break and should be left alone.

SCHEDULE A FAMILY MEETING TO DISCUSS TIME OUT

Tell the family that time out is a positive way to feel better (relax) and stay in control (i.e., of hands, feet, and mouth). Time out is best used when someone feels jumpy, irritated, sad, or overwhelmed, not just mad or after a major incident has occurred. The important part of time out is not the time taken (i.e., how long someone stays in time out) but that the person regains control of his or her hands, feet, or mouth (i.e., feels refreshed, better). A person can take a 10-minute time out or a 90-second time out. It is important to emphasize that time out is a good thing to do and is a privilege. The term *time out* should also be discussed during a calm and nonconfrontational moment. Discuss with the family members whether they want to call it *time out* or *break time.* The term *time out* may be viewed as negative or scary by some children, and it is important that caregivers acknowledge any negative feelings or thoughts when introducing this technique.

EXPLAIN THE RULES OF TIME OUT

The rules of time out should be explained during the family meeting. One rule many caregivers find useful is that both children and adults should take time outs. Caregivers who use time out in the home should model and reinforce a positive attitude about taking care of oneself (i.e., taking breaks). After caregivers model time out a few times in the home, they can begin to gently encourage children to take time outs. Children will typically begin to self-initiate time outs after they have observed their caregivers use it. If a child initiates a time out, the caregiver should immediately praise the child. For example, caregivers should inform the family when they are going to take a time out and say that they do not want to be interrupted. This needs to be explicitly communicated to the family each time. Caregivers should remind their family that everyone needs to take a break (from 2 to 5 minutes) each day. This offers caregivers an opportunity to wind down and teach their child good self-care skills. Some other rules for time out may include the following:

- When someone is taking a time out, she or he is not to be spoken to.
- Only one person at a time can be in time out.
- A time-out pass must be displayed each time a person uses it.
- After a person is done with time out, he or she should place the time-out pass next to the chair.

Time out can be used in different situations. For example, a person can take a time out when he or she is tired, overwhelmed, irritated, sad, or mad. Time outs can be used when someone's feelings or behaviors are mild, moderate, or severe. It is important that adults and children use time outs as a prevention intervention in which adults encourage children to take a time out early before their feelings or behavior get to a high level.

Practitioners should emphasize that caregivers should never threaten children with time out. If a caregiver tells a child to take a time out, he or she must follow through with intervention. What they say, they must do! This is important because not following through on time outs will inadvertently reinforce the child's undesired behavior. Also, caregivers should be aware that some children might display controlling (escape) behaviors during time outs (e.g., call caregivers' names, yell, cry, urinate in the chair, try to induce vomiting). Caregivers need to recognize that these are controlling behaviors and ignore them when appropriate. In addition, if children are not taking time out appropriately (e.g., violating agreed-on rules), caregivers can let them know that there will be a consequence. If a time out is initiated by an adult because the child refuses to comply with a direction (e.g., refuses to clean up toys, complete homework), it is important that the caregiver redirect the child to complete the original request (direction). The caregiver should not engage in a discussion (overprocess) with the child about the behavioral concern, but rather redirect the child to the requested activity. Caregivers should talk less and act more. Finally, caregivers should not hold a grudge after behavioral incidents. It is wise for them to move on, and help their child do the same.

Managing Children's Behavior in Public Places

Child and caregiver interactions in the community can be complex and challenging. Many times caregivers become embarrassed and stressed by their children's behavior and inadvertently use ineffective strategies that they would not otherwise use in public or private settings. It is best for caregivers and children to have a *shared approach* to behavior management. This approach needs to be specifically discussed (calmly) with the child before leaving the home. Obtaining the child's input helps to develop buy-in and motivation. It is important to review the behavioral goals, rewards for accomplishing the goals, and the consequences for not achieving the goals. The following steps are offered to help manage behavior.

- Caregivers should discuss the behavioral goals and rules for the outing. Goals and rules should be limited to three each and should be phrased in positive language (e.g., keep hands to self, stay an arm's length away from parent).
- An incentive (reward) should be established with the child for following the specific behavioral goals (rules). For example, let the child know that she or he can earn points toward a privilege (e.g., having ice cream, riding a bike, playing at a friend's house). Another incentive caregivers can use is snacks (cookies, chips). For long outings (i.e., more than an hour), the child can earn points or a small reward for each time interval (e.g., every half hour or hour) they adhere to the behavior goals. Rewarding the child at set time periods (intervals) during long outings can help sustain the child's motivation to adhere to the goals and make the outing a more positive experience for all.
- The consequence for not following the specific behavioral rules and goals should be discussed with the child as well. Examples of punishment can be the loss of television time (e.g., one show) or another privilege.
- Again, it is critically important that the three steps be outlined before leaving the home. Also, the three steps should be reviewed first inside the home, again in the car, and again outside the public place (shopping mall, restaurant, toy store).

CONCLUSION

This chapter has underscored the importance of caregiver involvement in children's group play interventions and emphasized that positive parent–child interactions foster and reinforce children's development of prosocial skills. Roles and approaches for practitioners to engage caregivers in their children's group experience were outlined. Additionally, caregiver techniques to promote and sustain skills learned from group play interventions were discussed in depth.

II

GROUP PLAY SKILL SEQUENCES

Group play skill sequences are a step-by-step behavior approach to teaching children prosocial skills through modeling, feedback, and role playing with adults and peers. Group play skill sequences are designed to prepare children *before* they participate in group play interventions. It is recommended that a practitioner implement one or two skill sequence(s) before implementing a group play intervention.

As outlined in Chapter 4, "Group Instructional and Behavioral Management Strategies," four instructional strategies are recommended for teaching group play skill sequences: (a) adult formal instruction (verbal and written review of skills); (b) adult and child modeling of skills; (c) role playing[1] (skill application; guided "mock play group situations"); and (d) performance feedback (coaching).

Part II includes 43 group play skill sequences for practitioners to select from that teach children specific prosocial skills for successfully participating in group play interventions.

---

[1]A three-phase role playing (modeling) approach is recommended: (1) adult-adult model, (2) adult-child model, and (3) child-child model with adult coaching and engagement.

1 COMMUNICATING WITH OTHERS

EVIDENCE FOR SKILL Effective communication fosters collaboration, trust, mutual respect, and knowledge of others (Lasky, 2000; McNaughton, Hamlin, McCarthy, Head-Reeves, & Schreiner, 2008). Talking with friends about problems can help children learn how to express and regulate their emotions and behavior (Jellesma, Rieffe, & Terwogt, 2008).

Group Skill Sequence 1: Communicating With Others

1. *Look* at the other person.

2. *Walk* up to the other person, staying an arm's length away from her or him.

3. *Wave* or *smile* at the person.

4. *Tell* the person your name. "Hi, my name is _____."

5. *Wait* and *listen* for other person to tell you his or her name or *ask* his or her name.

6. *Say*, "It's nice to meet you."

7. *Wait* for person to respond.

8. *Ask* the person a question. For example, "What do you like to do for fun?"

9. *Wait* and *listen* for his or her answer.

10. *Respond* by asking the person more about the topic. For example, "Is soccer your favorite sport?"

Social Contexts in Which to Role Play (Practice) the Skill Sequence

- Your friend told you about his or her birthday party plans and wants to know what you think about them.

- Your brother talks with you about some children teasing him at school.

- Your teacher wants the class to get to know each other and pairs you with a classmate.

2   USING NICE TALK

EVIDENCE
FOR SKILL

Friendships and positive child–adult relationships are developed through positive conversational exchanges that reflect the ability to cooperate in play, resolve conflicts, and explore feelings and shared experiences (Dunn, Cutting, & Fisher, 2002). Children who use prosocial skills such as *nice talk* are more likely to report that they enjoy making and maintaining friendships (Dunn et al., 2002).

Group Skill Sequence 2: Using Nice Talk

1. *Approach* the person in a friendly way (do not run into them or get in their face).

2. *Stand* an arm's length away from the person.

3. *Smile* at him or her!

4. *Talk* in a friendly way (with a low tone).

Social Contexts in Which to Role Play (Practice) the Skill Sequence

- You want to borrow a friend's baseball bat or Pokemon card.

- You want to ask your mom if you can bake cookies together.

- A new student joined your class today and you want him or her to feel welcome

3 INTRODUCING SELF TO OTHERS

Children use various communicative and interactive skills to establish friendships and forge peer acceptance (National Institute of Child Health and Human Development Early Child Care Research Network, 2008a). Peer social competence is associated with increased social and emotional adjustment and academic skills throughout childhood and adolescence (Boivin, Hymel, & Bukowski, 1995; Gifford-Smith & Brownell, 2003; Ladd, Buhs, & Troop, 2002; Vandell & Hembree, 1994).

Group Skill Sequence 3: Introducing Self to Others

1. *Look* at the other person.

2. *Walk* toward the person.

3. *Wait* until the other person looks at you.

4. *Tell* the person your name. "Hello, my name is _____."

5. *Pause* and *listen* to see if he or she tells you their name. If he or she forgets, ask, "What's your name?"

6. *Say*, "It was nice to meet you."

Social Contexts in Which to Role Play (Practice) the Skill Sequence

- You are at a friend's birthday party with kids you haven't met before.

- Your parents have neighbors over for dinner, and you want to meet their daughter.

- There is a new classmate at the playground, and you want to meet her.

4 INTRODUCING OTHERS

Research has found that high levels of positive peer interactions, such as introducing others, are a buffer against the development of peer aggression and problem behaviors (Howes & James, 2002). Young children (younger than 5 years old) who have consistent positive peer interactions are more likely to experience cooperative and prosocial peer play interactions during later childhood (Campbell, Lamb, & Hwang, 2000; Howes, 2000).

Group Skill Sequence 4: Introducing Others

1. *Look* at other people.

2. *Say* the name of one person, and *tell* her or him the name of the other person. "Mike, this is Amanda."

3. *State* the name of the other person, and *tell* him or her the name of other person. "Amanda, this is Mike."

4. *Say* something that they both enjoy, such as, "Both of you like chocolate ice cream."

Social Contexts in Which to Role Play (Practice) the Skill Sequence

- You are having a pool party and you want your old friends to meet your new friends.

- A friend of yours has moved into your neighborhood, and your parents want you to introduce your brother and sister to them.

- You are sitting at the lunch table with two friends who don't know each other.

5 JOINING IN A CONVERSATION

To effectively join in ongoing peer interactions, children must have good self-control and social skills (Sebanc, Pierce, Cheatham, & Gunnar, 2003). Engaging in complex peer play (i.e., getting along with peers) promotes the use of social skills necessary to resolve conflict, collaborate, and communicate ideas, which in turn relate to peer acceptance and less aggression and peer withdrawal in childhood (Howes & Phillipsen, 1998).

Group Skill Sequence 5: Joining in a Conversation

1. *Look* at the people having the conversation and smile.

2. *Wait* for the people to stop talking (pause).

3. *Talk* about something that is similar to what they are talking about.

4. If ignored, *walk* away and *do* something else.

Social Contexts in Which to Role Play (Practice) the Skill Sequence

- Your friends Stacey and Maria are talking about a new TV show.

- Your parents are talking about what to make for dinner.

- Two classmates are talking about the Mets baseball game.

6 JOINING A PLAY GROUP

EVIDENCE
FOR SKILL

When joining a play group, children tend to use a combination of prosocial/assertive, passive, and creative strategies (Green, Cillessen, Reichis, Patterson, & Hughes, 2008). Some children use group-centered strategies, such as making suggestions on how to extend a game so they can join in. Children's use of creative problem solving is particularly beneficial when dealing with challenging social situations such as negotiating turns and roles during games (Green et al., 2008)

Group Skill Sequence 6: Joining a Play Group

1. *Stand* near a group and *watch* the activity.

2. *Make* a positive comment about the game, such as "Good shot!" or "That looks like fun!"

3. *Engage* in similar activity alongside of the group game.

4. *Ask* to join group game; for example, "Can I play with you guys?"

Social Contexts in Which to Role Play (Practice) the Skill Sequence

- During recess, children are playing a game of kickball or soccer.

- Your older brothers or sisters are playing a game of basketball.

- Your classmates are playing a game of Uno.

7

SHARING ABOUT ONESELF

EVIDENCE
FOR SKILL Sharing about oneself can increase children's sense of well-being and attachment with others (Jellesma et al., 2008). Sharing interests, accomplishments, problems, and emotional experiences with a friend can increase emotional security and support, and buffer against negative affect (Jellesma et al., 2008).

Group Skill Sequence 7: Sharing About Oneself

1. *Look* at the person you want to talk to.

2. *Think* about what you want to say to the other person. "I really want to tell Rebecca about my new goldfish, Harry."

3. *Ask* your friend if it's OK to tell her or him something, "Hey Rebecca, want to hear something cool?"

4. *Wait* to see if it's OK to start talking.

5. *Do it!* Tell your friend what you want to share with him or her. "Rebecca, I just got a new pet this weekend!"

6. *Respond* with more information if your friend asks questions such as, "Wow that's neat, what kind of pet did you get?"

Social Contexts in Which to Role Play (Practice) the Skill Sequence

- Playing with dolls is your favorite thing to do, and you want your best friend to know.

- Your mom just had a new baby, and you want to tell your teacher about it.

- You received a good grade on a math quiz, and want to tell your parents.

8 SHARING YOUR THINGS WITH OTHERS

EVIDENCE
FOR SKILL

Children that exhibit prosocial behaviors such as sharing, helping others, and asking for help from others are more likely to be academically successful and better adjusted (Lim, Khoo, & Wong, 2007). Sharing personal possessions lets others know that you like them, and indicates your likes and dislikes. Sharing also has many extrinsic and intrinsic rewards.

Group Skill Sequence 8: Sharing Your Things With Others

1. *Decide* if you have something to share; for example, "I want to share my snack."

2. *Pick* who you want to share with; for example, "I want to share it with John."

3. *Think* about when you want to share; for example, "I will share it with John during lunchtime."

4. *Share* it! Tell John, "I want to share my animal crackers with you. Would you like some?"

Social Contexts in Which to Role Play (Practice) the Skill Sequence

- You ask a friend to play tennis. She doesn't have a racket, but you have an extra in your closet.

- Your parents bought a new goldfish for you and your brother to share.

- You brought in a box of goldfish crackers and want to share them with your classmates at lunch.

9 LEARNING ABOUT OTHERS

EVIDENCE FOR SKILL Children can learn about one another through sharing interests, telling jokes, and playing sports (Asher, Parker, & Walker, 1996; Savin-Williams & Berndt, 1990). Learning about others requires children to effectively listen to what others say, relate information to what they have previously learned, and use good self-control (e.g., not interrupting others while they are speaking and keeping hands and feet to themselves; Asher et al., 1996; Selman, 1980).

Group Skill Sequence 9: Learning About Others

1. *Look* at the person you want to talk to.

2. *Think* about what you want to know about the other person.

3. *Ask* the person questions such as, "What's your favorite food?" "What's your favorite video game?" or "Do you have any brothers or sisters?"

4. *Listen* to what they tell you.

5. *Wait* until they are finished talking.

6. *Ask* more questions if you want to know more. "Wow, you have five brothers, what are their names?" or "How old are your brothers?"

Social Contexts in Which to Role Play (Practice) the Skill Sequence

- You want to know what your best friend's favorite food is.

- Your big sister is dressed really fancy with makeup and jewelry on, and you want to know why.

- Your teacher has a picture of a dog on her desk, and you want to know the dog's name.

10 BEING AN ACTIVE LISTENER

EVIDENCE
FOR SKILL
The use of active listening helps establish trusting and positive relationships (Duhamel & Tabot, 2004). Children who are active listeners are motivated to ask appropriate questions and to offer empathetic statements toward others (McNaughton et al., 2008).

Group Skill Sequence 10: Being an Active Listener

1. *Stop* what you are doing.

2. *Have* quiet hands and feet!

3. *Look* at the person who is talking to you.

4. *Make* good eye contact.

5. *Nod* your head if you understand what the person said.

6. If you don't understand, ask the person to tell you more about it.

Social Contexts in Which to Role Play (Practice) the Skill Sequence

- Your friend wants to tell you about the movie she or he just saw.

- Before your mom leaves for work, she wants you to know the plans for after school.

- Your teacher is telling the class about an upcoming science project.

11 GIVING COMPLIMENTS

Giving compliments to others produces positive social interactions, outlooks, and adaptive coping strategies that help lower stress, anxiety, and depression (Bertera, 2007). Pointing out positive attributes or behaviors of others can foster social support from peers (Bertera, 2007).

Group Skill Sequence 11: Giving Compliments

1. *Pick* a person you want to say something nice to.

2. *Identify* something about the person that you like.

3. *Think* about what you are going to tell the person ("I really like your headband").

4. *Face* the person and *make* good eye contact.

5. *Say* the compliment to the person; for example, "Sasha, I really like your headband."

6. *Wait* for a response from the person.

7. *Respond* if you need to.

Social Contexts in Which to Role Play (Practice) the Skill Sequence

- Your friend is going to a party and looks nice.

- You like the pancakes that your mom made you.

- Your classmate has a neat-looking pencil case.

12 RECEIVING COMPLIMENTS

EVIDENCE
FOR SKILL
Receiving compliments from others can bolster children's sense of self and self-esteem and serve as a buffer against negative mood (Bertera, 2007). For example, children who report more positive social exchanges with peers in preschool exhibit better social and communicative skills and outcomes (e.g., sociable, cooperative, less aggressive, more peer acceptance and friendships) in third grade (National Institute of Child Health and Human Development Early Child Care Research Network, 2008b).

Group Skill Sequence 12: Receiving Compliments

1. *Face* the person and listen.

2. *Make* good eye contact.

3. *Respond* to the compliment by saying "thank you."

4. *Think* about whether the compliment is correct.

    a) If correct, *give* the person a compliment back.

    b) If incorrect, *correct* the person, and then *give* the person a compliment.

Social Contexts in Which to Role Play (Practice) the Skill Sequence

- A friend tells you that you have pretty hair.

- Your dad tells you that you did a good job cleaning your room.

- Your teacher tells you that you wrote a good paper.

- A friend tells you that you have a great sweatshirt, but it is not your sweatshirt.

13 RESPECTING OTHERS

EVIDENCE
FOR SKILL
Respecting others often requires children to be attentive, empathetic, sympathetic, kind, and supportive toward others. Being respectful to others deepens a sense of security with friendships and increases mutual trust in peer and child–adult relationships (Frei & Shaver, 2002).

Group Skill Sequence 13: Respecting Others

1. *Look* at the person you want to talk to or do something with.

2. *Wait* and *see* if that person is talking to someone else or is busy doing something.

3. If you can't tell, *say* "Excuse me, are you busy now?"

4. If they say yes, *decide* what to do:

    a) *Wait* patiently (do not speak, hands to self) until he or she is done; or

    b) *Come back* later when he or she is free.

5. *Do* what you decided to do.

Social Contexts in Which to Role Play (Practice) the Skill Sequence

- You know your friend likes funny movies and doesn't like scary movies, so you agree to see a funny movie.

- Your brother is eating his favorite snack. You do not ask for some of his snack or take any of his snack, but instead wait to see if he offers you some of it.

- Your father wants to talk with your mother alone about something important about work, and you decide to leave the room to give them some privacy.

14 RESPECT FOR OTHERS' PERSONAL SPACE

EVIDENCE
FOR SKILL

Personal space relates to an individual's representation of the self and the self in relation to others (Horner, 1983). Being aware of one's personal space relies heavily on an ability to regulate behaviors and emotions. Individuals tend to seek an optimal distance during interactions, and when this space has been compromised, discomfort or dissatisfaction occurs (Bar-Haim, Aviezer, Berson, & Sagi, 2002). Thus, teaching children ways to respect and manage personal space is a critical social skill.

Group Skill Sequence 14: Respect for Others' Personal Space

WHEN YOU INVADE OTHERS' SPACE

1. *Check* to see if you are touching a classmate.

2. *Move* away so that she or he is an arm's length away.

3. If you are too close, *say* you're sorry.

4. *Use* quiet hands and feet.

WHEN OTHERS INVADE YOUR SPACE

1. *Check* to *see* if someone is too close to you (e.g., look around or if you feel someone next to you).

2. If he or she is too close, *ask* him or her nicely to give you some space.

3. *Say* "thank you" to the person for giving you space.

Social Contexts in Which to Role Play (Practice) the Skill Sequence

- Your friend tells you that you are sitting too close to her or him.

- Your brother or sister pushes you away when you jump on top of him or her.

- You grab a classmate's pencil without asking for it.

15 NOT INTERRUPTING OTHERS

EVIDENCE
FOR SKILL

Children learn good conversational skills by observing adult conversations (e.g., parents, teachers, or coaches). As children mature, they learn that a conversation is a turn-taking activity that includes listening, attention, respect for others, and cooperation skills (Maroni, Gnisci, & Pontecorvo, 2008).

Group Skill Sequence 15: Not Interrupting Others

1. *Think* of the person you need to talk with.

2. *Find* the person.

3. *Wait* until he or she sees you.

4. *Smile* and *say,* "Excuse me, can I ask you something?"

Social Contexts in Which to Role Play (Practice) the Skill Sequence

- Your friend is on the phone, but you want to ask her if you can borrow her headband.

- Your mom is busy making dinner, and you need her to help you with your homework.

- You want to ask your teacher when your homework is due, but she is busy helping another student.

16 SELF-CONTROL

Self-control is associated with positive well-being and reductions in externalizing behaviors in the home and school. Exhibiting self-control can have positive effects on the development and maintenance of friendships, child–adult relationships, academic performance, and overall well-being (Wills, Ainette, Mendoza, Gibbons, & Brody, 2007).

Group Skill Sequence 16: Self-Control

1. *Pause* and *take* a few moments to cool off (relax).

2. *Ask* yourself, "How do I feel? Are my toes or fingers tingling?"

3. *Take* three slow, deep breaths.

4. *Reward* yourself by taking time to do something fun. Read a book, color, draw, or play a game.

5. *Think* of a person you can talk to about your feelings. It could be a teacher, friend, or classmate. See if they are available (not busy).

Social Contexts in Which to Role Play (Practice) the Skill Sequence

- Your friend borrows a toy and breaks it accidentally.

- Your parents won't let you go to a friend's house.

- A classmate takes your lunch from you and won't give it back.

17 IDENTIFYING FEELINGS AND EMOTIONS

Identifying and responding to peers' feelings are essential skills for developing and maintaining friendships. For example, recognizing when a friend is upset and knowing how and when to respond to his or her feelings are important skills for relationship development (Dunn et al., 2002).

Group Skill Sequence 17: Identifying Feelings and Emotions

1. *Look* at a person's facial expression or body movements.

2. *Decide* if she or he is frowning, crying, smiling, or laughing. Are her or his arms crossed tightly, or are they loose and moving around?

3. *Think* to yourself, "He must feel happy if he is laughing or smiling," or "She must feel sad or down if she is crying or frowning," or "He looks mad, I see his arms are crossed and he is frowning."

3. *Decide* if you want to ask the person if he or she is feeling sad or happy.

4. *Do it!* Say, "Are you sad about something?" or "You seem really excited. What are you excited about?"

Social Contexts in Which to Role Play (Practice) the Skill Sequence

- Your friend is rolling around on the ground giggling.

- Your dad is reading a letter from his brother and is smiling a lot.

- Your teacher is quiet, has her arms crossed, and is staring straight ahead.

18 EXPRESSING FEELINGS AND EMOTIONS

Expressing feelings and emotions is an important skill for promoting social and behavioral well-being (Shipman & Zeman, 2001). Being aware, managing, and coping with one's emotions are important components of emotion regulation (Zeman, Shipman, & Suveg, 2002). Children with poor or limited emotional awareness are more likely to display internalizing distress (e.g., anxiety, depression) and externalizing problems (e.g., acting out, impulsivity), and are less likely to access social support (Zeman et al., 2002).

Group Skill Sequence 18: Expressing Feelings and Emotions

1. *Wait* and *think* about how you feel.

2. *Think* about what's going on with your body and in your head. For example, "My legs feel heavy," "My fingers feel tingly," "I feel so torn up inside I could scream!" or "I'm so excited I could burst!"

3. *Pick* the emotion or feeling that matches what you feel inside.

4. *Decide* if you want to tell someone how you feel.

5. *Do it!* Talk with someone, such as a parent, teacher, friend, or classmate. Tell that person how you feel. "I feel sad about my bird or dog dying," or "I'm excited about going on vacation."

Social Contexts in Which to Role Play (Practice) the Skill Sequence

- Your best friend tells you that he is moving away.

- Your mom told you that you have to give away your dog because you are allergic to the dog.

- A classmate sitting next to you called you a geek.

19 UNDERSTANDING SOCIAL CUES

Children learn how to understand social cues by observing and monitoring interactions of others (Ackerman & Izard, 2004). When children engage in social interactions, they learn to infer and anticipate emotions expressed by others and themselves and build on their knowledge by regulating their own emotions during social exchanges (Ackerman & Izard, 2004). The ability to monitor and understand social cues is associated with greater social emotional adjustment (Fine, Izard, Mostow, Trentacosta, & Ackerman, 2003; Izard et al., 2001; Schultz, Izard, Ackerman, & Youngstrom, 2001).

Group Skill Sequence 19: Understanding Social Cues

1. *Look* at what the other person is doing.

2. *Watch* her facial expressions (is she happy, sad, or angry?).

3. *Watch* his body movements (arms crossed? body stiff, loose?).

4. *Decide* what you want to do.

    a) Does a friend look like she wants to talk to you?

    b) Does a friend look like he wants to be alone?

5. *Do* it! Make the best decision.

Social Contexts in Which to Role Play (Practice) the Skill Sequence

- A friend of yours just got into a fight with his brother.

- Your mom is motioning with her arms for you to come over and talk with her.

- Your teacher has a stern look on her face and is upset that the class is not quiet during reading time.

20 SHOWING CONCERN FOR OTHERS' FEELINGS

EVIDENCE FOR SKILL Children's empathy and concern for others are related to advanced prosocial behaviors, such as helping others and asking others (Goodvin, Carlo, & Torquati, 2006). Showing empathy toward peers is also associated with positive coping strategies, social competence, and peer acceptance (Goodvin et al., 2006).

Group Skill Sequence 20: Showing Concern for Others' Feelings

1. *Look* to see if a person is feeling a certain way (e.g., happy, sad, angry, scared).

2. *Ask* the person if she is feeling the way you think she may be feeling. "Are you feeling sad?"

3. *Wait* for the person to answer.

4. *Ask* why she is feeling that way.

5. *Show* concern by:

6. If he is feeling a good emotion (e.g., happy) say, "I am glad that you are feeling ___."

7. If he is feeling a bad emotion (e.g., sad, angry) say, "I am sorry that you are feeling ____."

Social Contexts in Which to Role Play (Practice) the Skill Sequence

- Your friend didn't get a good grade on the spelling test and he looks upset.

- Your grandma is upset because she dropped a plate and it broke.

- Your friend went to the school nurse and looks like she is feeling sick.

21 DEALING WITH STRESS

EVIDENCE
FOR SKILL
Stress management strategies can help build goal setting and goal attainment skills and positive self-concept. Techniques such as deep breathing, muscle relaxation, and physical exercises are ways children can manage stress. Practicing patience, understanding emotions, and expressing emotions are exercises children can use to effectively cope with stress (Gonzalez & Sellers, 2002).

Group Skill Sequence 21: Dealing With Stress

1. *See* how your body feels (nervous, excited, scared).

2. *Calm* down. Take a few moments and take three deep, slow breaths.

3. *Relax* parts of your body, one by one, until you feel better.

   a) Suggestion: Tighten your muscle in each body part slowly, and then release the muscle.

4. *Describe* how you feel afterward.

Social Contexts in Which to Role Play (Practice) the Skill Sequence

- You are really mad at a friend.

- Your family is going to an amusement park and you're excited.

- You have a big spelling test tomorrow and you are nervous about how you are going to do.

22 DEALING WITH ANXIETY

EVIDENCE
FOR SKILL
Children increasingly face high levels of anxiety and stress in their lives. Although techniques that help children navigate everyday anxieties and stressors are warranted, low to moderate levels of anxiety have been found to promote academic, social, and sports performance (Bradley, 2000). Thus, effective management of anxiety can lead to a greater sense of self-efficacy and empowerment, as well as enhanced positive peer affiliation (Bradley, 2000; Suveg & Zeman, 2004).

Group Skill Sequence 22: Dealing With Anxiety

1. *Stop* and *see* how your body feels (tense, jittery, upset stomach).

2. *Think* about what would make you feel better.

   a) *Take* three slow, deep breaths.

   b) *Talk* with a parent or teacher.

   c) *Relax* by squeezing and releasing parts of your body (hands or fists, feet, stomach, jaw).

3. *Do* it! *Make* the best choice or *do* all three!

4. *See* if you feel better (less anxious).

Social Contexts in Which to Role Play (Practice) the Skill Sequence

- Your friend wants you to go to the haunted house on Halloween, but you are afraid.

- Your older brother is making you go on a big roller coaster ride.

- You are attending a new school and are nervous about meeting new teachers and classmates.

23 DEALING WITH YOUR ANGRY FEELINGS

Anger is a natural and common feeling expressed by children and adults of all ages. Managing anger or disappointment is an essential skill for social development and social affiliation. Children can use several behavioral strategies, such as distracting themselves with another stimulus or activity to reduce feeling angry. Also, children can use cognitive strategies, such as reevaluating (reframing) situations before acting on their emotions (Miers, Reiffe, Terwogt, Cowan, & Linden, 2007).

Group Skill Sequence 23: Dealing With Your Angry Feelings

THE TURTLE

1. *Stop* and *think,* what is making me mad?

2. *Do* the Turtle!!!

   a) *Hold* legs firmly against your chest.

   b) *Take* three slow, deep breaths (blow a lot of air out of your mouth).

   c) Slowly *release* your legs from your chest.

3. *Repeat* steps 2a–2c.

4. *Reward yourself*—Do a fun activity or something relaxing.

THE PILLOW SQUEEZE

1. *Stop* and *think* about how you are feeling.

2. *Take* three slow, deep breaths.

3. *Squeeze* the pillow.

4. *Reward yourself*—Do a fun activity or something relaxing.

OTHER STRATEGIES TO DISCUSS

1. *Do* something relaxing; for example, read a book, color a picture, play with a pet, hold a stuffed animal.

2. *Ask* to talk with someone who is not busy. (Important—wait if your teacher is helping another student or your mom is talking on the telephone.)

3. *Take* a time out ("break").

4. *Play* a game by yourself, ride a bike, or take a walk.

Social Contexts in Which to Role Play (Practice) the Skill Sequence

- Your friend pushes you off your bike.

- Your dad tells you that you are not allowed to go your friend's house until you clean up your toys or room.

- Your best friend at school calls you a bad name.

24 DEALING WITH ANOTHER PERSON'S ANGRY FEELINGS

EVIDENCE
FOR SKILL
Coping with another person's anger is related to how well one regulates his or her emotions, cognitions, and behavioral responses to the event (Miers, Rieffe, Terwogt, Cowan, & Linden, 2007). Emotion regulation includes both cognitive and behavioral coping strategies (Miers et al., 2007). Examples of these strategies include a child's ability to express his or her feelings in response to another's anger, deflect the anger toward another stimulus or activity, or seek social support from friends, family, or other adults (Linden et al., 2003).

Group Skill Sequence 24: Dealing With Another Person's Angry Feelings

1. *Ask* the person if she feels like talking about what is making her angry.

2. *Think* about what to do (pick one):

   a) *Be* a good listener.

   b) *Ask* if you can help.

   c) *Come* back later if she wants some space.

3. *Do it!* Pick the best action.

Social Contexts in Which to Role Play (Practice) the Skill Sequence

- Your friend is angry with you because you did not want to play with him.

- Your mom is upset because she told you to clean up your toys, but you forgot.

- Your classmate is angry because he got a bad grade on the homework assignment.

25 Dealing With Rejection

EVIDENCE
FOR SKILL Teachers and parents who encourage and involve children in problem solving can improve children's abilities to navigate difficult social situations such as peer rejection and bullying (Kochenderfer-Ladd & Pelletier, 2008). When children inform adults about bullying incidents, it can prevent further incidents, reduce emotional distress, and strengthen their social support systems and coping skills (Hunter, Boyle, & Warden, 2004).

Group Skill Sequence 25: Dealing With Rejection

1. *Look* for someone you want to play with.

2. *Ask* that person, "Do you want to play with me?"

3. If the person says, "no," *decide* what you will do:

   a) *Walk* away.

   b) *Tell* yourself or think to yourself, "Maybe next time he will play with me."

   c) *Tell* the person, "Maybe some other time."

   d) *Do* something that's fun instead (e.g., color, play ball, ask someone else to play).

4. *Do it!* Make the best decision.

Social Contexts in Which to Role Play (Practice) the Skill Sequence

- You want to join a kickball game, but there are already enough players.

- You ask your dad if he wants to play a game, but he says that he doesn't have time today.

- Children at school are putting a puzzle together, but they tell you there is no more room at the table.

26 DEALING WITH BEING LEFT OUT

EVIDENCE
FOR SKILL

Dealing with being left out (peer rejection) challenges children to manage their emotions, thoughts (cognitions), and behaviors in the home and school (Reijntjes, Stegge, & Terwogt, 2006). Successfully managing negative emotions associated with peer rejection is related to psychological adjustment and wellness (Reijntjes et al., 2006).

Group Skill Sequence 26: Dealing With Being Left Out

1. *Think* about why you feel left out.

2. *Decide* what you want to do about it:

    a) *Decide* if you want to join in.

    b) *Decide* what to say.

    c) *Choose* a good time.

    d) *Say* it in a friendly way.

3. If you don't join in, *look* for someone else to play with.

4. *Think* of another game you can play.

Social Contexts in Which to Role Play (Practice) the Skill Sequence

- Your friend tells you that there isn't enough room in her car for you to go with her to the pool.

- Your big sister tells you that you are too young to go to the mall with her and her friends.

- A classmate asks two friends to sit with him at lunch, but you wanted to sit with him, too.

27 DEALING WITH BOREDOM

EVIDENCE
FOR SKILL

Feeling bored is a common experience for most school-age children and can be attributed to many factors. For example, children may verbalize that they are bored when they feel lonely, discouraged, confused, overwhelmed, or ambivalent about an activity or disappointed by the outcome of play activities. Dealing with these common feelings and situations is critically important to promote self-regulation and independence (Sharp, Caldwell, Graham, & Ridenour, 2006).

Group Skill Sequence 27: Dealing With Boredom

1. *Ask* yourself, "Am I bored?" or "Do I have nothing to do?"

2. If the answer is yes, *make* a list of activities you like to do.

3. *Pick* the activity you want to do.

4. *Do it!*

5. *Give* yourself a pat on the back for keeping busy.

Social Contexts in Which to Role Play (Practice) the Skill Sequence

- Your best friend went away for the weekend, and you have no one to play with.

- You were going to fly a kite with your dad, but it's raining and now you are stuck inside.

- Recess is indoors because it is snowing, and you don't have anything to do.

28 SETTING GOALS AND OBTAINING THEM

EVIDENCE
FOR SKILL

Children with high self-efficacy (i.e., those who believe in themselves and their abilities) persist at tasks longer and work harder to achieve their goals (Szente, 2007). When children are successful at setting and achieving their initial goals, they are motivated to set higher goals (Pintrich & Schunk, 2002) and are committed to following through with them (Bandura, 1993).

Group Skill Sequence 28: Setting Goals and Obtaining Them

1. *Think* about things you want to accomplish, such as

   a) Getting good grades.

   b) Trying out for the baseball team.

2. *Make* a list of your goals.

3. *Talk* to someone about your goals (teacher, friend, or parent).

4. *Ask* for advice on how to reach your goals.

5. *Write* down ways you can reach your goals.

6. *Try* your best to accomplish your goals.

   a) *Practice!*

   b) *Ask* others to help you reach your goals.

   c) *Think* of other things you can do to reach your goal.

7. *Give* yourself a pat on the back for reaching your goal.

Social Contexts in Which to Role Play (Practice) the Skill Sequence

- You and a friend want to build an airplane together.

- You and your mom want to win a prize for selling the most Girl Scout cookies this year in your troop.

- You want to earn an *A* in English this year.

29 SOLVING EVERYDAY PROBLEMS

Being successful at problem solving involves integrating various cognitive abilities that are critical for academic achievement and social success. For example, cognitive problem solving skills may include sustained attention, memory, object manipulation, and visual–motor processes (e.g., Colombo & Cheatham, 2006; Karpov, 2003). Children who approach learning by trying out potential solutions and persist until the problem is solved achieve later academic and social success (Greenwood, Walker, Carta, & Higgins, 2006).

Group Skill Sequence 29: Solving Everyday Problems

1. *Think* about what the problem is.

2. *Think* about the different ways you can deal with the problem.

3. *Make* the best choice.

4. *Think* about what happened after you acted.

   a) Did the problem get solved?

   b) If not, *try* another plan.

Social Contexts in Which to Role Play (Practice) the Skill Sequence

- You know your friend stole candy from the grocery store, but you are not sure what to do.

- Your dad let you borrow his baseball glove, but you lost it at the park.

- You left your math book at school and now you need it to complete your homework assignment.

30 SOLVING A PROBLEM AS A GROUP

EVIDENCE
FOR SKILL
Group problem solving is a collaborative interaction in which children work together to achieve a mutually acceptable goal (Garton & Pratt, 2001). During these interactions, children must work efficiently to define the task, share the responsibility, and share knowledge to accomplish their goal (Garton & Pratt, 2001). Communication and conscious awareness of other child participants are integral components of group problem solving and are necessary for success (Garton & Pratt, 2001).

Group Skill Sequence 30: Solving a Problem as a Group

1. *Listen* to what each group member has to say.

2. *Wait* until it is your turn to talk and *say* what you think.

3. *Decide* as a group what the problem is.

4. *Decide* as a group what the possible solutions could be.

5. *Decide* as a group what the best choice would be.

6. As a group, *make* the best choice!

Social Contexts in Which to Role Play (Practice) the Skill Sequence

- You and a group of friends want to go to the movies, but you can't decide which movie to see.

- You and your family want to choose a place to go for vacation this summer, but everyone wants to go to a different place.

- During recess, a group of kids are trying to choose which sport would be the most fun to play.

31 FOLLOWING DIRECTIONS

The ability to follow verbal or written directions is a fundamental skill needed for social, behavioral, and academic success (Valeski & Stipek, 2001). Directions or commands require good auditory, working memory, organization, and motor planning skills (Reddy, Weissman, & Hale, in press). This skill is essential for school, sports, work, and peer and family interactions.

Group Skill Sequence 31: Following Directions

1. *Look* at the person who is asking you to follow directions.

2. *Stop* what you are doing and *listen* to what was said.

3. *Say* the directions out loud or to yourself.

4. *Do* it! Follow what was asked of you.

Social Contexts in Which to Role Play (Practice) the Skill Sequence

- You are playing a board game with a friend, and she is reading the directions on how to play out loud.

- Your parents are telling you how to set the table for dinner.

- You are working on a drawing, and your teacher tells the class to start reading a book.

32 PAYING ATTENTION

EVIDENCE FOR SKILL Children's ability to focus and sustain attention is associated with social competence and prosocial behavior (Wilson, 2003). Attention skills (divided and sustained attention) can improve the likelihood of current and future success in school (Piker & Rex, 2008; Reddy & Hale, 2007) and contribute to lower levels of negative mood (Wilson, 2003).

Group Skill Sequence 32: Paying Attention

1. *Look* at the person who is talking.

2. *Listen* to what the person is saying to you.

3. *Think* about what he or she is saying or asking you to do.

4. *Write*, if you can, what is being said to help you remember the important parts.

5. *Do it!*

   a) If he or she tells you to do something.

   b) If he or she does not tell you to do something, remember the important parts of what he or she said.

Social Contexts in Which to Role Play (Practice) the Skill Sequence

- Your friend is telling you how to get to the park.

- Your mother is telling you the steps to complete a math problem you are working on.

- Your teacher is telling your class about a field trip to the zoo in 2 weeks.

33 STAYING ON TASK

Staying on task requires children to sustain effort and maintain self-control (Lauth, Heubeck, & Mackowiak, 2006). Staying on task strengthens academic skills, increases learning opportunities, and reduces possible conflicts with teachers or peers (Gest & Gest, 2005). The amount of time-on-task is an important contributor to academic success because learning is heavily dependent on the amount of time spent on a task (Bloom, 1974; Carroll, 1963).

Group Skill Sequence 33: Staying on Task

1. *Clear* your desk of things that are distracting (other homework, games, toys, and food).

2. *Work* in a quiet area if you can.

3. *Ask* your teacher or parent for help if you are having trouble.

4. *Do it!* Work on one topic and take breaks.

Social Contexts in Which to Role Play (Practice) the Skill Sequence

- A friend asks you to come over to help her with her science project.

- Your mom asks you to look for pictures of trees in magazines to help her make a collage.

- Your science class takes a trip to the library and you are asked to look up books on iguanas.

34 WORKING INDEPENDENTLY

Being self-reliant strengthens children's self-regulation skills, frustration management, and social competence (National Institute of Child Health and Human Development Early Child Care Research Network, 2008a). Working independently also illustrates children's effective use of time at school and home. When children work independently, they must also rely on their own ability to find solutions to problems, focus attention, and not give up (National Institute of Child Health and Human Development Early Child Care Research Network, 2008a).

Group Skill Sequence 34: Working Independently

1. *Listen* to or *read* directions.

2. *Follow* the instructions.

3. If a friend asks you for help, *tell* him or her politely that you need to work on the assignment by yourself and can talk with him or her later.

4. *Ask* your teacher or parent questions if you do not understand the assignment.

5. *Work* quietly on your assignment.

Social Contexts in Which to Role Play (Practice) the Skill Sequence

- You and a friend are working on different homework assignments before you go to the playground.

- Your mom tells you that it is time to start your homework in your room.

- Your art teacher wants students to paint a picture of their family.

35 COOPERATION

Cooperating with others is a skill that requires children to coordinate their behaviors with peers and work in partnerships with others to achieve a common goal. Cooperation is an important skill because it requires children to take other children's views into account and adjust their views to achieve a shared goal (Brownell, Ramani, & Zerwas, 2006).

Group Skill Sequence 35: Cooperation

1. *Listen* to what another person (or others) on your team say.

2. *Think* about what you want to say.

3. *Decide* what you want to say.

4. *Tell* them if you agree with what they said. "Good idea, John, that could really work."

5. If you don't agree with them, say, "That is a good idea, but maybe we could do it this way."

6. *Listen* to what the rest of the team says.

7. *Work* together to come up with group ideas. "Let's try to all work on John's idea to build the wheels first and then work on the wings."

8. *Do it!* Work as a team to complete the task.

Social Contexts in Which to Role Play (Practice) the Skill Sequence

- Your friend wants to play baseball, but first the two of you have to finish your homework together.

- Your mom wants you and your brother to work together to clean up the house.

- Your teacher has given the class an assignment to build a space ship as a group.

36 TAKING TURNS

EVIDENCE
FOR SKILL
Effective turn-taking can help the group obtain its goals and can enhance children's learning (Sommerville & Hammond, 2007). Collaborative exchanges (e.g., taking turns) have been shown to enhance children's performance on memory and planning tasks. Additionally, children who work together on a group project are more successful at completing a task than working independently (Sommerville & Hammond, 2007).

Group Skill Sequence 36: Taking Turns

1. *Look* around to see when it is your turn to _____.

2. *Think* about what you are going to say or do.

3. *Wait* to make sure you can start talking or do what the previous person was doing.

4. *Finish* what you are saying and then let the next person go, or *finish* what you are doing so that the next person can participate.

Social Contexts in Which to Role Play (Practice) the Skill Sequence

- Your friends are talking about what they did over the weekend, and you want to tell them what you did.

- You are using the family computer, and your brother wants to use it.

- Your teacher would like children in the classroom to talk about their favorite ice cream, activity, or vacation.

37 BEING A GOOD SPORT

EVIDENCE
FOR SKILL
When children engage in competitions, the outcome produces "winners" and "losers." Depending on the outcome, children may feel depressed, anxious, or good about themselves (Salvador, 2005). Children may also display different coping strategies and styles in response to winning, losing, playing well, and/or playing poorly (Salvador, 2005).

Group Skill Sequence 37: Being a Good Sport

1. *Think* about how well you and the other person played the game.

2. *Think* of nice things you can tell the other person:

   a) "Good game!"

   b) "You did a great job!"

   c) Give them a high five.

3. *Do it!* Tell the person something nice.

Social Contexts in Which to Role Play (Practice) the Skill Sequence

- Shake a friend's hand after losing a game.

- You lose to your brother in a game of soccer.

- You win a prize in the school spelling bee.

38 BEING PATIENT

EVIDENCE
FOR SKILL
Demonstrating patience requires emotion and behavior self-regulation, which help children attain goals and manage their emotions and behavior (e.g., Denham, 1998; Kopp, 1982; Saarni, 1999; Shoda, Mischel, & Peake, 1990). For example, children instructed to wait their turn need to have prosocial motivation and inhibitory control in order to comply with such a request (Dennis, 2006).

Group Skill Sequence 38: Being Patient

1. *Decide* whether you need to wait.

2. *Keep* your hands and feet quiet.

3. *Wait* until the person is finished with what he or she is doing or saying.

4. *Do* something else while you are waiting:

    a) *Draw* a picture.

    b) *Talk* with a friend.

    c) *Read* a book.

Social Contexts in Which to Role Play (Practice) the Skill Sequence

- Your friend is helping her little brother get dressed, but you want to go to the park now!

- You want to go to the movies, but your mom says you have to wait until she finishes reading the newspaper.

- Your teacher tells the class everyone will have to wait 5 minutes before they are allowed to go to recess.

39 BEING ASSERTIVE

EVIDENCE
FOR SKILL Children who use effective assertive strategies are more likely to successfully resolve conflicts with others (Duman & Margolin, 2007). Assertive skills have been associated with secure attachments and advanced developmental abilities such as social negotiation skills with parents and other adults (Duman & Margolin, 2007).

Group Skill Sequence 39: Being Assertive

1. *Decide* if something is bothering you (e.g., someone cuts in front of you in line).

2. *Think* about how to tell the person how you feel.

3. *Share* your feelings with the person. "Excuse me, I don't like it when you cut in front of me in line."

4. *Suggest* to the person another (alternate) behavior that is acceptable. "Please wait behind me until it is your turn."

Social Contexts in Which to Role Play (Practice) the Skill Sequence

- Your friend takes a ball that you were playing with.

- Your sister or brother pushes you.

- A child in your class begins coloring on your paper.

40 SAYING *NO*

Learning to say *no* can be useful when children face social situations such as adult requests, peer conflict, and bullying. Teachers advocate that children use assertive coping techniques to effectively deal with peer issues, including peer victimization (Kochenderfer-Ladd & Pelletier, 2008). Children may face adult or peer situations in which they must rely on independent problem solving to make decisions in response to tough situations (Kochenderfer-Ladd & Pelletier, 2008).

Group Skill Sequence 40: Saying No

1. *Ask* yourself if you want to do what is being asked.

2. *Decide* why you don't want to do it.

3. *Say:* "No, I'm sorry, I can't do that."

4. *Tell* them why you said no.

Social Contexts in Which to Role Play (Practice) the Skill Sequence

- A friend pressures you to take someone's baseball bat from the park.

- Your brother encourages you to draw a picture on the outside of the house.

- A classmate asks if he can copy your science homework.

41 ACCEPTING *No*

EVIDENCE FOR SKILL

Children often face situations in which they are told *no* by adults or peers in their lives. For children to accept or deal with being told *no*, they must be able to manage their disappointment and redirect their emotional and behavioral responses (Bridges & Grolnick, 1995; Thompson, 1994). As children age, they come to understand rules for expressing their emotions and behavior and begin to regulate their positive and negative emotions in accordance with societal and cultural norms (Cole, 1986; Saarni, 1984).

Group Skill Sequence 41: Accepting No

1. *Think* about why you were told *no*.

2. *Decide* what you want to do:

   a) *Do* another activity.

   b) *Tell* them how that made you feel in a nice way.

   c) If you can't tell them, *write* about what you want to say.

3. *Do it!* Pick the best option.

Social Contexts in Which to Role Play (Practice) the Skill Sequence

- Your friend said that you aren't allowed to come over on a school night.

- Your mom tells you that you aren't allowed to go to the park after school.

- The teacher tells you that you aren't allowed to go to recess today.

42 ASKING FOR HELP

Asking for help is an important coping strategy that children use when they are seeking information (advice) or emotional support (comfort; Compas, Connor-Smith, Saltzman, Thomsen, & Wadsworth, 2001; Skinner, Edge, Altman, & Sherwood, 2003). When children ask for help, they are resolving an immediate problem, learning strategies to deal with future problems, and reducing anxiety, anger, or fear (Newman, 2008). Children also develop their self-competence, self-efficacy, and emotional regulation skills in help-seeking situations (Newman, 2008).

Group Skill Sequence 42: Asking for Help

1. *Decide* what the problem is and if you need help.

2. *Decide* whom to ask (parent, teacher, or friend).

3. *Choose* what to say. "I need help figuring out this math problem."

4. *Wait* until you get the other person's attention and say, "Excuse me."

5. *Tell* the person what you need in a nice way.

Social Contexts in Which to Role Play (Practice) the Skill Sequence

- Your friend is getting picked on at school during lunch, and you want a teacher to come stop it.

- You want to clean your room, but you need your mom's help.

- You received a bad grade on your spelling test and need help to do better next time.

43 HELPING OTHERS

Helping others is a powerful protective factor (strength) related to academic and social success in children (Ryan & Patrick, 2001). Engaging in prosocial interactions, such as helping others, fosters future prosocial acts and opportunities for positive social engagement (Eisenberg & Fabes, 1998).

Group Skill Sequence 43: Helping Others

1. *Decide* what the problem is.

2. *Decide* if someone needs your help.

3. *Ask* your friend if you can help her. Say, "Can I help you?"

4. If your friend says yes, help her out!

Social Contexts in Which to Role Play (Practice) the Skill Sequence

- A classmate can't reach his lunchbox, but you can.

- Your sister is having difficulties playing a new video game.

- Your classmate looks as though he is having trouble carrying all his books.

III

GROUP PLAY INTERVENTIONS

As discussed in Part II, group play skill sequences are important *prerequisite* skills for successfully participating in group play interventions. Prior to selecting and implementing group play interventions, the reader is encouraged to read the chapters in Section 1. These chapters provide a thorough review of the "nuts and bolts" of creating and implementing effective group play training.

Part III includes 67 group play interventions conceptualized into eight teaching modules. The eight teaching modules are (1) making and maintaining friends; (2) identifying emotions and appropriately expressing emotions; (3) following directions and impulse control; (4) sharing, joining a group, and group cooperation; (5) anger management; (6) anxiety and stress management; (7) developing appropriate personal space; and (8) effective planning and time management. Each group play intervention includes a description of the targeted domain area, skills taught, required materials and resources, and detailed step-by-step instructions on the implementation and group facilitation process.

Teaching Module 1
Making and Maintaining Friends

1 GROUP PLAY INTERVENTION:
Swedish Meetball

OVERVIEW
Swedish Meetball allows children to have fun learning each other's names and interests. It also provides opportunities to share information about themselves.

GROUP PLAY INTERVENTION SKILLS TAUGHT
Primary: Introducing Self to Others, Listening to Others
Secondary: Following Directions, Self-Control

SKILL DIFFICULTY
Beginner

PREREQUISITE SKILLS
Children need to be able to introduce themselves to others, follow directions, and maintain self-control.

SUGGESTED GROUP SKILL SEQUENCES TO PRACTICE BEFORE GROUP PLAY INTERVENTION
No. 3. Introducing Self to Others
No. 36. Taking Turns
No. 16. Self-Control
No. 7. Sharing About Oneself

REQUIRED MATERIALS
Soft playground ball (approximately 23 inches in circumference).

ROOM SETUP
Children should have ample space to sit in a large circle on the floor.

GAME SYNOPSIS
Swedish Meetball involves children rolling the ball to one another and sharing information about themselves.

STEPS FOR IMPLEMENTING *SWEDISH MEETBALL*

1. Instruct children to sit in a circle.
2. Tell children that they need to roll the ball to other children in the circle. If a child bounces or throws the ball, the ball should be returned to him or her and he or she should be asked to redo the turn.
3. Give the first child the ball, tell him or her to state her or his name, and then roll the ball to another child in the circle.
4. The recipient of the ball should state his or her name and proceed to roll the ball to another child.
5. Repeat step 4 until all of the children have had an opportunity to have a turn.
6. Additional rounds can involve remembering others' names or stating interests.
7. Group process: Tell the children that the game is now over. Have them sit in their chairs or on the floor facing the front of the room and tell them it is time to discuss the game.

GROUP PROCESS QUESTIONS

1. Ask the children what they needed to do to play the game. Emphasize the importance of sharing information about themselves and using appropriate eye contact and tone of voice. Also emphasize the importance of listening to others and controlling their bodies.
2. Ask the children what they needed to do when they received the ball.
3. Ask the children how they felt introducing themselves at different points in the game (i.e., beginning, middle, and end).

2 GROUP PLAY INTERVENTION:
Parrot

OVERVIEW

Parrot is an icebreaker game that allows children to introduce themselves and to learn others' names.

GROUP PLAY INTERVENTION SKILLS TAUGHT

Primary: Introductions, Learning Others' Names
Secondary: Paying Attention, Listening to Others, Taking Turns

SKILL DIFFICULTY

Beginner

PREREQUISITE SKILLS

Children need to be able to listen to others, remember others' names, and speak clearly.

SUGGESTED GROUP SKILL SEQUENCES TO PRACTICE BEFORE GROUP PLAY INTERVENTION

No. 36. Taking Turns
No. 10. Being an Active Listener
No. 4. Introducing Others
No. 3. Introducing Self to Others

REQUIRED MATERIALS

None (chairs are optional).

ROOM SETUP

Children should sit in a circle. An empty area of a room with or without chairs for each group member to sit on can be utilized.

GAME SYNOPSIS

The group sits in a circle on the floor or in chairs. Each child goes around the room, states her or his name, and repeats the names of the children preceding her or him. This allows children to learn others' names. The difficulty of the game can be adjusted by increasing or decreasing the maximum number of names that the children need to remember.

    The leading therapist should ask children what a parrot does; eventually, the therapist answers that a parrot repeats the last few words a person says. Each child will then say his or her name as well as the names of the two previous people in the circle. For example, the first person would say, "My name is John," the second person would say, "My name is Jane, and this is John," and the third person would say, "My name is Scott, and this is Jane, and this is John." The fourth person would say his or her name in addition to the names of the *two* preceding people. This would continue around the circle twice so that everyone will say three names. The order could also be reversed after two times around the circle.

STEPS FOR IMPLEMENTING PARROT

1. Instruct children to sit in a circle and tell them they are going to play a game called *Parrot*. *Parrot* should be introduced to the children in a positive and playful manner. Tell children that they are about to play a special game in which they will be learning each other's names by acting like parrots.
2. Tell children that when they are the parrot, they are to introduce themselves and then act like a parrot by repeating the names of (all or a specified number of) people who came before them. For example, the first person would say, "My name is John," the second person would say, "My name is Jane, and this is

John," and the third person would say, "My name is Scott, this is Jane, and this is John." The fourth person would say his or her name as well as the names of the *two* preceding people.

3. The group facilitators should first introduce themselves and provide a demonstration of the game.
4. The group leader should call on the first child in the circle. That child should have an opportunity to introduce him- or herself and repeat the name of the preceding group facilitator.
5. The next child in the circle should be called on, and this process repeated until all children have had a turn and learned each other's names.
6. Group process: Tell the children that the game is now over. Have them sit in their chairs or on the floor facing the front of the room and tell them it is time to discuss the game.

GROUP PROCESS QUESTIONS

1. Ask the children what they needed to do to play the game. Emphasize the importance of introductions, listening, and remembering.
2. Ask the children what strategies they used to remember each other's names.
3. Ask the children how they felt when they were asked to recall each other's names.

3

GROUP PLAY INTERVENTION:
Name Planes

OVERVIEW

Name Planes allows children to have fun while learning each other's names and introducing themselves to others.

GROUP PLAY INTERVENTION SKILLS TAUGHT

Primary: Meeting Others, Introducing Self to Others
Secondary: Following Directions, Self-Control, Problem Solving, Cooperation

SKILL DIFFICULTY

Beginner

PREREQUISITE SKILLS

Children need to be able to introduce themselves to others. They must be able to follow simple directions and keep their bodies in control (maintain self-control).

SUGGESTED GROUP SKILL SEQUENCES TO PRACTICE BEFORE GROUP PLAY INTERVENTION

No. 16. Self-Control
No. 35. Cooperation
No. 3. Introducing Self to Others
No. 27. Dealing With Boredom

REQUIRED MATERIALS

8½ × 11 inch sheets of paper, writing instruments (crayons, markers, pens or pencils).

ROOM SETUP

Name Planes is an active game in which children need to move freely throughout the room. Therefore, the area in which the children are playing the game should be free from furniture or other objects that might become obstacles or cause injury.

GAME SYNOPSIS

Name Planes is an interactive game that includes two *launch groups*. One group of children flies their paper airplanes (containing their names on them) around the room. Each child in the second group retrieves a plane, identifies the name on the plane, and then attempts to locate the person whose name is on the plane. After the sender is located, both children formally introduce themselves to one another.

STEPS FOR IMPLEMENTING *NAME PLANES*

1. Instruct children to sit in a circle and give them a sheet of paper and a writing instrument.
2. Tell children to write their names on the sheet of paper (younger children and/or children with writing difficulties may need group facilitators to assist).
3. Teach children how to fold up the sheet of paper and make it into a paper airplane (see example paper plane).
4. Before the game starts, instruct children that during the game they need to
   a) Keep their arms in control—not hit or push others.
   b) Keep their feet in control—walk, not run, and stand and avoid bumping into objects and other group members.
   c) Pay attention to which *launch group* they are assigned to.
   d) Make sure that airplanes are thrown in the air into an empty area of the room. Children should avoid hitting others with their airplanes.

5. To start the game, divide children into two groups. Instruct the children to stand up with their airplanes in a launching position.
6. One of the group leaders counts down from five to one and then says, "Fly your airplanes (Group 1 or 2)." The children in the group that was called should launch their airplanes.
7. Once the planes have landed, instruct the children in the other group to retrieve one of the airplanes after they have all landed. The receivers should unfold the airplane they have retrieved and read the name of the sender on the inside of the airplane (younger children or children with reading difficulties may need assistance with reading the names).
8. Then tell the receivers to locate the sender whose name appears on the airplane. If they do not know what the sender looks like, they should ask others what their names are until they identify the sender. If they happen to get their own airplane or an airplane of someone that they already had, they should introduce themselves to the person next to them and trade airplanes with them.
9. Once the sender is located, the receiver and sender should introduce themselves to one another, and the receiver should return the airplane to the sender. Children can introduce themselves to each other simultaneously or one at a time (based on the group facilitators' preference and children's need for assistance/practice observing each other).
10. Continue to repeat Steps 6 through 9, but alternate between groups of launchers and receivers, until all of the children have had a chance to introduce themselves to one another. Each child should be provided with an opportunity to introduce him- or herself to everyone else in the group at least once.
11. *Name Planes* should be collected and stored (if playing *Conversation Planes*).
12. Group process: Tell the children that the game is now over. Have them sit in their chairs or on the floor facing the front of the room and tell them it is time to discuss the game.

GROUP PROCESS QUESTIONS

1. Ask the children what they needed to do to play the game. Emphasize the importance of identifying others and introducing yourself.
2. Ask the children what they needed to do to find the sender of the airplane.
3. Ask the children how they introduced themselves to the sender.
4. Ask the children how they felt introducing themselves at different points in the game (i.e., beginning, middle, and end).

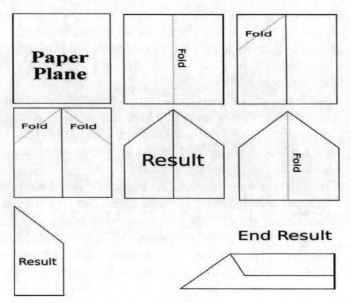

Example Paper Airplane

4 | GROUP PLAY INTERVENTION: *Conversation Planes (Continuation of Name Planes)*

OVERVIEW

Conversation Planes provides the opportunity for children to build on their introduction skills and target the necessary skills for initiating a conversation.

GROUP PLAY INTERVENTION SKILLS TAUGHT

Primary: Initiating Conversations With Others
Secondary: Following Directions, Self-Control

SKILL DIFFICULTY

Beginner–Intermediate

PREREQUISITE SKILLS

Children should have some experience with introducing themselves to others and beginning a conversation with others. They must be able to follow simple directions (e.g., one- to two-step directions) and keep their bodies in control.

SUGGESTED GROUP SKILL SEQUENCES TO PRACTICE BEFORE GROUP PLAY INTERVENTION

No. 3. Introducing Self to Others
No. 1. Communicating With Others
No. 2. Using Nice Talk
No. 5. Joining in a Conversation

REQUIRED MATERIALS

8½ × 11 inch sheets of paper (if applicable, *Name Planes* can be reused), writing instruments (crayons, markers, pens, or pencils).

ROOM SETUP

Conversation Planes is an active game in which children need to move freely throughout the room. Therefore, the area in which the children are playing the game should be free from furniture or other objects that might become obstacles or cause injury.

GAME SYNOPSIS

Conversation Planes is an interactive game that includes two *launch groups*. One group of children flies their paper airplanes (containing their names [from *Name Planes*] along with two to three written items about themselves) around the room. The other group retrieves the airplanes, locates the sender, greets the person, and then uses the interests written on the airplane to begin a conversation. At the end of the conversation, they return the airplane to the sender.

STEPS FOR IMPLEMENTING CONVERSATION PLANES

1. Instruct children to sit in a circle and give them either a blank sheet of paper or their paper airplane from *Name Planes* (if applicable) and a writing instrument.
2. Tell children to write two to three items about themselves under their name on a sheet of paper (younger children or children with writing difficulties may need group facilitators to assist). Group facilitators or children can choose item categories (e.g., favorite foods, television shows, sports).
3. Remind or teach children (if applicable) how to fold the sheet of paper to make it into a paper airplane.
4. Before the game starts, instruct children that during the game they need to
   a) Keep their arms in control—not hit or push others.
   b) Keep their feet in control—walk, not run, and stand and avoid bumping into objects and other group members.

c)   Pay attention to which *launch group* they are assigned.

d)   Make sure that airplanes are thrown into the air in an empty area of the room. Efforts should be made to avoid hitting others with their airplane.

5.   To start the game, divide children into two groups. Instruct children to stand up with their airplanes in a launching position.

6.   One group leader counts down from five to one and then says, "Fly your airplanes group (1 or 2)." Children in that group should then launch their airplanes.

7.   Once the planes have landed, instruct children in the other group to retrieve one of the airplanes after they have all landed. The receivers should unfold the airplane they have retrieved and read the name of the sender and the items below the name (younger children or children with reading difficulties may need assistance with reading the names).

8.   The receivers should then attempt to locate the sender whose name appears on the airplane. (The children should already be familiar with one another if *Name Planes* was played previously.) However, if they do not know or do not remember what the sender looks like, they should ask others what their names are until they identify the sender. If they happen to get their own airplane or an airplane of someone that they already had, they should trade airplanes with the person next to them.

9.   Once the sender is located, the receiver should begin a conversation with the sender about one or more of the items listed on the airplane. At the end of the conversation, the receiver should return the airplane to the sender. Children can begin conversations with each other simultaneously or one at a time (based on the group facilitators' preference and children's need for assistance/practice observing each other).

10.   Continue to repeat Steps 6 through 9, but alternate between groups of launchers and receivers until all children have had a chance to start a conversation with each another.

11.   Group process: Tell the children that the game is now over. Have them sit in their chairs or on the floor facing the front of the room and tell them it is time to discuss the game.

GROUP PROCESS QUESTIONS

1.   Ask the children what they needed to do to play the game. Emphasize the importance of beginning a conversation.

2.   Ask the children what they needed to do to greet the other person.

3.   Ask the children what they had to do to figure out how to begin a conversation.

4.   Ask the children how they felt about initiating a conversation at different points in the game (beginning, middle, and end).

5.   Ask the children how they felt when they were approached by someone.

6.   Ask the children how they felt when the person began a conversation with them at different points in the game (i.e., beginning, middle, and end).

5 GROUP PLAY INTERVENTION: *About Me Telephone*

OVERVIEW

About Me Telephone teaches children how to communicate effectively with others while allowing them to learn about each other. One child sends a message around the room from child to child. The goal is to maintain the integrity of the sender's message.

GROUP PLAY INTERVENTION SKILLS TAUGHT

Primary: Communication, Introductions
Secondary: Self-Control, Following Directions, Listening, Memory

SKILL DIFFICULTY

Beginner–Intermediate

PREREQUISITE SKILLS

Children should be able to sit quietly, whisper, follow simple directions, and share information about themselves.

SUGGESTED GROUP SKILL SEQUENCES TO PRACTICE BEFORE GROUP PLAY INTERVENTION

No. 36. Taking Turns
No. 10. Being an Active Listener
No. 32. Paying Attention
No. 2. Using Nice Talk
No. 7. Sharing About Oneself

REQUIRED MATERIALS

None (chairs are optional).

ROOM SETUP

Children should be sitting in a circle.

GAME SYNOPSIS

About Me Telephone is an adaptation of the standard telephone game and involves children whispering messages about themselves (e.g., "I am Pete and I love to play video games," or "My favorite game system is PSP and my favorite video game is *Space Invaders Extreme*") to other children around a circle. Message receivers repeat the message to the next person in the circle until all children have received the message. The last child in the circle to receive the message (i.e., child seated next to the sender) should repeat the message out loud. The sender should verify whether the message is accurate and correct the person if it is not. The next child in the group should provide the next message about her- or himself, and the game should continue until everyone has gotten an opportunity to send a message. For more advanced children, the last person to receive each message should appropriately respond to the content of the sender's message (e.g., "I also like PSP, but my favorite game is *Secret Agent Clank*").

STEPS FOR IMPLEMENTING *ABOUT ME TELEPHONE*

1. Instruct children to sit in a circle. Introduce *About Me Telephone* to the children in a positive and playful manner. Tell children that they are about to play a special game in which they will act as a human telephone, and that they will have an opportunity to send, pass, and receive messages.
2. Before the game starts, instruct children that during the game they need to:

a) Remain quiet while the message is being sent.

b) Listen carefully to the person telling the message.

c) State the message clearly in the receiver's ear.

3. Instruct the sender to come up with a message about him- or herself that he or she would like to share with the group. (Group facilitators should indicate how long the messages should be. Examples and topics may be provided.)

4. The sender should tell the message to a group leader for approval before sending it to other children.

5. Once the message has been approved, the rules of the game should be reviewed.

6. Have everyone repeat the directions (out loud) before beginning the game.

7. Instruct the first child to send the message to the receiver on his or her left. Facilitators assist the children with carrying the message around the entire circle.

8. Ask the final receiver to state the message out loud to all of the children so that it can be corrected by the sender.

9. Repeat Steps 3 through 8 until all children have had an opportunity to send a message.

10. Group process: Tell the children that the game is now over. Have them sit in their chairs or on the floor facing the front of the room and tell them it is time to discuss the game.

GROUP PROCESS QUESTIONS

1. Ask the children what they needed to do to play the game. Emphasize the importance of sharing information about themselves, listening, and communicating.

2. Ask the children how they felt when they had to generate a message.

3. Ask the children how they felt when their message went around the room.

4. Ask the children how they felt when their message was told back to them.

5. Ask the children how they felt when they had to listen for other children's messages.

6. Ask the children what they had to do to get the message around the room.

7. Ask the children how they felt when they had to say the message out loud to all the children.

6 GROUP PLAY INTERVENTION: *Interest Pictionary*

OVERVIEW

Interest Pictionary involves sharing and learning about the interests of others. Each child draws a picture of an item that other children have designated as their interests. Children attempt to identify what the item is and whose interest it was.

GROUP PLAY INTERVENTION SKILLS TAUGHT

Primary: Sharing About Oneself, Learning About Others, Verbal and Nonverbal Communication
Secondary: Paying Attention, Following Directions, Cooperation, Teamwork

SKILL DIFFICULTY

Beginner–Intermediate

PREREQUISITE SKILLS

Children should be familiar with the other children in the group, share information about themselves, and be able to follow simple rules of turn-taking.

SUGGESTED GROUP SKILL SEQUENCES TO PRACTICE BEFORE GROUP PLAY INTERVENTION

No. 7. Sharing About Oneself
No. 10. Being an Active Listener
No. 36. Taking Turns
No. 35. Cooperation
No. 9. Learning About Others

REQUIRED MATERIALS

Sheets of paper cut in squares or index cards, two containers to hold sheets of paper, writing instruments (crayons, markers, pens or pencils), easel, easel pad, and stopwatch or timer.

ROOM SETUP

An easel and easel pad with writing instruments should be set up in the front of the room. Children should be able to sit on the floor or in chairs facing the easel.

GAME SYNOPSIS

Children are divided into two teams. Children share one of their interests by either writing it down or telling it to a facilitator. All the children's interests are written down and placed into their group's container. One child at a time is called up to the front of the room to be the drawer. This child selects a card out of the opposing team's container and has 60 seconds to draw the item. Children on their team keep guessing out loud until someone gets it right or time runs out. If a child guesses the correct answer, his/her team gets a point. The child who guessed the item correctly can get a bonus point if he or she can correctly identify whose interest it is. If he or she is unable to guess the item or identify the child whose interest it is, a group leader shares this information with the children. A member from the other team should then be called up to be the drawer, and the process is repeated.

STEPS FOR IMPLEMENTING INTEREST PICTIONARY

1. Divide children into two groups.
2. Seat children on the floor or in chairs in their groups, facing the easel in the front of the room.

3. Give children an index card or sheet of paper and tell them to write down or tell a group facilitator one of their interests (e.g., favorite movie, game, or fictional character). Facilitators can provide topics, if necessary. Children should not share their interest with other children in the group. All interests should be written down with the children's name next to the items.

4. A group facilitator should then collect the cards and place them in the corresponding group's container.

5. Before the game starts, instruct children that during the game
   a) The child drawing should not begin until instructed to by a group facilitator.
   b) The child drawing cannot write words.
   c) The child drawing cannot talk or act.
   d) The child drawing should draw as fast as possible.
   e) The drawer's team is the only team that can speak.

6. To start the game, select a child to draw for the first team and have the child go to the easel. A group facilitator should provide the child with the other team's container and tell the child to select a card.

7. Review the instructions to ensure that the drawer knows what to do, each teams knows who is guessing, and what each teams' roles will be.

8. Ensure that the child understands the information on the card and is ready to draw the interest listed.

9. A group facilitator says the sequence, "ready–set–go," letting the child know to begin drawing and for his or her team to start guessing. A 60-second timer is started.

10. If a child on the drawer's team gets it right, ask the child to guess which member on the opposing team the characteristic belongs to.

11. If either or both are correct, the child is congratulated for getting the right answer. If either is wrong, the children are told the correct answers.

12. One point should be awarded for getting the item right and a second point is awarded for identifying the correct person. Scores are recorded and a summary of scores is shared with the children

13. Repeat Steps 6 through 12, alternating between members of the two groups. This should be done until all the children have had a chance to draw. Other rounds can be initiated at Step 3.

14. Group process: Tell the children that the game is now over. Have them sit in their chairs or on the floor facing the front of the room and tell them it is time to discuss the game.

GROUP PROCESS QUESTIONS

1. Ask the children what they needed to do to play the game. Emphasize the importance of sharing information about oneself, figuring out how to communicate nonverbally, and paying attention.

2. Ask the children how they felt when they were drawing.

3. Ask the children how they felt when they were trying to guess.

4. Ask the children how they felt when they were on the team that was not guessing.

7 GROUP PLAY INTERVENTION: *Common Traits in a Hat*

OVERVIEW

Common Traits in a Hat allows children to share information about themselves and identify commonalities among group members.

GROUP PLAY INTERVENTION SKILLS TAUGHT

Primary: Sharing About Oneself, Learning About Others
Secondary: Listening, Paying Attention, Following Directions, Relating to Others

SKILL DIFFICULTY

Beginner–Intermediate

PREREQUISITE SKILLS

Children should be able to generate information about themselves.

SUGGESTED GROUP SKILL SEQUENCES TO PRACTICE BEFORE GROUP PLAY INTERVENTION

No. 7. Sharing About Oneself
No. 9. Learning About Others
No. 32. Paying Attention
No. 1. Communicating With Others

REQUIRED MATERIALS

Sheets of paper cut in squares, writing instruments (crayons, markers, pens or pencils), and hat or container.

ROOM SETUP

Children should be sitting in a manner in which they can see one another. They can sit in chairs or on the floor.

GAME SYNOPSIS

Children share information about their likes and interests by either writing, drawing, or telling facilitators about them. All the items are placed in a hat or container. Items are pulled, one by one, out of the hat or container and read out loud by the group facilitator. Children are asked to raise their hands after they hear an object read aloud that they like or are interested in. This allows children to learn about other children's interests, share their interests with others, and see which children share their interests.

STEPS FOR IMPLEMENTING COMMON TRAITS IN A HAT

1. Seat children in a manner in which they can see each other. Tell children that they are going to play a game called *Common Traits in a Hat*.
2. Provide children with one piece of paper and a writing instrument.
3. Instruct children to write (or draw or tell a group facilitator) something about themselves or something they like on the sheet of paper. Group facilitators can provide a specific topic (e.g., favorite cartoon, favorite food) for the children to write about or leave the topic open-ended.
4. Tell children to fold the paper and drop it in the hat or container.
5. Repeat Steps 3 and 4 for a number of items (determined by the group facilitators).
6. The group facilitator selects an item out of the hat or container, one at a time, and reads it out loud. Children are asked to raise their hands if the item read aloud is something that they like or are interested in.

7. Acknowledge children who raise their hands for the interest that they all share. Then ask children to put their hands down and repeat Step 6 until all items are read.
8. Group process: Tell the children that the game is now over. Have them sit in their chairs or on the floor facing the front of the room and tell them it is time to discuss the game.

GROUP PROCESS QUESTIONS

1. Ask the children what they needed to do to play the game. Emphasize the importance of sharing information about oneself and recognizing that others share their interests.
2. Ask the children how they felt when the items that they liked or related to were called out.
3. Ask the children how they felt when they realized that others shared their likes and interests.

8 GROUP PLAY INTERVENTION: *Compliment Sticker*

OVERVIEW

Compliment Sticker allows children to learn about giving and receiving compliments in a fun, active, and exciting way.

GROUP PLAY INTERVENTION SKILLS TAUGHT

Primary: Giving Compliments, Receiving Compliments
Secondary: Self-Control, Following Directions

SKILL DIFFICULTY

Beginner–Intermediate

PREREQUISITE SKILLS

Children should have a basic understanding of what compliments are and why they are given. They should have the ability to move their bodies in a controlled fashion and be able to follow basic rules.

SUGGESTED GROUP SKILL SEQUENCES TO PRACTICE BEFORE GROUP PLAY INTERVENTION

No. 1. Communicating With Others
No. 11. Giving Compliments
No. 12. Receiving Compliments
No. 2. Using Nice Talk

REQUIRED MATERIALS

White labels (that can stick onto clothing), sheets of white paper, markers, and chairs (optional).

ROOM SETUP

Children should sit in a circle.

GAME SYNOPSIS

All children write a compliment for each child in the group on a sheet of paper. They then write the compliments on white labels and gently stick them on the back of the corresponding child in the group. After every child has had a turn, a child is selected to remove his or her first compliment from the child's back. He or she thanks the group for the compliment and guesses who gave the compliment. For every correct match, one point is awarded. The game continues with the next child in the circle removing one compliment from his or her back and guessing. This proceeds until all compliments have been received.

STEPS FOR IMPLEMENTING COMPLIMENT STICKER

1. Instruct children to sit in a circle. Introduce *Compliment Sticker* to the children in a positive and playful manner. Tell children that they are about to play a special game in which they will be giving and receiving compliments.
2. Before the game starts, instruct children that during the game they need to
    a) Prepare appropriate compliments for everyone in the group and only give them out when told to do so.
    b) Remain seated and face forward when being given compliments.
    c) Leave the compliments on their back until told to take them off.
    d) Stay quiet when a child is guessing or someone is responding to a guess.
3. Give children a sheet of paper, a label for each member of the group, and a marker.

4. Instruct children to write a compliment for each child in the group on the sheet of paper. They should copy these compliments onto the label. The name of the child they are giving the compliment to should also be written on the label.

5. The rules of the game should be reviewed. Have everyone repeat the directions out loud before beginning the game.

6. To start the game, instruct one child to give out his or her compliments by sticking the appropriate compliment on each child's back. Facilitators can assist the child with giving out the compliments and ensure that the other children remain seated and do not turn around.

7. After this child has given out all of his or her compliments, that child should return to his or her seat. Repeat Step 6 for each child in the group.

8. After all children have given out their compliments, instruct one child to pull a compliment off her or his shirt. The child should read the compliment out loud and thank the group for giving the compliment.

9. The same child should then guess who gave him or her the compliment.

10. The child who is named as the giver affirms or disconfirms whether he or she had given the compliment to this child and a point is recorded by one of the facilitators if he or she guesses correctly.

11. Repeat Steps 7 through 9 until all children have read and guessed all of their compliments.

12. Group process: Tell the children that the game is now over. Have them sit in their chairs or on the floor facing the front of the room and tell them it is time to discuss the game.

GROUP PROCESS QUESTIONS

1. Ask the children what they needed to do to play the game. Emphasize the importance of coming up with compliments and how to respond to receiving compliments.

2. Ask the children how they felt when they had to generate compliments.

3. Ask the children how they felt when they gave out the compliments.

4. Ask the children how they felt when they received the compliments.

5. Ask the children how they felt when they had to guess who gave them the compliment.

6. Ask the children how they felt when they guessed correctly.

7. Ask the children how they felt when they guessed incorrectly.

9 GROUP PLAY INTERVENTION:
Interviewing and Presenting

OVERVIEW

Interviewing and Presenting allows children to learn the skill of introducing others.

GROUP PLAY INTERVENTION SKILLS TAUGHT

Primary: Introducing Others
Secondary: Initiating and Maintaining Conversations, Listening, Paying Attention, Taking Turns, Working Collaboratively

SKILL DIFFICULTY

Intermediate

PREREQUISITE SKILLS

Children should have some experience introducing themselves to others, sharing information about themselves, and beginning and engaging in conversations.

SUGGESTED GROUP SKILL SEQUENCES TO PRACTICE BEFORE GROUP PLAY INTERVENTION

No. 3. Introducing Self to Others
No. 5. Joining in a Conversation
No. 9. Learning About Others
No. 2. Using Nice Talk
No. 4. Introducing Others

REQUIRED MATERIALS

Sheets of paper (depending on children's abilities sheets may contain interview questions, guidelines for interview questions, or may be blank) and a writing instrument.

ROOM SETUP

The room should be conducive to pairs of children sitting together and talking. There should be ample room for each dyad to be spread far enough apart so that one dyad's conversation does not disrupt another.

GAME SYNOPSIS

Interviewing and Presenting is an activity in which children are paired off and instructed to take turns asking each other questions. Following this, they are provided an opportunity to present their partner to the rest of the group.

STEPS FOR IMPLEMENTING INTERVIEWING AND PRESENTING

1. Introduce *Interviewing and Presenting* to the children in a positive and playful manner. Tell children that they are about to play a special game in which they will be asking each other questions to get to know one another.
2. Give each child a sheet of paper, either blank or prepared, and a writing instrument.
3. Match each child with a partner and assign to an area of the room.
4. Instruct one child from each pair to interview the other and record the information on the sheet of paper (this can be done verbally or using pictures). The goal is to obtain enough information about the other child in order to present that information to the group. The child should be provided with a specified amount of time (e.g., approximately 5 to 10 minutes) for the interviewing process.
5. After the specified amount of time has elapsed, children in each dyad should switch roles.

6. Then ask the children to return to the group and to sit quietly in a circle.
7. One at a time, children should be provided with an opportunity to introduce their partner to the group. They should introduce their partner by name and then provide a description of the person.
8. Repeat Step 7 until all children have had a chance to introduce someone to the group.
9. Group process: Tell the children that the game is now over. Have them sit in their chairs or on the floor facing the front of the room and tell them it is time to discuss the game.

GROUP PROCESS QUESTIONS

1. Ask the children what they needed to do to play the game. Emphasize the importance of learning about others and introducing others.
2. Ask the children what kinds of questions they needed to ask their partners to learn about them.
3. Ask the children how they felt when they were asking their partner questions.
4. Ask the children how they felt when they were being questioned.
5. Ask the children how they felt when they were introducing their partner to the group.
6. Ask the children how they felt when they werc being introduced to the group.

Teaching Module 2

Identifying Emotions and Appropriately Expressing Emotions

1 GROUP PLAY INTERVENTION: *Feelings Dice*

OVERVIEW
Feelings Dice allows children to practice expressing and identifying feelings.

GROUP PLAY INTERVENTION SKILLS TAUGHT
Primary: Expressing Feelings, Identifying Feelings
Secondary: Paying Attention, Following Directions

SKILL DIFFICULTY
Beginner

PREREQUISITE SKILLS
Children need to be able to identify and express basic emotions (happy, sad, mad, scared).

SUGGESTED GROUP SKILL SEQUENCES TO PRACTICE BEFORE GROUP PLAY INTERVENTION
No. 17. Identifying Feelings and Emotions
No. 18. Expressing Feelings and Emotions
No. 31. Following Directions
No. 19. Understanding Social Cues

REQUIRED MATERIALS
A large six-sided die created out of heavy paper (e.g., construction paper or poster board). Each side should be labeled with a different feeling (e.g., happy, sad, angry, scared, frustrated, confused).

ROOM SETUP
Children should be sitting in a circle. They can sit in chairs or on the floor.

GAME SYNOPSIS
One child at a time rolls the feelings die and acts out the feeling on the die for everyone else to see. The children observing are provided with opportunities to identify specific behaviors that the actor is doing to portray the feeling.

STEPS FOR IMPLEMENTING *FEELINGS DICE*

1. Seat children in a circle, show the feelings die, and tell them that they are going to play a game called *Feelings Dice*.
2. Instruct children that when they are given the feelings die, they are to roll the die and act out the feeling presented on the die using both their face and body. Inform them that that they cannot use words.
3. Tell children that while a child is acting, they are to attend to the actor, try to identify what the actor is doing, and raise their hand to share their answers with the group. Children should receive one point for every behavior that they correctly identify.
4. After all behaviors are identified, pass the die to the next child in the circle and repeat Step 3 until all children have had a turn.
5. Group process: Tell the children that the game is now over. Have them sit in their chairs or on the floor facing the front of the room and tell them it is time to discuss the game.

GROUP PROCESS QUESTIONS

1. Ask the children what they needed to do to play the game. Emphasize the importance of identifying and expressing emotions, taking turns, and following directions.

2. Ask the children what they needed to do when they were the actor.
3. Ask the children how they felt being the actor.
4. Ask the children what they needed to do to be the observer.
5. Ask the children how they felt when they were the observer.

2

GROUP PLAY INTERVENTION:
Stone Face Stevie/Samantha

OVERVIEW

Stone Face Stevie/Samantha is a game that allows children to practice the skills of identifying and expressing emotions through teaching these skills to others.

GROUP PLAY INTERVENTION SKILLS TAUGHT

Primary: Expressing Feelings, Identifying Feelings
Secondary: Communication, Collaboration, Following Directions

SKILL DIFFICULTY

Beginner–Intermediate

PREREQUISITE SKILLS

Children need to be able to identify and express basic emotions (happy, sad, mad, scared).

SUGGESTED GROUP SKILL SEQUENCES TO PRACTICE BEFORE GROUP PLAY INTERVENTION

No. 17. Identifying Feelings and Emotions
No. 18. Expressing Feelings and Emotions
No. 1. Communicating With Others

REQUIRED MATERIALS

Blanket, sheet, or shawl to cover the head and body of a group facilitator acting as *Stone Face* and chairs or open floor space for Stone Face and children to sit. Index cards or sheets of 8½ × 11 inch paper, cut into four pieces. Each card or piece of paper should have an emotion written on it.

ROOM SETUP

Children sit in a semicircle on the floor or in chairs facing the front of the room. A chair or floor space should be available for Stone Face.

GAME SYNOPSIS

Stone Face Stevie/Samantha is a game in which children have an opportunity to teach a seemingly emotionless "ogre" how to express emotions. Children use verbal and visual prompts and corrective feedback to get the ogre to express emotions listed on cards.

STEPS FOR IMPLEMENTING STONE FACE STEVIE/SAMANTHA

1. Introduce *Stone Face Stevie/Samantha* to the children in a positive, playful manner. Tell children that they are about to play a special game that involves expressing feelings, identifying feelings, communication, collaboration, and following directions.
2. One group facilitator should stand outside the room out of view from the children, with a blanket, sheet, or shawl covering his or her head. The facilitator should wait outside the room until given the signal to enter.
3. A different group facilitator in the room should begin reading the story of Stone Face to the children:

   Stone Face Stevie [or Samantha if the group facilitator (actor) is a female] is a simple ogre who has lived his whole life in the deepest, darkest cave somewhere in the Alaskan wilderness. He is not a mean ogre, nor is he an especially nice ogre. The problem with Stone Face Stevie is that he isn't any particular kind of ogre. He just *is*. He simply exists in his cave, eating raw fish out of an underground stream that he had discovered as a baby. Living alone his entire life, without any friends to play with, Stone Face Stevie never learned how to make facial expressions nor was even taught what facial expressions were. In fact, Stone Face Stevie got his name because his face never made any facial expressions. Sure, he has feelings, but because he lived alone for so many years, he never learned how to express his feelings to others. Today, he's had a chance to leave his cave to visit our group. He wants us to teach him about expressing feelings. Each of you will have a turn at teaching Stone Face Stevie about facial expressions and body language.

4. Once the story is finished, the group facilitators in the room should give Stone Face a signal to enter the room, and then introduce him. Stone Face should walk around the room grunting, showing no facial expression, and he should sit in a chair or on the floor in front of the group.
5. Select one child and give her or him a feeling card from the stack.
6. The child should then teach Stone Face how to make the facial expression and the accompanying body language of the emotion. Make sure that Stone Face really gets it before that child's turn is finished. Encourage the actor playing Stone Face to "get it wrong" before they get it right to force the child to emphasize and rehearse the facial expressions and body language.
7. Continue to repeat Steps 5 and 6 until all children have an opportunity to teach Stone Face how to express a feeling.
8. Group process: Tell the children that the game is now over. Have them sit in their chairs or on the floor facing the front of the room and tell them it is time to discuss the game.

GROUP PROCESS QUESTIONS

1. Ask the children what they needed to do to play the game. Emphasize the importance of expressing feelings, identifying feelings, communication, collaboration, and following directions.
2. Ask the children how they felt when they met Stone Face.
3. Ask the children how they taught Stone Face to express various emotions (have the children provide specific examples).
4. Ask the children how they felt when they were teaching Stone Face how to express feelings.
5. Ask the children how they felt when they were successful in getting Stone Face to express feelings correctly.

3

GROUP PLAY INTERVENTION:
Facial Expression Identification

OVERVIEW

Facial Expression Identification is a game that allows children to identify emotions by observing or labeling facial expressions.

GROUP PLAY INTERVENTION SKILLS TAUGHT

Primary: Linking Facial Expression to Emotions
Secondary: Paying Attention, Following Directions

SKILL DIFFICULTY

Beginner–Intermediate

PREREQUISITE SKILLS

Children need to be able to identify and express basic emotions (happy, sad, mad, scared).

SUGGESTED GROUP SKILL SEQUENCES TO PRACTICE BEFORE GROUP PLAY INTERVENTION

No. 17. Identifying Feelings and Emotions
No. 18. Expressing Feelings and Emotions
No. 19. Understanding Social Cues
No. 32. Paying Attention

REQUIRED MATERIALS

Large pictures of different facial expressions (happy, sad, scared, embarrassed, tired, angry) with blank lines for children to fill in the corresponding emotion. A word bank of emotions may be provided if necessary.

ROOM SETUP

Children sit in a circle on the floor or in chairs.

GAME SYNOPSIS

Children are given a worksheet in which they are to label emotions corresponding to pictures of facial expressions.

STEPS FOR IMPLEMENTING FACIAL EXPRESSION IDENTIFICATION

1. Seat children in a circle and tell them that they are going to play a game called *Facial Expression Identification.*
2. Provide children with a worksheet containing pictures of faces.
3. Tell children that they should try to identify and write down the emotions that correspond to the facial expressions displayed.
4. Encourage children to work as quickly as possible and tell them that they will be earning one point for each facial expression that they correctly identify. Bonus points should be awarded for finishing first, second, third, and so forth.
5. Tell children to begin and to let a group facilitator know when they finish. Group facilitators should check their answers for accuracy and indicate on each child's worksheet what place he or she finished in. Wrong answers should be explained and points for the game should be recorded.
6. Ask children to go around the circle, one at a time, and share their answers for each picture.
7. Announce the winners of the game.

8. Group process: Tell the children that the game is now over. Have them sit in their chairs or on the floor facing the front of the room and tell them it is time to discuss the game.

GROUP PROCESS QUESTIONS

1. Ask the children what they needed to do to play the game. Emphasize the importance of reading facial expressions and understanding their connection to people's emotions.
2. Ask the children what they did to identify the emotions. Allow children to provide specific examples.
3. Ask the children how they felt about racing each other.
4. Ask the children how they felt about sharing their answers with the group.

4 GROUP PLAY INTERVENTION: *Emotion Memory*

OVERVIEW

Emotion Memory teaches children how to recognize and identify emotional expressions by matching up pairs of cards that identify the same emotion.

GROUP PLAY INTERVENTION SKILLS TAUGHT

Primary: Identifying Feelings
Secondary: Following Directions, Paying Attention, Taking Turns

SKILL DIFFICULTY

Beginner–Intermediate

PREREQUISITE SKILLS

Children should be able to follow simple verbal instructions and have basic self-control and attention skills.

SUGGESTED GROUP SKILL SEQUENCES TO PRACTICE BEFORE GROUP PLAY INTERVENTION

No. 17. Identifying Feelings and Emotions
No. 31. Following Directions
No. 32. Paying Attention

REQUIRED MATERIALS

Memory cards that include names of emotions (e.g., angry, sad, happy) and simple facial pictures of emotions on each card.

ROOM SETUP

A space for children to sit in a circle on the floor or around a table.

GAME SYNOPSIS

Emotion Memory teaches children to recognize and identify emotional expressions. Children take turns selecting two memory cards. Children try to match up pairs of cards that identify the same emotion.

STEPS FOR IMPLEMENTING EMOTION MEMORY

1. Tell children they are going to play a matching game about different emotions. Ask the children to identify different types of emotions that they are aware of (e.g., happy, sad, angry, lonely).
2. Then instruct children to sit in a circle around the memory cards. (The memory cards should be placed face down ahead of time by the group facilitator.)
3. Tell children they will select two memory cards when it is their turn. Encourage children to find two cards with the same emotion. Also tell children to pay attention and remember all the cards selected so they can make a match when it is their turn. If a child makes a match, she or he takes another turn and should be given verbal praise by the adult(s) and group members.
4. Repeat Step 3 until each child has taken a turn and has successfully made a match.
5. Group process: Tell the children that the game is now over. Have them sit in their chairs or on the floor facing the front of the room and tell them it is time to discuss the game.

1. Ask the children what they needed to do to play the game.
2. Ask the children how they felt when they made a match with the memory cards.
3. Ask the children how they felt when they were not able to find memory cards that matched.
4. Ask the children how they felt when other children found memory cards that matched.
5. Ask the children how they felt when they knew where the same memory cards were when it was not their turn.
6. Ask the children how they felt after the game was over.

5 GROUP PLAY INTERVENTION: *Emotional Vocabulary Competition*

OVERVIEW

Emotional Vocabulary Competition encourages children to recall different emotions and expand on their current emotional vocabularies.

GROUP PLAY INTERVENTION SKILLS TAUGHT

Primary: Expanding Emotional Vocabulary
Secondary: Cooperation, Respect for Others, Listening to Others, Following Directions

SKILL DIFFICULTY

Beginner–Intermediate

PREREQUISITE SKILLS

Children should have a basic knowledge of feeling words. Children need to be able to identify and express basic emotions (e.g., happy, sad, mad, scared).

SUGGESTED GROUP SKILL SEQUENCES TO PRACTICE BEFORE GROUP PLAY INTERVENTION

No. 17. Identifying Feelings and Emotions
No. 35. Cooperation
No. 13. Respecting Others

REQUIRED MATERIALS

Large floor space or chairs for several small groups to sit; several sheets of paper and writing instruments.

ROOM SETUP

Children sit in one large circle on the floor when receiving initial directions.

GAME SYNOPSIS

Small groups of children compete to come up with feeling words and group facilitators document these words on sheets of paper. Points are awarded for unique contributions.

STEPS FOR IMPLEMENTING EMOTIONAL VOCABULARY COMPETITION

1. Seat children in a circle and ask them to count from one to four (this number will vary depending on the number of children present in the large group).
2. Ask children, accompanied by a group leader, to move to different areas of the room by number.
3. Give directions to all children after they are seated quietly. Tell the children that, as a small group, they have 10 minutes to come up with as many feeling words as possible.
4. Facilitators can help guide the group if the group is struggling. For example, by using phrases such as, "If you went to bed late and had to wake up early for school, you might be feeling . . . "
5. After the allotted time, have each group share the number of feeling words that they came up with. The group with the least number of feeling words shares their list first.
6. While the first group is sharing their list of words, instruct other groups to cross out feeling words from their list if they have come up with the same words.
7. The group with the most unique feeling words wins the game.

8. Group process: Tell the children that the game is now over. Have them sit in their chairs or on the floor facing the front of the room and tell them it is time to discuss the game.

1. Ask the children what they needed to do to play the game. Emphasize the importance of expanding their emotional vocabularies and maintaining respect for other group members and their ideas.
2. Ask the children how they felt coming up with different emotions.
3. Ask the children how they felt when they scored a point for a unique feeling word.
4. Ask the children how they felt when another group had the same word they did.

6 GROUP PLAY INTERVENTION: *Feelings Tag*

OVERVIEW

Feelings Tag encourages children to recall different emotions and expand on their current emotional vocabularies.

GROUP PLAY INTERVENTION SKILLS TAUGHT

Primary: Emotional Vocabulary
Secondary: Self-Control, Following Directions

SKILL DIFFICULTY

Beginner–Intermediate

PREREQUISITE SKILLS

Children should have a basic knowledge of feeling words. Children should be able to keep their bodies in control and follow directions.

SUGGESTED GROUP SKILL SEQUENCES TO PRACTICE BEFORE GROUP PLAY INTERVENTION

No. 17. Identifying Feelings and Emotions
No. 16. Self-Control
No. 31. Following Directions
No. 13. Respecting Others

REQUIRED MATERIALS

Radio with a CD or cassette tape player and a CD or cassette with dance music (child appropriate).

ROOM SETUP

Large, open, unobstructed floor space for children to move around.

GAME SYNOPSIS

Children move around the room to music while a group leader or selected child attempts to tag them before they can recall a new feeling word.

STEPS FOR IMPLEMENTING *FEELINGS TAG*

1. Seat children in a circle and ask them to raise their hands to share examples of feeling words with the group. After three or four different feelings are mentioned, give children directions for the game.
2. Tell children that the game begins when the music starts. A group facilitator or child will be designated as *it*. *It* will walk around the room attempting to tag children and make them *it* before they can name a feeling word. Instruct children to walk around the room without being tagged *it* by saying a feeling word that has not already been mentioned. Children are rewarded with a point for each round that they complete without being *it*. The game continues until all children have been tagged because they were unable to identify a new feeling word. When all group members have the opportunity to be tagged, the final child tagged becomes the new *it* and the round ends.
3. Turn the music on and begin the game.
4. After a new *it* is tagged, turn the music off, and award all the other children a point. A group facilitator should make an announcement about the new *it*.
5. Repeat Steps 3 and 4 for several rounds until group facilitators have determined that the children have achieved sufficient expansion of their emotional vocabularies.

6. Group process: Tell the children that the game is now over. Have them sit in their chairs or on the floor facing the front of the room and tell them it is time to discuss the game.

1. Ask the children what they needed to do to play the game. Emphasize the importance of expanding their emotional vocabularies and keeping their bodies in control.
2. Ask the children how they came up with different emotions.
3. Ask the children how they felt when *it* was coming to get them.
4. Ask the children how it felt to be *it*.

7 GROUP PLAY INTERVENTION:
Emotional Charades

OVERVIEW

Emotional Charades allows children to practice expressing and identifying emotions.

GROUP PLAY INTERVENTION SKILLS TAUGHT

Primary: Expressing Emotions, Identifying Emotions
Secondary: Paying Attention, Listening, Taking Turns, Working Collaboratively, Impulse Control

SKILL DIFFICULTY

Intermediate

PREREQUISITE SKILLS

Children need to have knowledge of basic emotions and have the ability to identify and express basic emotions (happy, sad, mad, scared). They should be able to follow simple directions, pay attention, work collaboratively, and take turns.

SUGGESTED GROUP SKILL SEQUENCES TO PRACTICE BEFORE GROUP PLAY INTERVENTION

No. 18. Expressing Feelings and Emotions
No. 17. Identifying Feelings and Emotions
No. 10. Being an Active Listener
No. 19. Understanding Social Cues

REQUIRED MATERIALS

Index cards or sheets of 8½ × 11 inch paper, cut into four pieces, and a stopwatch or timer. Each card or piece of paper should have an emotion written on it.

ROOM SETUP

Children should be sitting with their team in an area where they can see the front of the room and where the actors will be acting. They can sit in chairs or on the floor.

GAME SYNOPSIS

Emotional Charades is a game in which children nonverbally act out various emotions that are listed on cards, with the goal of getting their teammates to guess what they are.

STEPS FOR IMPLEMENTING EMOTIONAL CHARADES

1. Separate children into two groups (teams) and instruct them to sit with their teammates, facing the front of the room.
2. Before the game starts, instruct children that during the game
    a) The child acting should not begin until instructed by a group facilitator.
    b) The child acting is not allowed to talk.
    c) The actor's team should continuously call out guesses until either someone gets it right or time runs out.
    d) Children on the other team should sit quietly while trying to figure out what emotion is being acted out (they could have a chance to steal a point).
3. To start the game, call on a child from the first team to be the actor and give him or her one of the emotion cards.
4. Tell the child to act out the emotion on the card when given a signal. Remind the actor's teammates to guess, and encourage the other team to think of possible responses while remaining silent.
5. If a child guesses correctly within a predetermined amount of time, a point should be awarded to the actor's team. If time runs out before one of the actor's

teammates correctly identifies the emotion, the opposing team gets a chance to steal the points. This team should huddle together and come up with a single answer. If they guess incorrectly, the round ends and no points are awarded.

6. Once the round is over, select a child from the other team to be the actor. Continue this step until either all of the children have had a turn to act or until the children have successfully mastered the skill.

7. Group process: Tell the children that the game is now over. Have them sit in their chairs or on the floor facing the front of the room and tell them it is time to discuss the game.

GROUP PROCESS QUESTIONS

1. Ask the children what they needed to do to play the game. Emphasize the importance of identifying and expressing emotions, observing each other, taking turns, and following directions.

2. Ask the children what they needed to do when they were the actor.

3. Ask the children how they felt being the actor.

4. Ask the children what they needed to do to be the guesser.

5. Ask the children how they felt when they were the guesser.

8 GROUP PLAY INTERVENTION: *Feelings–Experience Dice*

OVERVIEW — *Feelings–Experience Dice* allows children to practice linking or relating feelings to events in their lives. Children also practice listening to others' emotionally charged experiences and learn to formulate socially appropriate questions to help others expand on their feelings.

GROUP PLAY INTERVENTION SKILLS TAUGHT — Primary: Linking Feelings to Experiences
Secondary: Following Directions, Paying Attention, Listening to Others

SKILL DIFFICULTY — Intermediate

PREREQUISITE SKILLS — Children should have an understanding of basic feelings and be able to link them to personal experiences. Children should be able to formulate socially appropriate questions to ask the presenter.

SUGGESTED GROUP SKILL SEQUENCES TO PRACTICE BEFORE GROUP PLAY INTERVENTION — No. 17. Identifying Feelings and Emotions
No. 31. Following Directions
No. 7. Sharing About Oneself
No. 20. Showing Concern for Others' Feelings

REQUIRED MATERIALS — A large, six-sided die created out of heavy paper (e.g., construction paper or poster board). Each side should be labeled with a different feeling (e.g., happy, sad, angry, scared, frustrated, confused).

ROOM SETUP — Children should be sitting in a circle on the floor or in chairs.

GAME SYNOPSIS — Children roll the die and describe an experience when they felt the specific emotion displayed on the die. As an added activity to the game, children can also act out the feeling that was experienced. The children observing are provided with opportunities to identify the feeling that the actor (child) displays.

STEPS FOR IMPLEMENTING FEELINGS–EXPERIENCE DICE

1. Seat children in a circle, show them the feelings die, and tell them that they are going to play a game called *Feelings–Experience Dice.*
2. Instruct each child to roll the feelings die. Ask the child to discuss an experience in which he or she felt the particular feeling presented on the die.
3. Group members should listen to each child's experience and formulate an appropriate question to ask the presenter.
4. Once the child finishes describing his or her experience, allow group members to take turns raising their hands and asking the presenter socially appropriate questions to help the presenter expand on her or his feeling.
5. Then instruct the child to act out the feeling presented on the die using both face and body. To increase the difficulty, group facilitators may impose the challenge that the group is not allowed to use words.

6. Tell children that while a child is acting, they are to attend to the actor and try to identify what the actor is doing and how the emotion relates to the experience the actor shared. Children should be encouraged to raise their hands and share their answers with the group.

7. Have the actor pass the die to the next child in the circle, and repeat Steps 2 through 6 until all children have a chance to be the actor.

8. Group process: Tell the children that the game is now over. Have them sit in their chairs or on the floor facing the front of the room and tell them it is time to discuss the game.

GROUP PROCESS QUESTIONS

1. Ask the children what they needed to do to play the game. Emphasize the importance of identifying and describing emotions, taking turns, and following directions.

2. Ask the children what they needed to do after they rolled the die.

3. Ask the children how they felt describing a personal experience.

4. Ask the children what they needed to do as a group member when the presenter was describing an experience.

5. Ask the children how they felt coming up with an appropriate question to ask the presenter.

Teaching Module 3
Following Directions and Impulse Control

1

GROUP PLAY INTERVENTION:
Red Light, Green Light

OVERVIEW   *Red Light, Green Light* is a game in which one child at a time is the leader of the game and plays the stoplight, while the rest of the children try to touch him or her.

GROUP PLAY INTERVENTION SKILLS TAUGHT

Primary: Self-Control, Patience
Secondary: Taking Turns, Paying Attention

SKILL DIFFICULTY   Beginner

PREREQUISITE SKILLS

Children should be able to follow simple verbal instructions and have basic self-control and cooperative play skills.

SUGGESTED GROUP SKILL SEQUENCES TO PRACTICE BEFORE GROUP PLAY INTERVENTION

No. 16. Self-Control
No. 38. Being Patient
No. 36. Taking Turns

REQUIRED MATERIALS

A large open space.

ROOM SETUP

At the beginning of the game, all the children should form a line about 15 ft from the stoplight. The stoplight faces away from the line of children.

GAME SYNOPSIS

Red Light, Green Light involves children taking turns, acting like a stoplight. The other children form a line behind the stoplight. The children start moving toward the stoplight when he or she says, "green light." At any point, the stoplight may say "red light" and turn around to face the other children. If any of the children are caught moving after "red light" has been called, they go back to the starting line and begin again. The first player to touch the stoplight earns the right to take a turn as the stoplight for the next game.

STEPS FOR IMPLEMENTING RED LIGHT, GREEN LIGHT

1. Select one child to be the leader or the stoplight. Instruct the stoplight to face away from the other children.
2. Tell all of the other children to form a line about 15 ft away from the stoplight.
3. Instruct children to start moving toward the stoplight when the stoplight says, "green light," and stop moving when the stoplight calls out, "red light" and turns around.
4. If any of the children are caught moving after the stoplight has said, "red light," instruct them to return to the starting line and begin again. This game is good for building impulse control and dealing with rejection.
5. Continue the game by having the stoplight call out either "red light" or "green light." The first player to touch the stoplight earns the right to take a turn as the stoplight for the next game.
6. Repeat the game until each child has had a turn to be the stoplight.

7. Group process: Tell the children that the game is now over. Have them sit in their chairs or on the floor facing the front of the room and tell them it is time to discuss the game.

GROUP PROCESS QUESTIONS

1. Ask the children what they needed to do to play the game. Emphasize the importance of self-control and patience that was required to play this game.
2. Ask the children how they felt when they were the stoplight.
3. Ask the children how they felt when they were not the stoplight.
4. Ask the children how they felt when they were sent back to the starting line.

2 GROUP PLAY INTERVENTION: *Islands*

OVERVIEW

Islands places children in an imaginary dangerous situation. This game requires children to ask for help, help others, share, cooperate, control their hands and feet (i.e., self-control), and manage stress effectively.

GROUP PLAY INTERVENTION SKILLS TAUGHT

Primary: Asking for Help, Helping Others
Secondary: Following Directions, Self-Control, Stress Management

SKILL DIFFICULTY

Beginner

PREREQUISITE SKILLS

Children should possess basic abilities to follow simple directions and keep their bodies in control with some redirection or reminders.

SUGGESTED GROUP SKILL SEQUENCES TO PRACTICE BEFORE GROUP PLAY INTERVENTION

No. 42. Asking for Help
No. 43. Helping Others
No. 16. Self-Control

REQUIRED MATERIALS

Bath towels (three or four) and a radio, tape, or CD player.

ROOM SETUP

Towels are placed on the floor of the room and evenly spaced out. There should be ample room for children to comfortably move in between the towels. A radio should be set up near a group facilitator so that the group facilitator can easily turn the radio's volume *slowly* up and down. The radio should not be abruptly shut off, like in the game of musical chairs, because this will induce unnecessary anxiety and impulsivity in the children. An age-appropriate radio station, CD, or tape with dance music should be identified before the game is started. As the game progresses, towels are gradually folded and later removed.

GAME SYNOPSIS

Islands is an interactive game in which children are told to pretend that they live on islands, which are represented by towels. Imaginary crocodiles share the islands and water with the children. The group facilitator instructs the children about how to live peacefully with the crocodiles and how to avoid being bitten or eaten. While the music is playing, the crocodiles go to sleep on the islands, allowing the children to swim freely in the water. However, when the music stops, the crocodiles wake up, go into the water, and become aggressive. As a result, the children should swim around the islands while the music is playing. After the music stops, they should go onto the islands. However, if a child is found to be in the water for more than a couple of seconds after the music stops, they must ask one of the other children for help getting onto an island. As the game progresses, the tide comes in and the islands get smaller (towels are folded and are eventually removed), thereby increasing the number of children asking for help.

1. Introduce *Islands* to the children in a positive and playful manner. Tell children that they are about to play a special game that involves following directions, asking for help, helping others, controlling their hands and feet, and managing their stress.

2. A group facilitator should read the story of *Islands* to the children:

> You are the islanders who live on a beautiful group of islands. The water around the islands is warm and blue. You like to swim every day, but there is one problem: There are crocodiles that travel together that also live in the water and on the islands. When the wind blows over the water and through the trees, a musical sound starts. The music causes the crocodiles to go onto the islands and fall asleep, leaving the waters peaceful. But when the music stops, the crocodiles wake up [make a yawning gesture and sound], go into the water, and look for food. So when the music is playing, you should swim around in the water by walking, floating, or dancing slowly around the islands. Make sure that when the music is playing you are not on an island because you do not want to disturb the peaceful crocodiles. When the music stops, you must leave the water and climb onto an island. If you are not on an island right away, you need to ask someone on an island for help. One of the other islanders will help you onto an island to safety. If you are on an island and someone asks you for help, you should put out your arm and help them onto the island. When the tide comes in, the water covers some of the beaches on the islands, and then you need to share the islands with your friends or find another island to stay on. Sharing islands and helping others will keep you safe and happy.

3. Before the game starts, instruct children that during the game they need to
   a) Keep their arms in control—not hit or push others.
   b) Keep their feet in control—walk, not run, and stand and avoid bumping into objects and other group members.
   c) Listen carefully for the music to start or stop.
   d) Not run or jump onto islands.

4. Have everyone repeat the directions (out loud) before beginning the game.

5. Start playing the music. While the music is playing, encourage the children to walk slowly, (pretend) swim, and dance around the islands without stepping on them. Group facilitators should encourage the children to keep moving around all the islands and avoid stepping on or touching the islands. After approximately a minute, *slowly* turn the music down. After a few seconds, tell the children to "freeze." Remind children who are not on an island that they should ask someone who is on an island for help. Children on an island who are asked for help should extend one of their arms to help others onto the island. If children jumped onto an island after they were told to "freeze," tell those children to step off the island and ask others for help onto one. The children should ask for help loudly enough for the entire group to hear.

6. Continue to repeat Step 5. After a couple of times, fold the towels, signifying to the children that the tide is coming in. After a couple of additional times, fold the towels again to make the islands even smaller. Then remove one towel at a time, until only a single towel is left. All the children should have at least one opportunity to ask others for help during the game.

7. Group process: Tell the children that the game is now over. Have them sit in their chairs or on the floor facing the front of the room and tell them it is time to discuss the game.

1. Ask the children what they needed to do to play the game. Emphasize the importance of asking for help and helping others.
2. Ask the children how they felt when the music was playing.
3. Ask the children how they felt when the music was becoming lower and lower.
4. Ask the children how they felt when the music was off.
5. Ask the children when they needed help from others.
6. Ask the children how they felt when they needed help.
7. Ask the children how they felt when others helped them.
8. Ask the children how they felt when they helped others.

3 GROUP PLAY INTERVENTION: *Impulse Control Drawing*

OVERVIEW

Impulse Control Drawing is a game in which children draw a picture as fast as they can, and then draw another picture slowly and carefully. The children are asked to compare the two pictures and discuss why there may be differences between the two pictures.

GROUP PLAY INTERVENTION SKILLS TAUGHT

Primary: Identifying the Effects of Impulse Control
Secondary: Following Directions, Paying Attention

SKILL DIFFICULTY

Beginner–Intermediate

PREREQUISITE SKILLS

Children should be able to follow simple verbal instructions, have a degree of hand–eye coordination, and have basic self-control and attention skills.

SUGGESTED GROUP SKILL SEQUENCES TO PRACTICE BEFORE GROUP PLAY INTERVENTION

No. 16. Self-Control
No. 31. Following Directions
No. 32. Paying Attention
No. 34. Working Independently

REQUIRED MATERIALS

Drawing paper and pencils.

ROOM SETUP

An open space for children to sit on the floor or a table for children to sit around.

GAME SYNOPSIS

Impulse Control Drawing is a game in which children are asked to draw two pictures. Children are asked to draw the first picture as fast as they can; then they are asked to draw the second picture slowly and carefully. Children are taught to recognize and identify the differences between a drawing that was done impulsively and one that was done with impulse control.

STEPS FOR IMPLEMENTING *IMPULSE CONTROL DRAWING*

1. Tell children they are going to play a drawing game about impulse control. Group facilitators should describe examples of good impulse control. Children should also be encouraged to share their stories or examples of good impulse control.
2. Ask children to draw a picture of a person as fast as they can ("quick as bunny").
3. Next, ask the children to stop, think, and then draw a picture of a house, as slowly and carefully as they can ("slow as a turtle or snail"). After the children have drawn both pictures, give each child a turn to discuss what she or he thinks about the two pictures. First, encourage the children to describe each of their pictures to the group. Examples may include "Tell us about your person," or "Tell us about your house."
4. Then ask the children the following questions:
   a) What are some of the differences between the two pictures?
   b) Which picture are you most proud of? Why are you most proud of that picture?
   c) Which picture do you like better?

5. Group process: Tell the children that the game is now over. Have them sit in their chairs or on the floor facing the front of the room and tell them it is time to discuss the game.

GROUP PROCESS QUESTIONS

1. Ask the children what they needed to do to play the game.
2. Ask the children how they felt when they were drawing the picture of the person as fast as they could.
3. Ask the children how they felt when they were drawing the picture of the house slowly and carefully.
4. Ask the children how they felt after the game was over.

4 GROUP PLAY INTERVENTION:
The Freeze

OVERVIEW

The Freeze involves children moving to music. Children must stay in control of their bodies and their actions while moving around the room. This game allows children with varying abilities many opportunities to interact with each other. In our experience, children will start to encourage each other.

GROUP PLAY INTERVENTION SKILLS TAUGHT

Primary: Self-Control, Cooperation, Following Directions
Secondary: Group Problem Solving, Auditory and Visual Acuity

SKILL DIFFICULTY

Intermediate

PREREQUISITE SKILLS

Children should be able to follow simple verbal instructions and have basic self-control and cooperative play skills.

SUGGESTED GROUP SKILL SEQUENCES TO PRACTICE BEFORE GROUP PLAY INTERVENTION

No. 16. Self-Control
No. 35. Cooperation
No. 30. Solving a Problem as a Group

REQUIRED MATERIALS

A large open space, and a CD player to play music.

ROOM SETUP

The game begins with the group standing in a circle a few feet apart from each other.

GAME SYNOPSIS

When the music starts, each child moves slowly around the room. When the music stops, each child must freeze like a statue. The music can be varied at different speeds to emphasize staying in control to the children. Children who are able to move around the general space without bumping into others should be praised. A group challenge can be introduced after the children become more experienced with these skills. For example, the group can be challenged to move around the room for 2 minutes without bumping into each other.

STEPS FOR IMPLEMENTING *THE FREEZE*

1. Instruct children to stand in a circle a few feet apart from each other.
2. Instruct children to begin moving slowly around the room when the music starts. Then turn the music on and begin the game. When the music stops, each child must freeze like a statue. The music can be varied at different speeds to emphasize staying in control. Tell children they are not to bump into each other. Children who are able to move in the general space without bumping into each other are praised.
3. As the children become more adept at these skills, a group challenge can be introduced. For example, the group can be challenged to move to the music and freeze after 2 minutes without touching each other. If there are three touches during the time, the group receives three points. The challenge is to move around again for 2 minutes and try to decrease the number of touches or points.

4. Other group challenges can be presented. For example, groups who become competent in moving under control can have the size of the general area decreased.
5. Group process: Tell the children that the game is now over. Have them sit in their chairs or on the floor facing the front of the room and tell them it is time to discuss the game.

GROUP PROCESS QUESTIONS

1. Ask the children what they needed to do to play the game. Emphasize the importance of how staying in control of their bodies and actions led to success in the game.
2. Ask the children how they felt when they were praised for not bumping into other children during the game. Ask the children how they felt when they were able to avoid bumping into each other during the 2-minute period and decrease the number of points the team received.
3. Ask the children how they felt when they were not able to keep themselves from bumping into other children. Ask the children how they felt when they bumped into other children and received points.

5 GROUP PLAY INTERVENTION:
The Cotton Ball

OVERVIEW

The Cotton Ball teaches children that they can affect their environment. Children take turns gently blowing through a straw to move a cotton ball onto the other team's side of the table.

GROUP PLAY INTERVENTION SKILLS TAUGHT

Primary: Self-Control, Taking Turns, Following Directions
Secondary: Group Problem Solving, Fine Motor Skills

SKILL DIFFICULTY

Intermediate

PREREQUISITE SKILLS

Children should be able to follow simple verbal instructions and have basic self-control and cooperative play skills.

SUGGESTED GROUP SKILL SEQUENCES TO PRACTICE BEFORE GROUP PLAY INTERVENTION

No. 16. Self-Control
No. 36. Taking Turns
No. 30. Solving a Problem as a Group
No. 37. Being a Good Sport

REQUIRED MATERIALS

A large open space, a table, tape to divide the table in half, cotton balls, and straws.

ROOM SETUP

The group facilitator should begin with the group standing around a table, a few feet apart from each other. As the game is about to begin, the children should be divided into two teams, standing on opposite sides of the table.

GAME SYNOPSIS

The Cotton Ball involves children using and controlling their breathing to use a straw to blow a cotton ball across the table. The group facilitator demonstrates how one's breathing can impact one's environment. The facilitator shows the children slow and fast breathing through a straw. Instruct children to practice moving the cotton ball by breathing through the straw. Next, the children are divided into two teams, with each standing on opposite ends of the table. Each child tries to get his or her cotton ball onto the other team's side of the table. Group challenges include trying to get all of the cotton balls onto one side of the table, having an even amount of cotton balls on both sides, or keeping all of the cotton balls on the table during a specified period of time. Children participate at their own level of ability, blowing as many or as few cotton balls as they are comfortable with.

STEPS FOR IMPLEMENTING *THE COTTON BALL*

1. Instruct children to stand around the table. A group facilitator should demonstrate how one's breathing can impact one's environment. The facilitator should show slow and fast breathing through a straw.
2. Give each child a straw and cotton ball and tell them to practice moving the cotton ball by breathing through the straw.
3. Then divide the group into two teams, standing on opposite sides of the table. A line of tape or a line should be drawn down the middle of the table.

4. Instruct children to try to get their cotton balls onto the other team's side of the table. Because cotton balls are continuously moving back and forth, the children are constantly trying to get rid of the cotton balls on their side. If a child runs out of breath, he or she can take a short break. The children can only blow their own cotton ball with their straw. If a child purposely blows another child's cotton ball off the table, he or she must go and pick up the cotton ball and apologize to the other child.

5. Group challenges can also be presented. For example, the teams could try to get all the cotton balls onto one side of the table, have an even amount of cotton balls on either side, or keep all the cotton balls on the table during a specified period of time. Children participate at their own level of ability, blowing as many or as few cotton balls as they are comfortable with. The team and group challenges allow children of different abilities to have many opportunities to positively interact.

6. Group process: Tell the children that the game is now over. Have them sit in their chairs or on the floor facing the front of the room and tell them it is time to discuss the game.

GROUP PROCESS QUESTIONS

1. Ask the children what they needed to do to play the game. Emphasize the importance of controlling their breathing and how it affected where their cotton balls went.

2. Ask the children what skills they needed to use to get their cotton balls onto the other team's area of the table. Ask the children how they needed to work as a team in the group challenge to keep all the cotton balls on the table for the specified amount of time.

3. Ask the children how they felt when they were able to successfully get their cotton balls onto the other team's area of the table.

4. Ask the children how they felt if they were having trouble getting their cotton balls onto the other team's area of the table.

5. Ask the children how it felt to control the direction and force of their cotton balls.

6 GROUP PLAY INTERVENTION: *Dance Jam*

OVERVIEW
Dance Jam involves learning and teaching a 10-step dance.

GROUP PLAY INTERVENTION SKILLS TAUGHT
Primary: Following Directions, Paying Attention
Secondary: Self-Control, Cooperation

SKILL DIFFICULTY
Intermediate

PREREQUISITE SKILLS
Children should be able to have basic self-control and attention skills. They must also be able to follow simple verbal instructions.

SUGGESTED GROUP SKILL SEQUENCES TO PRACTICE BEFORE GROUP PLAY INTERVENTION
No. 31. Following Directions
No. 32. Paying Attention
No. 35. Cooperation

REQUIRED MATERIALS
A radio, tape player, or CD player with appropriate dance music and an open space, without obstacles, that is conducive to having children move around freely.

ROOM SETUP
Children are divided into two groups, with each group standing on opposite sides of the room. Children will initially be sitting with their group facing the front of the room. They should have enough room to move about freely.

GAME SYNOPSIS
Children in each of the two groups are taught a 10-step dance by a group facilitator. Following this, each child in one group is paired off with a child in the other group. Each child must teach his or her partner the dance they learned.

STEPS FOR IMPLEMENTING *DANCE JAM*

1. Divide children into two groups, and send the groups to opposite sides of the room. Tell children that they are going to play a game called *Dance Jam* that involves learning and teaching.
2. Group facilitators should work with each group separately to teach them a unique, 10-step dance. The two groups should be taught different dances.
3. Turn the music on, review dance moves, and have members of the respective groups practice the moves until each child has learned his or her group's dance.
4. Then pair off children with members from the other group and instruct them to teach each other the dances that they learned. Tell children to work as quickly as possible and to let a facilitator know when both children in a pair know both dances.
5. After all pairs have finished, allow all children to dance one of the dances and check them for accuracy. Then, have everyone dance the second dance and check them for accuracy. Whichever pair finishes first and has danced both dances correctly should be the winner.

6. Group process: Tell the children that the game is now over. Have them sit in their chairs or on the floor facing the front of the room and tell them it is time to discuss the game.

1. Ask the children what they needed to do to play the game. Emphasize the importance of following directions, paying attention, and listening to others.
2. Ask the children how they felt when they were being taught the dance by group facilitators.
3. Ask the children how they felt when they were told that they needed to teach the dance to one of their peers.
4. Ask the children how they felt when they needed to demonstrate both dances to the group.
5. Ask the children how they felt about the place they finished in.

7 GROUP PLAY INTERVENTION: *All Mixed Up*

OVERVIEW	*All Mixed Up* involves learning a set of novel rules to respond to visual cues.
GROUP PLAY INTERVENTION SKILLS TAUGHT	Primary: Following Directions, Paying Attention Secondary: Self-Control
SKILL DIFFICULTY	Intermediate–Advanced
PREREQUISITE SKILLS	Children should be able to distinguish between playing cards, have basic self-control and attention skills, and should be able to follow simple verbal instructions.
SUGGESTED GROUP SKILL SEQUENCES TO PRACTICE BEFORE GROUP PLAY INTERVENTION	No. 31. Following Directions No. 32. Paying Attention No. 16. Self-Control
REQUIRED MATERIALS	Several cards from an oversize deck of playing cards, an open space that is conducive to children moving around freely and in which they can easily see the playing cards being displayed in the front of the room.
ROOM SETUP	Children sit on the floor or in chairs facing the front of the room.
GAME SYNOPSIS	Children are taught behavioral rules that correspond to playing cards. As specific playing cards are displayed, children are to follow the associated rules.

STEPS FOR IMPLEMENTING *ALL MIXED UP*

1. Seat children in a manner in which they have space around them so they can move freely in place. Tell children that they are going to play a game called *All Mixed Up* that involves paying attention and following directions.
2. Tell children that they will be taught rules instructing them to perform various behaviors corresponding to specific playing cards. Each card corresponds to a specific behavior. When a card is displayed, they are to quietly perform the corresponding behavior.
3. The group facilitator provides the rules that correspond to each card and shows them how the game works. For example

   10—Put Hands on Head
   J—Jumping Jack
   Q—Touch Your Feet
   K—Sit Down
   A—Turn Around

   (The number of cards should be adjusted based on children's abilities.)
4. Tell children to stand up in their spot. Then hold up a card, one at a time, for practice. Provide coaching to correct mistakes and ensure proper acquisition of

the information. This should be done until the majority of the children can recall and perform the behaviors corresponding to each card.

5. Tell children that the game will now formally begin. If a child makes a mistake, he or she should sit down and become a judge by helping group facilitators identify other group members who have made errors.

6. Group facilitators should start with a single card, then present two cards, then three cards, simultaneously, and children should perform the appropriate behaviors according to the sequence in which the cards appear. Initially, cards should be held up until the commands are completed. However, as the game continues, group facilitators should hold cards up for shorter and shorter durations.

7. The round ends when only one child is left standing and performing the behaviors. This child should be designated the winner of the round.

8. Repeat Steps 3 through 7 for several rounds until children have mastered the skills or time allocated for the game has elapsed.

9. Group process: Tell the children that the game is now over. Have them sit in their chairs or on the floor facing the front of the room and tell them it is time to discuss the game.

GROUP PROCESS QUESTIONS

1. Ask the children what they needed to do to play the game. Emphasize the importance of following directions, paying attention, and learning to respond to nonverbal cues.

2. Ask the children what they needed to do when a card was displayed. Allow children to provide some specific examples of behaviors corresponding to playing cards.

3. Ask the children how they felt when they knew what to do in response to seeing a certain playing card.

4. Ask the children how they felt when they did not know what do in response to seeing a certain playing card.

5. Ask the children how they felt when they made a mistake.

6. Ask the children how they felt when they saw their peers make a mistake.

8 | GROUP PLAY INTERVENTION: *Blindfold Madness*

OVERVIEW

Blindfold Madness is a relay race that involves children providing verbal instructions to guide their blindfolded teammates in placing a ball in the intended canister across the room.

GROUP PLAY INTERVENTION SKILLS TAUGHT

Primary: Verbal Communication, Following Directions, Active Listening
Secondary: Self-Control, Trust Building

SKILL DIFFICULTY

Advanced

PREREQUISITE SKILLS

Children should possess the ability to follow simple verbal directions and keep their bodies in control.

SUGGESTED GROUP SKILL SEQUENCES TO PRACTICE BEFORE GROUP PLAY INTERVENTION

No. 1. Communicating With Others
No. 10. Being an Active Listener
No. 43. Helping Others
No. 42. Asking for Help
No. 2. Using Nice Talk
No. 39. Being Assertive

REQUIRED MATERIALS

Two small rubber or plastic balls, two canisters (small buckets), and four blindfolds.

ROOM SETUP

Blindfold Madness is an active game in which children need to move freely throughout the room. Therefore, the area in which the children are playing the game should be free from furniture or other objects that might become obstacles or cause injury.

GAME SYNOPSIS

Blindfold Madness is a relay race in which each child stays in a single-file line, is blindfolded, and is verbally instructed to walk over and place a small ball into a canister held by a teammate approximately 10 ft across the room. The goal of the game is for each entire team to successfully drop the ball in the container as fast as possible. When everyone on a team has taken a turn, the round ends and the fastest team wins the round.

STEPS FOR IMPLEMENTING BLINDFOLD MADNESS

1. Begin *Blindfold Madness* by separating children into two teams. Instruct each team to stand in a single-file line on opposite corners of the same end of the room. Select one child from each team to stand 10 ft across from the single-file line.
2. Blindfold the children at the front of each line of each team and give them a ball. The teammate standing directly across the room should be holding a canister.
3. Before the game begins, instruct the children holding the canisters that they will verbally direct their blindfolded teammate to *walk* across the room and place the ball inside the canister that they are holding as quickly as possible. After the blindfolded child has successfully dropped the ball into the canister, she or he should remove her or his blindfold and begin holding the canister for the next teammate. The child originally holding the canister should then go to

the end of her or his team's line, and the game continues until all members of the team have had a chance to be blindfolded. Tell children that if they run, they will have to return to the beginning of their line to start over.

4. Give a signal to begin the race.

5. After all children on a team have completed their turn, make an announcement that the round has ended and that the next round has begun.

6. Group process: Tell the children that the game is now over. Have them sit in their chairs or on the floor facing the front of the room and tell them it is time to discuss the game.

GROUP PROCESS QUESTIONS

1. Ask the children what they needed to do to play the game. Emphasize the importance of verbal communication, following directions, trust, and self-control.

2. Ask the children how they felt when they were blindfolded.

3. Ask the children how they felt when they were directing their blindfolded teammate.

4. Ask the children how they felt when their team won the race.

5. Ask the children how they felt when their team lost the race.

Teaching Module 4

Sharing, Joining a Group, and Group Cooperation

1

GROUP PLAY INTERVENTION:
The Spider Web

OVERVIEW

The Spider Web involves creating a spider web with each group member as a piece of the web.

GROUP PLAY INTERVENTION SKILLS TAUGHT

Primary: Cooperation, Following Directions, Sharing About Oneself
Secondary: Self-Control, Paying Attention

SKILL DIFFICULTY

Beginner

PREREQUISITE SKILLS

Children should be able to follow simple verbal instructions and have basic self-control and attention skills.

SUGGESTED GROUP SKILL SEQUENCES TO PRACTICE BEFORE GROUP PLAY INTERVENTION

No. 35. Cooperation
No. 31. Following Directions
No. 32. Paying Attention
No. 7. Sharing About Oneself

REQUIRED MATERIALS

A ball of string or yarn and a large, open space that is big enough to create the spider web, where children can move about freely.

ROOM SETUP

Children sit on the floor in a circle.

GAME SYNOPSIS

In *The Spider Web*, children roll a ball of string or yarn to each member of their group to create a spider web with the string or yarn. Children select one group member and slowly roll the ball of string or yarn to him or her. If the child throws the string or does not gently roll it, the string is returned to him or her, and he or she is directed to roll it again according to the established rules. The child who received the ball of string or yarn tells the group something he or she likes to do for fun. Each child must have a turn and must end up holding a part of the string in order for the game to be complete. Children are to stay seated on the floor throughout the game so that the spider web can be created.

STEPS FOR IMPLEMENTING *THE SPIDER WEB*

1. Instruct children to sit in a circle.
2. Tell children they need to call out another child's name in the circle and toss the ball of string or yarn to him or her. Also tell children that they need to hold on to the end of the string.
3. Encourage the first child who is handed the ball of string to tell the group something he or she likes to do for fun. Then ask the child to call out another child's name and toss the ball of string gently to that child. Remind the first child to hold onto the end of the string.
4. Instruct the child who catches the ball of string to call out another child's name and gently toss the ball of string to him or her. He or she should also hold onto the end of the string.

5. Repeat Step 4 until all the children have had the chance to catch the ball of string and are holding onto the string. The spider web is now complete.
6. Group process: Tell the children that the game is now over. Have them sit in their chairs or on the floor facing the front of the room and tell them it is time to discuss the game.

GROUP PROCESS
QUESTIONS

1. Ask the children what they needed to do to play the game. Emphasize the importance of cooperation and that *The Spider Web* would not have been such a great success if everyone did not follow directions, exhibit cooperation and self-control, and pay attention.
2. Ask the children what they needed to do when they received the ball of string. Emphasize that they each succeeded by following directions and list each of the steps they followed to achieve success (i.e., selecting a child, calling out her or his name, tossing the string to her or him, and holding onto the end of the string).
3. Ask the children how they felt when they saw the spider web they created.
4. Ask the children how they felt when it was their turn to add to the spider web and how they felt about working together with the other children to achieve this goal. Emphasize that each child made up a part of the web and the web would not have been completed without each child's contribution.
5. Ask the children what they learned about each other's favorite activities. Were their favorite activities similar to or different from other children's favorite activities?

2 GROUP PLAY INTERVENTION: *Monkey in the Blanket*

OVERVIEW

Monkey in the Blanket involves children working together in two groups to guess which child is hiding behind a blanket. This game helps children get to know each other's names.

GROUP PLAY INTERVENTION SKILLS TAUGHT

Primary: Cooperation, Impulse Control, Following Directions
Secondary: Taking Turns, (Visual) Memory, Number Recognition, Counting, Group Problem Solving, Language Skills

SKILL DIFFICULTY

Beginner

PREREQUISITE SKILLS

Children must be able to control their body's movements and follow simple verbal instructions. Children also should have a basic understanding of number comprehension skills.

SUGGESTED GROUP SKILL SEQUENCES TO PRACTICE BEFORE GROUP PLAY INTERVENTION

No. 35. Cooperation
No. 30. Solving a Problem as a Group
No. 36. Taking Turns
No. 43. Helping Others

REQUIRED MATERIALS

Open space in a room for children to stand, a blanket, and a marker to write each child's number on his or her hand if necessary.

ROOM SETUP

A large, open room.

GAME SYNOPSIS

Divide children into two teams. The first team stands with their backs to the second team at the start of the game. One team holds up a blanket as a wall and a member of same team hides behind it. The other team has to guess who the "monkey in the blanket" is. The team that is guessing who is behind the blanket must do so quietly by working together cooperatively and reaching a consensus before giving their final answer (guess). After each correct decision, the other team receives the blanket and follows the same procedure. The game ends when each child has been the monkey in the blanket.

STEPS FOR IMPLEMENTING MONKEY IN THE BLANKET

1. The group facilitator assists the children in forming two groups.
2. Give each child a number in secret. If the children have difficulty remembering their numbers, they can be written on the palm of one hand. The numbers should not be revealed to the other team.
3. Instruct the children on the first team to stand with their backs to the second team.
4. Tell each child on the second team to hold up the blanket as a wall. Instruct the child assigned the number *one* to go behind the blanket.
5. Tell the other team to turn around, face the team holding up the blanket, and decide who the *monkey in the blanket* is. The decision should be based on a team consensus with the help of the group facilitator. Instruct children *not to*

shout out their guesses. A group facilitator should help the children with this by instructing them to quietly discuss their answer before making their final decision. If they are incorrect, allow them to guess again after a team consensus until they are correct.

6. After each correct decision, the other team should receive the blanket and follow the procedure described in Steps 3 through 6. The game ends when each child has been the monkey in the blanket.

7. Group process: Tell the children that the game is now over. Have them sit in their chairs or on the floor facing the front of the room and tell them it is time to discuss the game.

GROUP PROCESS QUESTIONS

1. Ask the children what they needed to do to play the game. Emphasize the importance of making a group decision and how following directions and not shouting out individual answers assisted in making a group decision.

2. Ask the children how they felt when it was their turn to be the monkey in the blanket.

3. Ask the children how they felt when it was not their turn to be the monkey in the blanket.

4. Ask the children how they felt when they were helping the group reach a joint decision about who the monkey in the blanket was.

3 GROUP PLAY INTERVENTION:
The Blob is Spreading

OVERVIEW

The Blob is Spreading is a cooperative version of the classic game of tag, in which children who are tagged become part of a *blob* instead of being eliminated from the game. The game also encourages team cohesion and cooperation.

GROUP PLAY INTERVENTION SKILLS TAUGHT

Primary: Cooperation, Following Directions
Secondary: Self-Control, Paying Attention, Taking Turns

SKILL DIFFICULTY

Beginner

PREREQUISITE SKILLS

Children should be able to follow verbal instructions, display good self-control, and attend to tasks.

SUGGESTED GROUP SKILL SEQUENCES TO PRACTICE BEFORE GROUP PLAY INTERVENTION

No. 35. Cooperation
No. 31. Following Directions
No. 6. Joining a Play Group
No. 36. Taking Turns
No. 37. Being a Good Sport

REQUIRED MATERIALS

None.

ROOM SETUP

An open area, either indoors or outdoors.

GAME SYNOPSIS

One child is selected by the group facilitator to be *it*. The child designated as *it* must chase and tag the other children involved in the game. Instead of being eliminated from the game, each person who is tagged joins hands with the person who is *it* to form a blob. The blob becomes bigger and bigger as more children are tagged. As the blob gets larger, it becomes more difficult to maneuver, but with the use of cooperation, teamwork, self-control, and following directions, the blob moves smoothly as a cohesive unit. The game is over when the last child is tagged and becomes part of the blob. Children must stay in control of their bodies and actions during the game. They must use slow, controlled running while they are chasing and tagging other children.

STEPS FOR IMPLEMENTING *THE BLOB IS SPREADING*

1. Instruct children to find an open spot on the floor (or on the ground if the game is being played outdoors).
2. Select one child to be *it*. Instruct this child that he or she will be chasing the other participants and trying to tag them once the game begins.
3. Tell the children who are *not it* that they should avoid getting tagged by running away. The children must keep control over their bodies and cannot bump into anyone else while they are running in a slow, controlled manner.
4. Give a signal for the game to begin. Instruct the first child tagged to join hands with the person who is *it*, thus forming the beginning of the blob. Instruct them to work together to try to tag other children in the game.

5. Each subsequent child tagged should become part of the blob.
6. The game continues until all of the children have been tagged and have become part of the blob.
7. Group process: Tell the children that the game is now over. Have them sit in their chairs or on the floor facing the front of the room and tell them it is time to discuss the game.

GROUP PROCESS QUESTIONS

1. Ask the children what they needed to do to play the game. Emphasize the importance of cooperation and teamwork involved in being part of the blob.
2. Ask the children how they think the child who was *it* felt.
3. Ask the children how they felt when the blob was chasing them.
4. Ask the children what they needed to do when they became part of the blob. Emphasize that they succeeded in allowing the blob to function as a single unit by following directions and paying attention as they moved around the room.
5. Ask the children how they felt at the end of the game when each child in the group was part of the blob. Emphasize that each child played a role in allowing the blob to function and allowing the game to continue.

4 GROUP PLAY INTERVENTION: *Picture Puzzle*

OVERVIEW

Picture Puzzle involves children drawing a picture on a large piece of oak tag (poster paper). The children are to fill up the entire piece with their drawings. The group facilitator then cuts the oak tag into puzzle pieces, and the group works together to put the puzzle together.

GROUP PLAY INTERVENTION SKILLS TAUGHT

Primary: Cooperation, Problem Solving
Secondary: Paying Attention, Following Directions, Sharing

SKILL DIFFICULTY

Beginner–Intermediate

PREREQUISITE SKILLS

Children should be able to follow simple verbal instructions and have basic self-control and attention skills.

SUGGESTED GROUP SKILL SEQUENCES TO PRACTICE BEFORE GROUP PLAY INTERVENTION

No. 8. Sharing Your Things With Others
No. 30. Solving a Problem as a Group
No. 35. Cooperation
No. 38. Being Patient

REQUIRED MATERIALS

Large pieces of oak tag for children to draw on, markers, crayons, and scissors.

ROOM SETUP

Children sit at a table or on the floor. The children should be provided with enough space to comfortably work on their drawings.

GAME SYNOPSIS

Picture Puzzle involves children coming up with a picture to draw on a big piece of oak tag. First, the children spend 10 minutes drawing a picture, making sure the entire piece is filled up (the group facilitator can help). Second, the group facilitator cuts puzzle pieces out of the oak tag, handing one piece to each group member. Last, the group works on putting the puzzle together.

STEPS FOR IMPLEMENTING PICTURE PUZZLE

1. Tell the children they are going to play a game called *Picture Puzzle* that involves drawing a picture, cutting it up into puzzle pieces, and then putting the pieces together to make a puzzle.
2. Ask the children to come up with an idea for a picture to draw.
3. A group facilitator should give each child a large piece of oak tag and drawing supplies to draw his or her picture. Allow the children to spend 10 minutes drawing a picture, making sure the entire piece of oak tag is filled up (the group facilitator can help).
4. Next, a group facilitator cuts puzzle pieces out of the oak tag, handing one piece to each group member.
5. Group members should then work together on putting the puzzle together.

6. Group process: Tell the children that the game is now over. Have them sit in their chairs or on the floor facing the front of the room and tell them it is time to discuss the game.

GROUP PROCESS QUESTIONS

1. Ask the children how they decided what picture to draw on their piece of oak tag. Ask the children how they felt when they were drawing.
2. Ask the children how they felt when they were trying to fill up their entire piece of oak tag within the 10-minute time period.
3. Ask the children how they felt when the group facilitator cut their picture into pieces for the puzzle. Did they feel good or bad when the picture was cut into puzzle pieces?
4. Ask the children how they felt when they were working together to put the pieces of the puzzle together.

5 GROUP PLAY INTERVENTION: *Pyramid*

OVERVIEW

Pyramid is a game in which children work together in pairs and use listening and cooperation skills. There are 15 categories to choose from, and five clue words are provided for each category.

GROUP PLAY INTERVENTION SKILLS TAUGHT

Primary: Cooperation, Listening, Taking Turns
Secondary: Paying Attention, Following Directions

SKILL DIFFICULTY

Intermediate

PREREQUISITE SKILLS

Children should be able to follow simple verbal instructions and have basic self-control and attention skills. Children should have basic reading skills.

SUGGESTED GROUP SKILL SEQUENCES TO PRACTICE BEFORE GROUP PLAY INTERVENTION

No. 1. Communicating With Others
No. 2. Using Nice Talk
No. 10. Being an Active Listener

REQUIRED MATERIALS

15 cards, each with a different word that relates to the same chosen category, and five cards with cues that offer hints as to what the category words are (there should be one set of category and cue cards for each pair of children).

ROOM SETUP

Children sit in pairs at tables or on the floor.

GAME SYNOPSIS

Children are divided into pairs. One partner picks a card and provides clues to his or her partner about the card. The other child tries to guess the words on the cards. For each word he or she guesses correctly, a point is given to the child. The child with the most points wins.

STEPS FOR IMPLEMENTING *PYRAMID*

1. Tell children they are going to play a game called *Pyramid* that involves being given clues and trying to guess what a word is.
2. Divide the children into pairs.
3. Ask one child in the pair to pick out one of the 15 category cards. These cards should each contain a simple word for a specific category (e.g., animals, food, toys) or a simple picture for younger children who may not be able to read well.
4. Instruct the child with the category card to give clues to the other child based on the five cue cards. The same cue cards can be used for each of the 15 category word cards. These cards should be in a separate pile and should look different from the category cards. Examples of cues for the category "farm animals" are
   a) What type of animal is on the category card?
   b) How is this animal cared for?
   c) What does this animal do on the farm?

5. Tell the other child in the pair to begin guessing the words on the cards based on the clues given. A point should be given to the child for each word he or she guesses correctly. Once the child guesses correctly, or if he or she is unable to figure out the word after all five clues are given, then the round ends and it is the other child's turn to guess the next category word. The child with the most points wins.

6. Repeat Steps 4 and 5 until the children have attempted to guess all 15 category words.

7. Group process: Tell the children that the game is now over. Have them sit in their chairs or on the floor facing the front of the room and tell them it is time to discuss the game.

GROUP PROCESS QUESTIONS

1. Ask the children what they needed to do to play the game.
2. Ask the children how they felt when they were being given clues and were trying to guess the words on the cards.
3. Ask the children how they felt when they guessed the word correctly. Ask them how they felt when they guessed incorrectly.
4. Ask the children how they felt when they were giving the clues and their partners had to guess the words.

6

GROUP PLAY INTERVENTION:
Exclusion Air Ball

OVERVIEW

Exclusion Air Ball involves cooperation and assistance from each member of the group in order to keep a ball in motion and prevent it from touching the ground.

GROUP PLAY INTERVENTION SKILLS TAUGHT

Primary: Management of Emotions (i.e., rejection), Self-Control, Cooperation
Secondary: Following Directions, Taking Turns

SKILL DIFFICULTY

Intermediate

PREREQUISITE SKILLS

Children should be able to follow simple verbal instructions and have basic self-control and cooperative play skills.

SUGGESTED GROUP SKILL SEQUENCES TO PRACTICE BEFORE GROUP PLAY INTERVENTION

No. 25. Dealing With Rejection
No. 26. Dealing With Being Left Out
No. 21. Dealing With Stress
No. 38. Being Patient
No. 16. Self-Control
No. 27. Dealing With Boredom

REQUIRED MATERIALS

A ball. A large, open space in which to play the game.

ROOM SETUP

Instruct children to sit in the open play area, spaced out evenly.

GAME SYNOPSIS

Exclusion Air Ball involves children passing a ball to each other and catching it without the ball touching the ground. If the ball drops, the group stands up, and a trait or characteristic is chosen by which to reject (exclude) players (i.e., hair color, eye color, age). The goal of the game is for children to learn how to work together and deal with rejection. Group facilitators should be prepared to help children deal with their rejections.

STEPS FOR IMPLEMENTING EXCLUSION AIR BALL

1. Instruct children to sit on the floor or ground, spaced out evenly. Tell them they are going to play a game called *Exclusion Air Ball* and will learn how to work together.
2. Instruct children to keep the ball in motion by preventing it from touching the ground. Each child should pass the ball to someone else as soon as he or she receives it. The receiving person must try to catch the ball and not let it fall.
3. Tell children they need to call out something they like (e.g., pizza, video games, basketball) each time they catch the ball before they throw it to the next person. This step allows the children to playfully share something they like with the group. If the ball drops, the whole group has to stand up and identify a characteristic or trait of the child that dropped the ball (e.g., blonde hair, green eyes, wearing red shorts).
4. Any players who share the same characteristic or trait should then be rejected from the game. After a couple of rounds, the group facilitators should then

allow excluded (rejected) players a chance to rejoin the others participating in the game.

5. Those children who are rejected during the game should sit to the side and quietly watch the game being played. The group facilitator should have a negative reaction to the rejections at certain points during the game so children can see how to deal with the emotions that accompany rejection. Group facilitators should be prepared to help the children deal with their rejections.

6. Repeat Steps 2 through 5 until all the children have had a turn to catch and throw the ball.

7. Group process: Tell the children that the game is now over. Have them sit in their chairs or on the floor facing the front of the room and tell them it is time to discuss the game.

GROUP PROCESS QUESTIONS

1. Ask the children what they needed to do to play the game. Emphasize the importance of working together as a group.

2. Ask the children how they felt when they successfully caught the ball and threw it to the next player without the ball touching the ground.

3. Ask the children how they felt when they were excluded from the game based on the selected characteristic.

4. Ask the children how they felt when they excluded other children from the game.

5. Ask the children how they felt when they saw the group facilitator have a poor reaction to the rejection occurring in the game.

7 GROUP PLAY INTERVENTION: *Goodnight Rover*

OVERVIEW

Goodnight Rover involves cooperation and assistance from each member of the group in order to successfully get the dog (Rover) in his bed for the night without harming him or waking him up.

GROUP PLAY INTERVENTION SKILLS TAUGHT

Primary: Self-Control, Taking Turns, Cooperation
Secondary: Following Directions

SKILL DIFFICULTY

Intermediate

PREREQUISITE SKILLS

Children should be able to follow simple verbal instructions and have basic self-control and cooperative play skills.

SUGGESTED GROUP SKILL SEQUENCES TO PRACTICE BEFORE GROUP PLAY INTERVENTION

No. 16. Self-Control
No. 36. Taking Turns
No. 35. Cooperation

REQUIRED MATERIALS

A bed for Rover (e.g., small towel or folded blanket), an uncooked egg decorated to look like a dog (a dog made out of Legos can be used for children with egg allergies; tell children the Lego dog is delicate and could break if mishandled or dropped on the floor), and an open space or room large enough so children can move about freely.

The group facilitator can decorate the egg using magic markers. The children can also decorate the egg before the game begins, which provides them with an opportunity to take turns and work cooperatively. Each child could have the chance to draw one item on Rover (e.g., hair, eyes, mouth, fur). If the Lego dog is used, the children can work to put him together before the game.

ROOM SETUP

Children should start out sitting in a group. The group facilitator should call each child, one by one, and ask him or her to select a spot to stand for the beginning of the activity.

GAME SYNOPSIS

Goodnight Rover involves each child taking a turn to carry Rover safely to the next child without waking him up (e.g., by handling him roughly or dropping him). Rover's bed can be a small folded towel or blanket placed somewhere in the room by the group facilitator. Children are to call out the name of another group member and slowly walk over to that group member with Rover. The child holding Rover is to carefully hand him to the next child. If Rover is not handled carefully and he wakes up, the two children involved in the interaction are asked to go back to their original positions and repeat the interaction more carefully so Rover does not wake up. Each child must have a turn holding Rover and handing him to another group member. The last child handed Rover puts him to sleep in his bed for the night.

1. Instruct children to sit in a group.
2. Instruct each child individually to get up and select a spot on the floor where she or he will stand for the start of the game. Another variation is to have chairs set up in various locations in the room and instruct each child to select a chair to sit in for the start of the game. Chairs may encourage some level of competition, especially if there are children with social skills deficits. The group facilitator will need to be mindful of this and intervene when appropriate.
3. Tell children that they need to call out another child's name and carefully walk, not run, over to that child and hand Rover to him or her carefully so that he does not wake up.
4. Hand Rover to the first child. This child should be instructed to call out another child's name, and carefully walk, not run, to that child and hand Rover to him or her carefully so that Rover does not wake up.
5. Instruct the child who now has Rover to call out another child's name and take Rover to that child.
6. Repeat Step 5 until all the children have had a chance to hold and carry Rover.
7. The last child should be responsible for carrying Rover to his bed (e.g., a small folded towel or blanket) and put him to sleep for the night.
8. Group process: Tell the children that the game is now over. Have them sit in their chairs or on the floor facing the front of the room and tell them it is time to discuss the game.

**GROUP PROCESS
QUESTIONS**

1. Ask the children what they needed to do to play the game. Emphasize the importance of controlling their hands and feet and taking turns. Remind the group that Rover might have woken up or gotten hurt if everyone did not follow directions and abide by the rules.
2. Ask the children what they needed to do when they received Rover.
3. Ask the children how they felt about their contribution toward getting Rover safely in his bed for the night without waking him up or hurting him.

8 GROUP PLAY INTERVENTION: *The Mummy*

OVERVIEW

The Mummy encourages children to work together, as each child is assigned a special job or task to create the illusion of a spooky (mummy) atmosphere.

GROUP PLAY INTERVENTION SKILLS TAUGHT

Primary: Cooperation, Understanding Social Cues, Goal Setting and Obtainment
Secondary: Self-Control, Following Directions, Taking Turns

SKILL DIFFICULTY

Intermediate

PREREQUISITE SKILLS

Children should be able to understand and perform simple social cues (i.e., perform an assigned part of a group task), follow verbal instructions, display self-control, and attend to tasks.

SUGGESTED GROUP SKILL SEQUENCES TO PRACTICE BEFORE GROUP PLAY INTERVENTION

No. 19. Understanding Social Cues
No. 28. Setting Goals and Obtaining Them
No. 21. Dealing With Stress
No. 16. Self-Control

REQUIRED MATERIALS

A mid-size room or space, a chair, and a CD player to play music or "spooky" sounds. Additional materials for this game can vary depending on the imagination of the children involved in the group. For example, a chain or other similar object that will make a rattling noise, props such as a ghost or another spooky character, or a sheet to use to dress up as a ghost.

ROOM SETUP

A mid-size room or space.

GAME SYNOPSIS

The Mummy is a cooperative game that involves creating a spooky atmosphere. This game requires some planning before the actual game is played. Children sit in a circle or at a table with the group facilitator. Through cooperative discussions, each child selects a special job that will contribute to the spooky atmosphere. For example, one group member is selected to flicker the lights on and off, another group member is selected to start and stop the music or spooky sounds from playing, one member is selected to rattle a chain, or another is selected to dress up as a ghost and "float" by. Another child or an adult sits in a chair in the middle of the room and plays the role of the person who is "scared" by the spooky atmosphere. Each child must perform his or her assigned job to make the game a success.

STEPS FOR IMPLEMENTING *THE MUMMY*

1. Ask children to sit in a circle or at a table with the group facilitator and instruct them to plan out and determine each group member's role in the game (e.g., playing the music, flickering the lights).
2. After each child has selected his or her role in the game, group members should create a spooky atmosphere and prepare for their individual roles.

3. A volunteer should sit in the designated chair in the middle of the room. He or she should be encouraged to act scared once the game begins.

4. Instruct each child to perform her or his task to create the spooky atmosphere and scare the unwitting volunteer. This form of pretend play allows children to develop creativity skills. Instruct children to stay focused on the timing of their tasks, so they are performed at the appropriate time. If a child forgets to perform her or his task or performs it incorrectly, the group facilitator should discuss it with the group afterward and come up with a solution for how to make it work when she or he scares the next volunteer.

5. After each child has performed her or his assigned task, tell all the children to come to the center of the room where the volunteer is sitting and surround her or him, pretending to be mummies. The mummies should make scary moaning sounds and walk toward the volunteer, holding their arms out to look like mummies. The children must walk slowly and not run. Finally all of the mummies should give the volunteer a big group mummy hug!

6. Group process: Tell the children that the game is now over. Have them sit in their chairs or on the floor facing the front of the room and tell them it is time to discuss the game.

GROUP PROCESS QUESTIONS

1. Ask the children what they needed to do to plan and prepare for this game to be a success. Emphasize the importance of cooperation, self-control, and following instructions.

2. Ask the children what they needed to do to play the game. Emphasize how each person had a very special individual role, but it was the combination of all the individual roles that created the very spooky atmosphere.

3. Ask the children how they felt when the spooky music was playing and when they turned into mummies.

4. Ask the children how they felt when they tried to scare the volunteer.

5. Ask the children how they felt at the end of the game after they successfully created the spooky atmosphere and turned into mummies. Emphasize that each child played a role in making it a success.

9

GROUP PLAY INTERVENTION:
Creating A Story Together

OVERVIEW

Creating a Story Together involves children working collaboratively to invent a continuous narrative on a given topic.

GROUP PLAY INTERVENTION SKILLS TAUGHT

Primary: Cooperation, Paying Attention, Asking for Help, Helping Others
Secondary: Sharing, Self-Control, Staying on Topic, Working Independently, Following Directions

SKILL DIFFICULTY

Intermediate

PREREQUISITE SKILLS

Children should be able to work with other children, keep their bodies in control, and follow simple directions.

SUGGESTED GROUP SKILL SEQUENCES TO PRACTICE BEFORE GROUP PLAY INTERVENTION

No. 42. Asking For Help
No. 43. Helping Others
No. 33. Staying on Task
No. 34. Working Independently
No. 8. Sharing Your Things With Others
No. 15. Not Interrupting Others

REQUIRED MATERIALS

Open space for children to sit, pencils and crayons, and blank sheets of paper.

ROOM SETUP

Children sit at a table with a piece of blank paper, pencils, and crayons in front of them.

GAME SYNOPSIS

Group facilitators provide children with a topic and children are given 5 minutes to draw a picture relating to that topic. After they are finished, the group facilitator begins to tell a story based on the topic. Each child provides details about his or her drawing and helps to create a story.

STEPS FOR IMPLEMENTING *CREATING A STORY TOGETHER*

1. After the group facilitator has chosen a topic (e.g., a time . . . at the beach, at a playground, at an amusement park, in a classroom), tell children that they have 5 minutes to draw a picture that relates to that topic. Children should be designing their pictures independently. No further instruction is given.
2. After the 5-minute time period has elapsed, instruct children to form a circle and sit with their pictures on their laps.
3. When everyone is seated, the group facilitator starts a story by saying something like, "Once upon a time, there was a boy named . . . " The child sitting next to the facilitator on the right is instructed to use his or her picture to add to the story.
4. Tell children that their contribution must relate to their individual pictures and be relevant to the story line. If they feel stuck at any point, children should ask another group member for help.
5. The game continues until all children have a chance to add to the story line.

6. Group process: Tell the children that the game is now over. Have them sit in their chairs or on the floor facing the front of the room and tell them it is time to discuss the game.

GROUP PROCESS QUESTIONS

1. Ask the children what they needed to do to play the game. Emphasize the importance of listening to each other and asking for help when needed.
2. Ask the children how they felt when they were drawing their pictures.
3. Ask the children how they felt when it was their turn to add to the story.
4. Ask the children how they felt when they needed to ask others in the group for help.
5. Ask the children how they felt when they were helping another group member.

Teaching Module 5

Anger Management

1 GROUP PLAY INTERVENTION:
Let It Out Art

OVERVIEW
Let It Out Art allows children to express anger through free-form art.

GROUP PLAY INTERVENTION SKILLS TAUGHT
Primary: Anger Management
Secondary: Following Directions, Controlling Self-Expression (e.g., managing paints, brushes, paper in an appropriate way)

SKILL DIFFICULTY
Beginner

PREREQUISITE SKILLS
Children need to be able to draw and understand emotions.

SUGGESTED GROUP SKILL SEQUENCES TO PRACTICE BEFORE GROUP PLAY INTERVENTION
No. 23. Dealing With Your Angry Feelings
No. 34. Working Independently
No. 18. Expressing Feelings and Emotions

REQUIRED MATERIALS
Large pieces of paper to cover an entire wall, different colored paints, paint brushes, cups of clean water to rinse paint brushes in, and smocks.

ROOM SETUP
A large part of a wall should be completely covered with paper for the children to paint on.

GAME SYNOPSIS
Children are given a scenario that is likely to cause anger or frustration, and they are asked to express how they feel using paint. For example, a child might be told, "An older boy comes up to you at recess, steals the ball you are playing with, and runs away. Use the paints to express how this makes you feel." The group facilitator can explain the value of using art as an effective anger management technique by emphasizing that art is an acceptable way to express anger and let frustration out. During the Group Process Questions at the end, the group facilitator can ask how the children felt during and after painting. Children of different ages can express their anger at whatever level of artistic ability they possess.

STEPS FOR IMPLEMENTING *LET IT OUT ART*
1. Instruct children to sit on the floor in a group or circle. The group facilitator can ask preliminary questions and discuss them with the children. Sample questions might be
   a) What do you do when you are angry? Encourage the children to identify specific behaviors that they may exhibit such as crying, not wanting to talk, yelling, hitting things, throwing objects, and so forth.
   b) What do you think about when you are angry? Encourage the children to identify specific thoughts that they may have such as, "I am so angry," "Sam is so mean. I just want to hit him!" or "Jill is a jerk to say that to me!"
   c) How do you feel when you are angry? Encourage the children to identify specific feelings such as feeling jumpy, anxious, hot, tense, sick, and so forth.
   d) What do you do to make yourself feel better when you are angry?

2. Explain to the children that they are going to play a game called *Let It Out Art* using paint that provides a cool and acceptable way to express their anger. Tell children that they will be given a scenario that will likely make them angry or frustrated and that they will then be given the opportunity to "let it out" and express how they feel using art.

3. Select one child from the group to come up to the papered wall and read one of the anger- or frustration-inducing scenarios to the child. Then ask the child to express how she or he feels using the paints in any way she or he chooses, as long as the paint stays on the paper and there is no danger that anyone will get hurt.

4. Repeat Step 3 until each child has had a turn to "let it out."

5. Group process: Tell the children that the game is now over. Have them sit in their chairs or on the floor facing the front of the room and tell them it is time to discuss the game.

GROUP PROCESS QUESTIONS

1. Ask the children what they needed to do to play the game.

2. Ask the children how they felt after the group facilitator read them their anger- or frustration-inducing scenarios.

3. Ask the children how they felt while they were painting.

4. Ask the children how they felt when they were done with their paintings. Emphasize how expressing their anger or frustration through art allowed them to "let it out" in an acceptable way to release the anger.

2 GROUP PLAY INTERVENTION: *Anger Management Brainstorming Competition*

OVERVIEW

Anger Management Brainstorming Competition involves children working together as a group to generate a list of anger management strategies that can be used to make one feel better.

GROUP PLAY INTERVENTION SKILLS TAUGHT

Primary: Anger Management
Secondary: Cooperation, Listening to Others

SKILL DIFFICULTY

Beginner

PREREQUISITE SKILLS

Children should have been exposed to some anger management techniques (e.g., pillow squeeze, turtle, controlled breathing). Skill sequences should be used to illustrate how novel techniques are used.

SUGGESTED GROUP SKILL SEQUENCES TO PRACTICE BEFORE GROUP PLAY INTERVENTION

No. 23. Dealing With Your Angry Feelings
No. 10. Being an Active Listener
No. 30. Solving a Problem as a Group
No. 15. Not Interrupting Others
No. 24. Dealing With Another Person's Angry Feelings

REQUIRED MATERIALS

Paper and writing instruments.

ROOM SETUP

Children should be sitting on the floor or in chairs.

GAME SYNOPSIS

Children are divided into two (or three) teams, and a group facilitator works with each team to generate a list of as many appropriate activities that one can use to cope with anger.

STEPS FOR IMPLEMENTING ANGER MANAGEMENT BRAINSTORMING COMPETITION

1. Tell children that they are going to play a game called *Anger Management Brainstorming Competition* that involves working together to come up with activities that will help anyone feel better when he or she is angry.
2. Divide children into two (or three) teams and are told to go as a team to a designated area of the room.
3. Tell the groups to begin and give them a specified amount of time (e.g., 5 minutes) to generate a list of anger management strategies. A facilitator should assist each group to ensure that they are completing the activity appropriately and provide hints and guidance (as necessary). If children need assistance writing, the facilitator can write the strategies that the children come up with.
4. Let the groups know when time is up. Each group stops the activity.
5. Instruct groups to count the number of strategies they came up with. The group with the most strategies should read their list first.
6. Instruct children in the other groups to check off the items that match their list. Group facilitators should determine whether strategies are appropriate and practical.

7. The next group(s) should then read their items out loud one at a time while Step 6 is repeated.
8. Count the number of unique items for each group. The group that has the most unique items wins the game. Unique items for each group are reread out loud.
9. Group process: Tell the children that the game is now over. Have them sit in their chairs or on the floor facing the front of the room and tell them it is time to discuss the game.

GROUP PROCESS QUESTIONS

1. Ask the children what they needed to do to play the game. Emphasize the importance of working together, listening to each other, and coming up with anger management strategies.
2. Ask the children how they felt when they were able coming up with anger management strategies.
3. Ask the children how they felt if they were unable to generate strategies.
4. Ask the children how they felt when time ran out.
5. Ask the children what new strategies they had heard.
6. Ask the children which strategies they would use if they were angry.

3   GROUP PLAY INTERVENTION: *Bean Bag Toss*

OVERVIEW   *Bean Bag Toss* involves simulating a frustrating situation while encouraging the use of an anger management technique to make one feel better.

GROUP PLAY INTERVENTION SKILLS TAUGHT   Primary: Anger Management
Secondary: Self-Control, Following Directions

SKILL DIFFICULTY   Beginner–Intermediate

PREREQUISITE SKILLS   Children should have knowledge of basic emotions and the ability to identify and express their feelings verbally or nonverbally.

SUGGESTED GROUP SKILL SEQUENCES TO PRACTICE BEFORE GROUP PLAY INTERVENTION   No. 23. Dealing With Your Angry Feelings
No. 21. Dealing With Stress
No. 16. Self-Control
No. 17. Identifying Feelings and Emotions

REQUIRED MATERIALS   Bean bag, small bucket or container, and props that can be used for anger management strategies (books, crayons, stuffed animals, pillows, etc.).

ROOM SETUP   Children sit in two single-file lines facing each other. A small bucket or container is placed on the floor in the middle of the two lines. Props for anger management strategies are placed behind each of the lines so that children can easily reach them.

GAME SYNOPSIS   Children have to complete the difficult task of throwing a bean bag in a small bucket or container from a distance. When a child is unable to get the bean bag in the bucket or container, he or she must perform an effective anger management strategy.

STEPS FOR IMPLEMENTING BEAN BAG TOSS

1. Introduce *Bean Bag Toss* to children as an exciting game that involves throwing a bean bag into a container. If they get it in, a point is awarded. If they miss, they will have to perform an effective anger management technique to help them feel better.
2. Review several anger management techniques.
3. Instruct the first child in one of the lines to attempt to throw the bean bag into the container. If the first child tosses it in, she or he receives two points and goes to the end of the line. If she or he misses, she or he must decide on an anger management strategy that has not already been used and perform it before proceeding to the end of the line. If the child is successful in coming up with a unique strategy, she or he should receive one point.
4. Instruct the first child in the second line to take a turn and follows Step 3. The lines should continue alternating until all the children had the opportunity to observe or use a variety of anger management techniques.

5. Group process: Tell the children that the game is now over. Have them sit in their chairs or on the floor facing the front of the room and tell them it is time to discuss the game.

GROUP PROCESS
QUESTIONS

1. Ask the children what they needed to do to play the game. Emphasize the importance of appropriately coming up with and using effective anger management strategies, following directions, and staying in control.
2. Ask the children how they felt when they got the bean bag into the container.
3. Ask the children how they felt when they missed the container.
4. Ask the children how they felt when they had to come up with an anger management strategy.
5. Ask the children how they felt after using the anger management strategy.

PLAY INTERVENTION:
Angry Hot Potato

OVERVIEW

Angry Hot Potato involves simulating a frustrating situation while encouraging the use of anger management techniques to make one feel better.

GROUP PLAY INTERVENTION SKILLS TAUGHT

Primary: Anger Management
Secondary: Following Directions, Self-Control

SKILL DIFFICULTY

Basic–Intermediate

PREREQUISITE SKILLS

Children should have knowledge of basic emotions and the ability to identify and express their emotions.

SUGGESTED GROUP SKILL SEQUENCES TO PRACTICE BEFORE GROUP PLAY INTERVENTION

No. 23. Dealing With Your Angry Feelings
No. 16. Self-Control
No. 31. Following Directions
No. 37. Being a Good Sport

REQUIRED MATERIALS

Soft playground ball (approximately 23 inches in circumference), stuffed animals, pillows, books, crayons, and any other appropriate props that can be used to deal effectively with anger.

ROOM SETUP

Children sit in a circle on the floor or in chairs. Materials for anger management strategies are placed in the center of the circle (or in front of each child if deemed necessary).

GAME SYNOPSIS

Children gently pass the ball to different people in the circle with the goal of not letting it hit the floor. If the ball falls, this simulates a situation that makes the children angry, which requires that they engage in an anger management technique to make themselves feel better.

STEPS FOR IMPLEMENTING ANGRY HOT POTATO

1. In a positive, playful manner, tell children that they are going to play a special game called *Angry Hot Potato*, which involves following directions, controlling their hands and feet, and finding ways to make themselves feel less angry.
2. Before starting the game, review the rules:
    a) Children should pass a ball to others in the circle in a controlled manner.
    b) The goal is to pass the ball to as many children as possible without letting it hit the floor.
    c) If the ball falls, the whole group must sit down and the round ends. This makes everyone angry.
3. Children should repeat the directions to ensure that they know them.
4. The game begins, and the ball is gently passed to the first child. Children proceed to pass the ball until it touches the floor.
5. When the ball touches the floor, tell all the children to sit and to show their angry faces.

6. Instruct children to think of an anger management strategy that they can use to calm themselves down. Tell them that they can use one of the props from the center of the circle, if necessary.
7. After a few seconds, tell children to stand up and use the anger management strategy that they have chosen. After all the children have successfully used an anger management strategy and all props have been returned to the middle of the circle, the next round can begin.
8. Repeat Steps 4 through Step 7 until children have demonstrated knowledge of various anger management strategies.
9. Group process: Tell the children that the game is now over. Have them sit in their chairs or on the floor facing the front of the room and tell them it is time to discuss the game.

1. Ask the children what they needed to do to play the game. Emphasize the importance of appropriately dealing with anger, following directions, and staying in control.
2. Ask the children how they felt when they caught or passed the ball.
3. Ask the children how they felt when someone else dropped the ball.
4. Ask the children how they felt when they dropped the ball.
5. Ask the children what they did that they made themselves feel better.

5 GROUP PLAY INTERVENTION: *Go Samantha the Squirrel!*

OVERVIEW
Go Samantha the Squirrel! involves children helping Samantha the squirrel race to the finish line on her bicycle by answering questions correctly. When a child answers a question incorrectly, Samantha is forced to go backwards, creating a frustrating situation. Children must use an anger management technique to make them feel better if they get angry.

GROUP PLAY INTERVENTION SKILLS TAUGHT
Primary: Anger Management
Secondary: Self-Control, Following Directions

SKILL DIFFICULTY
Intermediate–Advanced

PREREQUISITE SKILLS
Children should have knowledge of basic emotions and the ability to identify and express their emotions (anger).

SUGGESTED GROUP SKILL SEQUENCES TO PRACTICE BEFORE GROUP PLAY INTERVENTION
No. 23. Dealing With Your Angry Feelings
No. 16. Self-Control
No. 37. Being a Good Sport

REQUIRED MATERIALS
- A set of small cards on which to write questions. The cards can be from a game such as *Trivial Pursuit Junior,* or the cards can be made by the group facilitator ahead of time. Index cards and a writing instrument are necessary if the group facilitator will create his or her own cards.
- A 2- × 3-ft poster board (can be purchased at any office supply store). The poster board serves as the bicycle race route for Samantha the Squirrel and should be set up by the group facilitator. It should have a track drawn with increments clearly indicated on it for moving forward and backward.
- A drawing of Samantha on her bicycle.
- Velcro (the Velcro is placed on the back of Samantha and on each designated step on the racing route so Samantha can be moved along the route).
- Scissors (the group facilitator will use scissors to cut out the drawing of Samantha on her bicycle).
- Props that can be used for anger management strategies (e.g., books, crayons, stuffed animals, pillows).

ROOM SETUP
Children sit in a group on the floor or in chairs. The poster board is placed in front of the children so they can come up and work with it when they are selected. Props for anger management strategies are placed so that children can reach them easily.

GAME SYNOPSIS
Children are asked a series of questions. When a child answers a question correctly, he or she is asked to come to the front of the room and move Samantha the Squirrel's bicycle forward two spaces. When a child misses the question, he or she is asked to move

Samantha's bicycle backward one space. The goal is to get Samantha to the finish line! The child must perform an effective anger management strategy if he or she feels frustrated or angry after answering a question incorrectly and having to move Samantha backwards on the bicycle route.

STEPS FOR IMPLEMENTING *GO SAMANTHA THE SQUIRREL!*

1. Instruct children to sit in a group on the floor or in chairs. Show them the poster board with Samantha the Squirrel on the racetrack. Tell them they will be playing a game called *Go Samantha the Squirrel!* that involves answering questions and moving Samantha forward or backward on the racetrack, based on whether they answer questions correctly or incorrectly.
2. Review several anger management techniques.
3. Select a child from the group to come up and answer a question from the set of cards. If the child answers the question correctly, she or he moves Samantha forward two spaces on the racetrack. If the child answers the question incorrectly, she or he moves Samantha back one space. The child should perform an effective anger management technique to help feel better if she or he feels angry after giving an incorrect answer.
4. The game continues until the group gets Samantha to the finish line.
5. Group process: Tell the children that the game is now over. Have them sit in their chairs or on the floor facing the front of the room and tell them it is time to discuss the game.

GROUP PROCESS QUESTIONS

1. Ask the children what they needed to do to play the game. Emphasize the importance of using effective anger management strategies, following directions, and staying in control.
2. Ask the children how they felt when they answered a question correctly.
3. Ask the children how they felt when they got to move Samantha forward in the race to the finish line.
4. Ask the children how they felt when they answered a question incorrectly.
5. Ask the children how they felt when they had to move Samantha backward.
6. Ask the children how they felt when Samantha reached the finish line. Emphasize that it is possible to feel angry or frustrated while working on a task (e.g., if they answered a question incorrectly), but they should work through their feelings and keep going in order to finish the task.
7. Ask the children how they felt while they were using an anger management strategy.
8. Ask the children how they felt after using the anger management strategy.

6

GROUP PLAY INTERVENTION:
Hot or Cool

OVERVIEW

Hot or Cool involves rolling a die and moving around a poster board. Children can land on various categories and must come up with or recall different methods for managing anger.

GROUP PLAY INTERVENTION SKILLS TAUGHT

Primary: Anger Management
Secondary: Paying Attention, Following Directions, Cooperation, Working as a Team

SKILL DIFFICULTY

Intermediate–Advanced

PREREQUISITE SKILLS

Children should have knowledge of basic emotions and the ability to identify and express their emotions (anger).

SUGGESTED GROUP SKILL SEQUENCES TO PRACTICE BEFORE GROUP PLAY INTERVENTION

No. 23. Dealing With Your Angry Feelings
No. 30. Solving a Problem as a Group
No. 42. Asking for Help
No. 43. Helping Others

REQUIRED MATERIALS

Die, playing pieces, and a 2- × 3-ft poster board (can be purchased at any office supply store). The poster board should be created by the group facilitator ahead of time. It should contain the following categories to land on: *Hot, Cool,* or *You Decide.*

ROOM SETUP

A group of three to five children should be seated around the poster board, either at a table or on the floor.

GAME SYNOPSIS

Children roll the die and move the specified number of spaces around the poster board. A child can land on one of three categories: *Hot, Cool,* or *You Decide.* If a child lands on *Hot,* he or she must state one way that is *not* acceptable to react when you become angry. If he or she lands on *Cool,* he or she must state one acceptable way to calm down (cool down), when he or she is angry. If a child lands on *You Decide,* he or she can choose to state a *Hot* or *Cool* answer. If the child cannot come up with an answer, the group facilitator calls on the group to provide some suggestions to help the child come up with an answer. The first player to get all the way around the board wins.

STEPS FOR IMPLEMENTING THE HOT OR COOL

1. Tell children they are going to play a game called *Hot or Cool* about acceptable and unacceptable ways to react to situations that make one angry. Several anger management techniques are reviewed.
2. Tell children to sit evenly spaced around the poster board. Children are each given a chance to roll the die. The child with the highest number goes first. The game proceeds clockwise from the first player.
3. The first child rolls the die and moves the specified number of spaces. He or she must state one acceptable or unacceptable way to react to a situation that induces anger, depending on what category he or she lands on. If the child pro-

vides the answer, he or she goes again. If the child has trouble thinking of an answer on his or her own, the group facilitator calls on the group to provide suggestions to help the child come up with an answer.

4. Repeat Step 3 until the first player gets all the way around the poster board.
5. Group process: Tell the children that the game is now over. Have them sit in their chairs or on the floor facing the front of the room and tell them it is time to discuss the game.

GROUP PROCESS QUESTIONS

1. Ask the children what they needed to do to play the game. Emphasize the importance of appropriately coming up with effective and ineffective anger management strategies, following directions, and staying in control.
2. Ask the children how they felt when they answered a question appropriately.
3. Ask the children how they felt when they had trouble answering the question and the group provided some suggestions to help come up with an answer. Ask the children if it felt good when their friends helped them. Emphasize that cooperation and teamwork leads to success.
4. Ask the children how they felt when they had to come up with an anger management strategy.
5. Ask the children how they felt when the game was over.

7

GROUP PLAY INTERVENTION:
Returning the Book

OVERVIEW

Returning the Book is a role-play game that involves children taking turns returning a book to a shopkeeper because it is missing a page. This game demonstrates to children the effect that their anger has on others and teaches them appropriate strategies for handling situations that induce anger.

GROUP PLAY INTERVENTION SKILLS TAUGHT

Primary: Anger Management, Assertiveness
Secondary: Following Directions, Self-Control

SKILL DIFFICULTY

Intermediate–Advanced

PREREQUISITE SKILLS

Children should have attention skills, self-control, and the ability to following directions. Children should have knowledge of basic emotions and the ability to identify and express their emotions (anger).

SUGGESTED GROUP SKILL SEQUENCES TO PRACTICE BEFORE GROUP PLAY INTERVENTION

No. 23. Dealing With Your Angry Feelings
No. 39. Being Assertive
No. 40. Saying No
No. 41. Accepting No
No. 21. Dealing With Stress
No. 24. Dealing With Another Person's Angry Feelings

REQUIRED MATERIALS

None.

ROOM SETUP

Children sit in a group on the floor or in chairs. A medium-size open space should be available for the children to role play the scenarios in small groups.

GAME SYNOPSIS

Children take turns (role play) being a customer returning a book to the shopkeeper because it's missing a page. There are three roles for the customer to play: Mr. or Mrs. Wimpy (submissive), Mr. or Mrs. Angry (aggressive), and Mr. or Mrs. Strong (assertive). After each role play, the group facilitator asks the shopkeeper how she or he felt, asks the customer how he or she felt, and asks the children who observed how they felt. Usually Mr. or Mrs. Wimpy makes everybody feel as though they do not want to change the book, and Mr. or Mrs. Angry gets everybody angry. The Mr. or Mrs. Strong approach means that the customer asserted him- or herself in a positive way and successfully came away from the shop with a new book.

STEPS FOR IMPLEMENTING *RETURNING THE BOOK*

1. Instruct children that they are going to play a game called *Returning the Book* that involves pretending to be a customer trying to return a book to a bookstore because it is missing a page. The group facilitator should also review with children the effect their anger has on others.
2. The group facilitator instructs the children that there are three possible roles for the customer: Mr. or Mrs. Wimpy (submissive), Mr. or Mrs. Angry (aggres-

sive), and Mr. or Mrs. Strong (assertive). Review what each role means with the children before playing the game.

3. Select a child to play the customer and a child to play the shopkeeper. The other children in the group should observe the scenario. Then direct the customer to take on the role of either Mr. or Mrs. Wimpy (submissive) or Mr. or Mrs. Angry (aggressive). A group facilitator should model the correct behavior if the children are struggling. After each role play, a group facilitator should ask the shopkeeper how she or he felt, ask the customer how he or she felt, and ask the children who observed how they felt.

4. Repeat Step 3 until each child has had a turn to play one of the roles.

5. Next, select a child to play the role of shopkeeper. Another child should model the customer role of Mr. or Mrs. Strong (assertive).

6. Group process: Tell the children that the game is now over. Have them sit in their chairs or on the floor facing the front of the room and tell them it is time to discuss the game.

GROUP PROCESS QUESTIONS

1. Ask the children what they needed to do to play the game. Emphasize the importance of appropriately dealing with anger and the effect that being angry has on other people.

2. Ask the shopkeeper how she or he felt when Mr. or Mrs. Wimpy was trying to return the book. Mr. or Mrs. Angry? Mr. or Mrs. Strong?

3. Ask the customer how he or she felt while playing the role of Mr. or Mrs. Wimpy? Mr. or Mrs. Angry? Mr. or Mrs. Strong?

4. Ask the observers how they felt while they were observing the customer play the role of Mr. or Mrs. Wimpy? Mr. or Mrs. Angry? Mr. or Mrs. Strong? Emphasize to all the children the effect being angry has on other people and that there are better ways to interact with people. Also, emphasize to the children that Mr. or Mrs. Strong is assertive in a positive way and that people will want to help him or her. Tell the children that when someone reacts angrily to a situation, people will become angry with that person and may not want to help him or her.

8 GROUP PLAY INTERVENTION:
Angries in the Bin

OVERVIEW

Angries in the Bin is a game that involves children brainstorming and creating a list as a group about things or situations that make them angry.

GROUP PLAY INTERVENTION SKILLS TAUGHT

Primary: Anger Management
Secondary: Self-Control, Following Directions, Paying Attention

SKILL DIFFICULTY

Intermediate–Advanced

PREREQUISITE SKILLS

Children should have basic attention skills and the ability to follow directions. Children should have knowledge of basic emotions and the ability to identify and express their emotions (anger).

SUGGESTED GROUP SKILL SEQUENCES TO PRACTICE BEFORE GROUP PLAY INTERVENTION

No. 7. Sharing About Oneself
No. 23. Dealing With Your Angry Feelings
No. 18. Expressing Feelings and Emotions

REQUIRED MATERIALS

Bin (e.g., a small wastebasket), a notepad or flip chart, and a writing instrument.

ROOM SETUP

Children sit in a circle on the floor, with the bin in the center. The group facilitator, with the notepad, should sit in the circle with the children. Alternatively, the facilitator can have a flip chart set up.

GAME SYNOPSIS

Children are asked to brainstorm a list of things or situations that make them angry (e.g., "Johnny cut in front of me in the lunch line," or "My Mom made me clean my room"). Next, each child is asked to discuss something that makes him or her angry and how he or she could handle it. After the child has stated something that makes him or her angry and how to handle it appropriately, he or she is encouraged to get rid of the *Angries* by tossing them gently into the bin.

STEPS FOR IMPLEMENTING *ANGRIES IN THE BIN*

1. Instruct children to sit in a circle on the floor. Tell them they are going to play a game called *Angries in the Bin* about understanding what makes them angry and finding good ways to deal with being angry. Tell children they will be able to toss their *Angries* in the bin to get rid of them after they find a good way to deal with their anger.
2. Ask the children to brainstorm and come up with a list of things or situations that make them angry. The group facilitator should encourage the children to come up with a wide range of things, letting them know it's all right to talk about what really makes them angry. The group facilitator keeps track of the items on a notepad or flip chart.
3. After the group has created the list, select a child to share with the group something that makes him or her angry and how he or she could handle it.

4. Next, encourage the child to get rid of the *Angries* by tossing them into the bin in the center of the circle.
5. The game continues until each child has had a chance to share something that makes him or her angry and to toss the *Angries* into the bin.
6. Group process: Tell the children that the game is now over. Have them sit in their chairs or on the floor facing the front of the room and tell them it is time to discuss the game.

GROUP PROCESS QUESTIONS

1. Ask the children what they needed to do to play the game. Emphasize the value of acknowledging what makes them angry and finding effective anger management strategies to deal with anger.
2. Ask the children how they felt when they shared with the group what makes them angry.
3. Ask the children how they felt when they tossed the *Angries* into the bin.

Teaching Module 6

Anxiety and Stress Management

1 GROUP PLAY INTERVENTION:
Cool Cat

OVERVIEW
Cool Cat involves teaching children how to relax and manage stress by closing their eyes and gently stroking the soft fur of a stuffed animal cat.

GROUP PLAY INTERVENTION SKILLS TAUGHT
Primary: Managing Stress and Anxiety
Secondary: Following Directions, Paying Attention

SKILL DIFFICULTY
Beginner

PREREQUISITE SKILLS
Children should be able to follow simple verbal instructions and have basic self-control and attention skills.

SUGGESTED GROUP SKILL SEQUENCES TO PRACTICE BEFORE GROUP PLAY INTERVENTION
No. 21. Dealing With Stress
No. 22. Dealing With Anxiety
No. 32. Paying Attention

REQUIRED MATERIALS
A soft, stuffed toy cat.

ROOM SETUP
An open space for children to sit in a circle.

GAME SYNOPSIS
Cool Cat provides children with relaxation, stress, and anxiety management skills. The group facilitator guides children in closing their eyes and relaxing as they gently stroke the soft fur of a stuffed toy cat. The facilitator uses guided imagery to take the children into a relaxed place as they pet their cat (or other stuffed animal). Children have been asked to bring along their favorite soft stuffed animal from home.

STEPS FOR IMPLEMENTING *COOL CAT*
1. Tell children they are going to play a game using the group facilitator's friend, *Cool Cat*. A group facilitator should sit in a circle with the children and ask everyone to cross their legs. The facilitator should introduce her friend, Cool Cat. She places Cool Cat in her lap, closes her eyes, and strokes Cool Cat's fur slowly and gently. She tells the children how soft Cool Cat is and how relaxing it is to feel the soft fur between her fingers.
2. Children should have been asked ahead of time to bring their favorite soft stuffed animal from home (it can be a cat or any other animal they are fond of, as long as it is very soft!). Ask the children to bring out the stuffed animals they have brought from home and to place them on their laps.
3. Then ask the children to close their eyes and begin to slowly and gently stroke the soft fur of their stuffed animal. The group facilitator should guide the children through a relaxing sensory experience by making such statements as
   a) Do you feel the fur between your fingers as you pet your animal?
   b) Do you feel how soft the fur of your animal is?
   c) Do you feel yourself beginning to relax?

4. Group process: Tell the children that the game is now over. Have them sit in their chairs or on the floor facing the front of the room and tell them it is time to discuss the game.

GROUP PROCESS QUESTIONS

1. Ask the children what they needed to do to play the game.
2. Ask the children how they felt while they were gently stroking the fur of the soft cat (or other favorite soft stuffed animal).
3. Ask the children if they felt more relaxed or less anxious after playing the game.

2 GROUP PLAY INTERVENTION: *Changing Seasons*

OVERVIEW

Changing Seasons is a stress- or anxiety-reducing game that involves children acting out what they think each season of the year feels like to a plant or flower.

GROUP PLAY INTERVENTION SKILLS TAUGHT

Primary: Managing Stress and Anxiety
Secondary: Following Directions, Paying Attention

SKILL DIFFICULTY

Beginner–Intermediate

PREREQUISITE SKILLS

Children should be able to follow simple verbal instructions and have basic self-control and attention skills. Children should also be familiar with the distinctive characteristics of each season of the year.

SUGGESTED GROUP SKILL SEQUENCES TO PRACTICE BEFORE GROUP PLAY INTERVENTION

No. 21. Dealing With Stress
No. 22. Dealing With Anxiety
No. 18. Expressing Feelings and Emotions

REQUIRED MATERIALS

None.

ROOM SETUP

The children should be seated in a circle, 2 to 3 ft apart. A medium-size open area with enough room for the children to move their bodies freely is warranted.

GAME SYNOPSIS

The *Changing Seasons* game involves children acting out different seasons of the year as if they were a plant or flower. For example, in the spring, plants and flowers grow slowly as they open up their petals. A child could slowly rise from the ground, as if extending his or her stem, and then open up his or her arms, one at a time, like the petals of the flower.

STEPS FOR IMPLEMENTING *CHANGING SEASONS*

1. Instruct children to sit in a circle in chairs or on the floor, 2 to 3 ft apart from each other.
2. Tell children they are going to play a game called *Changing Seasons* in which they will act out how the different seasons of the year feel to a plant or flower. The group facilitator shows the children examples of how a plant or flower might feel during each season of the year:
   a) Fall: The plants begin to shrivel and the petals and leaves fall from the trees. The group facilitator can slowly get closer to the ground and act as if leaves are falling.
   b) Winter: The plant is small and weak. The group facilitator can huddle close to the ground.
   c) Spring: The sun is shining, and the plants and flowers are just beginning to grow. The group facilitator can slowly open up her or his arms and let the sunshine in.

d) Summer: The sun shines very brightly, and the plants and flowers blossom. The group facilitator can act as if he or she is a flower and the petals (his or her arms) are opening up and blooming.

3. Select a child to come to the center of the circle and ask her or him to act out what a certain season would feel like to a plant or flower. Emphasize how the plants and trees move and grow slowly and gently. Encourage children to tense their muscles as they move slowly and stretch out their arms and legs.

4. Repeat Step 3 until each child has taken a turn. A group facilitator can designate a child in the center to select whose turn is next throughout the game.

5. Group process: Tell the children that the game is now over. Have them sit in their chairs or on the floor facing the front of the room and tell them it is time to discuss the game.

GROUP PROCESS QUESTIONS

1. Ask the children what they needed to do to play the game.
2. Ask the children how they felt while they were pretending to be the plant or flower. Emphasize that plants and flowers grow slowly and gently.
3. Ask the children how they felt after the game was over.
4. Ask the children how they felt when they were watching the child in the center acting out the seasons.

3

GROUP PLAY INTERVENTION:
I Am a Balloon

OVERVIEW

I Am a Balloon involves teaching children how to relax at home and school by pretending to be a balloon that is slowly inflating and deflating.

GROUP PLAY INTERVENTION SKILLS TAUGHT

Primary: Managing Stress and Anxiety, Self-Control
Secondary: Following Directions, Paying Attention, Visual and Auditory Acuity, Fine/Gross Motor Skills

SKILL DIFFICULTY

Beginner–Intermediate

PREREQUISITE SKILLS

Children should be able to follow simple verbal instructions and have basic self-control and attention skills.

SUGGESTED GROUP SKILL SEQUENCES TO PRACTICE BEFORE GROUP PLAY INTERVENTION

No. 21. Dealing With Stress
No. 22. Dealing With Anxiety
No. 32. Paying Attention

REQUIRED MATERIALS

None.

ROOM SETUP

An open space in which children can move around.

GAME SYNOPSIS

I Am a Balloon provides children with relaxation and stress and anxiety management skills. The group facilitator guides children into pretending that they are balloons being inflated and deflated.

STEPS FOR IMPLEMENTING *I AM A BALLOON*

1. Introduce the idea of feeling relaxed and demonstrate hard and soft arms and legs. Ask the children to identify ways they can relax at home and school.
2. Instruct children to stand far enough apart so they can extend their limbs and move about freely without touching others.
3. Next, tell children they are balloons with no air in them and they are to shake loose and collapse. The group facilitator should model the skills to the children. The group facilitator can check a few children for muscle looseness by doing the *limp noodle test.* The limp noodle test involves lifting a child's finger or arm slowly and dropping it. If the child's finger or arm falls quickly down, then the child's muscles are relaxed and he or she has passed the limp noodle test.
4. The group facilitator should announce that he or she has an air pump that can blow up each balloon. The adult makes the "ssshhhh" sound, indicating that the air is being pumped into the balloons.
5. The balloons (children) begin to fill up with air. The group facilitator should point out how each child can choose a different shape and way to blow up.

6. To engage the group, ask the following questions while the children fill up with air:
   a) Are you completely filled up with air?
   b) Using your arms, could you show me how filled up your balloon is?
   c) Do you feel like you are going to float away?
7. Next, announce that the balloon has a small leak, using the "ssssss" sound to indicate air being released from the balloon. The facilitator should model letting the air out as the balloon (children) slowly deflate and collapse on the ground. The facilitator can also include scenarios such as putting patches on each balloon and blowing them up again, balloons mirroring each other, and having children pretend to be air pumps.
8. Group process: Tell the children that the game is now over. Have them sit in their chairs or on the floor facing the front of the room and tell them it is time to discuss the game.

GROUP PROCESS QUESTIONS

1. Ask the children what they needed to do to play the game. What did they need to do when they were pretending to inflate? What did they need to do when they were pretending to deflate?
2. Ask the children how they felt while they were inflating like a balloon.
3. Ask the children how they felt while they were deflating. Emphasize that this can be a technique the children can use when they need to relax or reduce stress.

4 GROUP PLAY INTERVENTION: ZZZZZ...

OVERVIEW

ZZZZZ... involves children learning the difference between how they feel when they are going to sleep and when they wake up.

GROUP PLAY INTERVENTION SKILLS TAUGHT

Primary: Managing Stress and Anxiety
Secondary: Following Directions, Impulse Control, Paying Attention, Fine/Gross Motor Skills

SKILL DIFFICULTY

Beginner–Intermediate

PREREQUISITE SKILLS

Children should be able to follow simple verbal instructions and have basic self-control and attention skills.

SUGGESTED GROUP SKILL SEQUENCES TO PRACTICE BEFORE GROUP PLAY INTERVENTION

No. 21. Dealing With Stress
No. 22. Dealing With Anxiety
No. 16. Self-Control
No. 17. Identifying Feelings and Emotions

REQUIRED MATERIALS

A book that describes a short bedroom story.

ROOM SETUP

An open space in which children can move around.

GAME SYNOPSIS

ZZZZZ... provides children with relaxation and with stress and anxiety management skills. Children are read a story about going to sleep. The adult reading the story makes the sound, *zzzzz*, indicating that it is time for the group to go to sleep. The group facilitator guides the children in pretending to go to sleep. Next, the group facilitator makes a *rrrrrriinngggg!!* sound, indicating that an alarm clock is going off. Encourage children to slowly get up and move about.

STEPS FOR IMPLEMENTING ZZZZZ...

1. A group facilitator introduces the idea of feeling relaxed versus feeling stressed and anxious. Tell children they will be read a story about going to sleep. The group facilitator then reads a short bedtime book to the group. When the facilitator makes a *zzzzz* sound while reading the story, tell the group that it is time to go to sleep.
2. Instruct each child to find a safe spot on the ground where they can "go to sleep." The group facilitator can ask children:
   a) How does your body feel when you are asleep?
   b) How do your arms and legs feel?
   c) How do your arms and legs move?
3. Next, the group facilitator mimics an alarm clock going off—*rrrrrriinngggg!!*
4. Encourage the children to get up and move around the room when the alarm clock goes off. The children should move around and select another safe spot to slowly fall back asleep again to the sound of *zzzzz*.

5. Group process: Tell the children that the game is now over. Have them sit in their chairs or on the floor facing the front of the room and tell them it is time to discuss the game.

GROUP PROCESS QUESTIONS

1. Ask the children what they needed to do to play the game. What did they need to do when they were pretending to go to sleep? What did they need to do when they were pretending to wake up to the alarm clock?
2. Ask the children how they felt while they were sleeping. Emphasize that periods of quiet time and relaxation such as going to sleep can help them relax or reduce stress.
3. Ask the children how they felt when the alarm clock went off.
4. Ask the children how their bodies felt when they were pretending to sleep and when they heard the alarm.

5

GROUP PLAY INTERVENTION:
Imagine You Are Here

OVERVIEW

In *Imagine You Are Here,* children close their eyes and imagine they are having calming, relaxing experiences. Entering this relaxed state of mind can help reduce stress and anxiety.

GROUP PLAY INTERVENTION SKILLS TAUGHT

Primary: Managing Stress and Anxiety
Secondary: Following Directions, Paying Attention

SKILL DIFFICULTY

Beginner–Intermediate

PREREQUISITE SKILLS

Children should be able to follow simple verbal instructions and have basic self-control and attention skills.

SUGGESTED GROUP SKILL SEQUENCES TO PRACTICE BEFORE GROUP PLAY INTERVENTION

No. 21. Dealing With Stress
No. 22. Dealing With Anxiety
No. 31. Following Directions

REQUIRED MATERIALS

None.

ROOM SETUP

An open space for children to move their bodies and limbs freely. Children should be seated comfortably in chairs or on the floor.

GAME SYNOPSIS

Imagine You Are Here involves children taking off their shoes, closing their eyes, and being guided to imagine a series of relaxation-inducing scenarios common to elementary school children.

STEPS FOR IMPLEMENTING *IMAGINE YOU ARE HERE*

1. Tell children they are going to play a game called *Imagine You Are Here* that will help them relax when they are feeling stress or anxiety.
2. Instruct children to take off their shoes and socks and close their eyes. They should be sitting with their legs crossed and hands on their knees.
3. The group facilitator asks the children to listen carefully and imagine themselves doing the following:

   Imagine that you begin to walk slowly without your shoes. Focus very closely on what you feel beneath your feet. You are walking across high grass. Now you come to a gravel path, and the stones prick at the bottom of your feet. You leave the path and come to a forest where there are patches of mushy, wet moss. After a long walk you start to feel soft, warm sand beneath your feet.

4. Group process: Tell the children that the game is now over. Have them sit in their chairs or on the floor facing the front of the room and tell them it is time to discuss the game.

1. Ask the children what they needed to do to play the game.
2. Ask the children how they felt while they were imagining themselves walking. How did they feel when they were walking through the grass? Through mushy, wet moss? Through soft, warm sand?
3. Ask the children how they felt after the game. After everyone answers, then ask whether they felt relaxed.
4. Ask the children if they thought this would be a good technique to use when they felt stressed or anxious.
5. Ask the children other situations they could think about that would make them feel relaxed.

6 GROUP PLAY INTERVENTION: *Musical String Drawing*

OVERVIEW

Musical String Drawing involves teaching children a way to relax by listening to soft, relaxing music and creating an expression of the music through art.

GROUP PLAY INTERVENTION SKILLS TAUGHT

Primary: Managing Stress and Anxiety
Secondary: Following Directions, Paying Attention, Fine/Gross Motor Skills

SKILL DIFFICULTY

No. 21. Dealing With Stress
No. 22. Dealing With Anxiety
No. 18. Expressing Feelings and Emotions

PREREQUISITE SKILLS

Beginner–Intermediate

SUGGESTED GROUP SKILL SEQUENCES TO PRACTICE BEFORE GROUP PLAY INTERVENTION

Children should be able to follow simple verbal instructions and have basic self-control and attention skills.

REQUIRED MATERIALS

CD player; CD of soft, relaxing music; 4 ft of yarn or thick string; newspaper; large sheets of drawing paper; pencils; and oil pastels (or other artistic mediums such as markers, paints).

ROOM SETUP

A large table with chairs.

GAME SYNOPSIS

Musical String Drawing provides children with relaxation and with stress and anxiety management skills. Children are guided by a group facilitator to create musical expression through art by allowing the music to flow through their bodies and out of their hands onto the paper. Instruct children to arrange pieces of yarn on the paper so it looks the way the music sounds to them. After they have the yarn in place, they trace the path of the yarn on their papers and remove the yarn. The children then color in the shapes created by the yarn.

STEPS FOR IMPLEMENTING MUSICAL STRING DRAWING

1. A group facilitator turns on soft, relaxing music and has the children practice deep breathing before the game begins. Tell children that they are going to play a game called *Musical String Drawing* that teaches them to relax. Discuss with the children what *relaxing* means and present examples (e.g., reading, drawing, lying in bed).
2. Instruct children to pick up their piece of yarn and play around with it on their piece of paper, allowing it to move wherever the music takes it!
3. Tell children they should place one end of the string at the edge of the paper and slowly arrange the yarn on their paper so it looks the way the music sounds to them. Tell children to imagine what relaxing music would look like if it came flowing through their bodies, into their hands, and out onto the paper.

4. After they have created their artistic representation of the music, they finish by placing the other end of the string on another edge of the paper.

5. Next, instruct children to slowly trace the pattern of the yarn on their papers and to remove the yarn after they have traced the pattern. Children are left with an artistic representation of what the relaxing music looked and felt like to them.

6. Instruct children to use oil pastels (or other artistic media such as markers or paints) to color in their music. The colors can represent how the music made them feel.

7. Group process: Tell the children that the game is now over. Have them sit in their chairs or on the floor facing the front of the room and tell them it is time to discuss the game.

GROUP PROCESS QUESTIONS

1. Ask the children what they needed to do to play the game. What did they need to do when they were creating the music with the string?

2. Ask the children how they felt while they were listening to the music and allowing it to flow through their bodies, into their hands, and out onto the paper.

3. Ask the children how they felt while they were coloring in the music they created.

4. Ask the children if they felt more relaxed after playing the game. Did they feel the music flowing from their bodies out onto the paper?

7 GROUP PLAY INTERVENTION: *Swaying Boat*

OVERVIEW

Swaying Boat teaches children relaxation and stress and anxiety management skills. It involves children cooperatively working as a group on a boat floating in the sea. Imagery is used to create a relaxing experience in which the "boat" sways back and forth in the water.

GROUP PLAY INTERVENTION SKILLS TAUGHT

Primary: Managing Stress and Anxiety, Cooperation
Secondary: Following Directions, Paying Attention, Self-Control

SKILL DIFFICULTY

Intermediate

PREREQUISITE SKILLS

Children should be able to follow simple verbal instructions and have basic self-control and attention skills. They should have an understanding of what a relaxing situation is versus a stressful or anxious situation.

SUGGESTED GROUP SKILL SEQUENCES TO PRACTICE BEFORE GROUP PLAY INTERVENTION

No. 21. Dealing With Stress
No. 22. Dealing With Anxiety
No. 16. Self-Control
No. 35. Cooperation
No. 6. Joining in a Play Group

REQUIRED MATERIALS

None.

ROOM SETUP

A large, open space in which children can move around.

GAME SYNOPSIS

Children get on their hands and knees next to each other on the ground. The group facilitator guides them in pretending they are a boat on the sea that slowly and gently sways and rocks in the warm, blue water. One child (the boat) lays down facing others and closes his or her eyes. The boat must remain safely on the water through the cooperation of the sea. Scenarios such as an approaching storm in which the sea slowly gets rougher can be introduced after the children have become skilled at keeping the boat safely afloat in the sea.

STEPS FOR IMPLEMENTING SWAYING BOAT

1. Introduce the idea of feeling relaxed and ask children to give examples of situations in which they felt relaxed and situations that made them feel anxious or stressed.
2. Tell the children they are going to play a game called *Swaying Boat* in which they pretend they are the sea and the boat. Then ask the children to close their eyes and imagine that a boat is drifting slowly and gently over the waves of the sea.
3. Select one child to be the boat. Instruct the rest of the children to get on their hands and knees next to each other in a line and pretend they are the sea.

4. Tell the child (the boat) to lie close to others (the sea) facing up and to close his or her eyes.
5. The children who are the sea slowly start to swing and rock the boat gently. The group facilitator can ask the children, "Does it make you feel relaxed to have the sea moving slowly and gently?"
6. Next, introduce the idea that a storm is coming and the sea becomes a little bit rougher. The sea can start to move a little faster, but still moving in a safe, controlled manner. The facilitator can ask the children, "How did you feel when the sea got rougher and started moving faster?"
7. Repeat Steps 3 through 6 until each child has taken a turn as the boat.
8. Group process: Tell the children that the game is now over. Have them sit in their chairs or on the floor facing the front of the room and tell them it is time to discuss the game.

GROUP PROCESS QUESTIONS

1. Ask the children what they needed to do to play the game. What did they need to do when they were pretending to be the sea? What did they need to do when they were pretending to be the boat?
2. Ask the children how they felt when they were the boat. How did they feel while they had their eyes closed and were drifting gently and slowly on the sea? Emphasize how this technique can be used when children need to relax or are feeling stressed.
3. Ask the children how they felt when they were the boat and the sea started getting rough and they began moving faster.
4. Ask the children how they felt when they were the sea and it was moving slowly and gently? Moving faster?
5. Ask the children how they felt after the game was over.

<table>
<tr><td>**8**</td><td colspan="2"># GROUP PLAY INTERVENTION:
Color by Number</td></tr>
</table>

OVERVIEW	*Color by Number* involves children coloring in pictures to the best of their ability in a certain amount of time. The game seeks to reduce the stress and anxiety associated with perfectionism.
GROUP PLAY INTERVENTION SKILLS TAUGHT	Primary: Managing Stress and Anxiety, Reducing Need for Perfectionism Secondary: Following Directions, Paying Attention
SKILL DIFFICULTY	Intermediate
PREREQUISITE SKILLS	Children should be able to follow simple verbal instructions have basic self-control and attention skills. They should also be familiar with numbers so that they are able to complete the color-by-number pictures.
SUGGESTED GROUP SKILL SEQUENCES TO PRACTICE BEFORE GROUP PLAY INTERVENTION	No. 21. Dealing With Stress No. 22. Dealing With Anxiety No. 32. Paying Attention No. 34. Working Independently No. 8. Sharing Your Things With Others
REQUIRED MATERIALS	Color-by-number pictures, crayons and markers, a stopwatch or timer.
ROOM SETUP	The children should be seated at tables.
GAME SYNOPSIS	Children are required to color in a picture in a specified time period. During the first color-by-number task, children are timed but are not told about the timing. Fully colored pictures are recognized. When the children do the second color-by-number task, they are told they will be timed. They are told to fill in as much of the picture as possible. The game is designed to help children overcome perfectionism.
STEPS FOR IMPLEMENTING COLOR BY NUMBER	1. Tell children they are going to do color-by-number pictures. 2. Give each child his or her own color-by-number picture, as well as crayons and markers. The children are timed but are not told about the timing. Instruct the children to color the picture to the best of their ability. When the time is up, the group leader should give recognition to fully colored pictures. 3. Next, give each child a second color-by-number picture and ask them to color in as much as possible. This time, tell them that they will be timed. 4. Group process: Tell the children that the game is now over. Have them sit in their chairs or on the floor facing the front of the room and tell them it is time to discuss the game.
GROUP PROCESS QUESTIONS	1. Ask the children what they needed to do to complete the entire color-by-number picture within the time period allowed.

2. Ask the children how they felt while they were coloring their first picture (when they did not know they were being timed).
3. Ask the children how they felt while they were coloring their second picture (when they did know they were being timed). Did they feel stress or anxiety?
4. Ask the children what strategies they used to reduce any stress or anxiety they felt while coloring their pictures.

Teaching Module 7

Developing Appropriate Personal Space

1 GROUP PLAY INTERVENTION: *Dodging in Personal Space*

OVERVIEW

Dodging in Personal Space teaches children about personal space.

GROUP PLAY INTERVENTION SKILLS TAUGHT

Primary: Respect for Personal Space
Secondary: Paying Attention, Following Directions

SKILL DIFFICULTY

Beginner

PREREQUISITE SKILLS

Children should be able to follow simple verbal instructions and have basic self-control and attention skills.

SUGGESTED GROUP SKILL SEQUENCES TO PRACTICE BEFORE GROUP PLAY INTERVENTION

No. 14. Respect for Others' Personal Space
No. 32. Paying Attention
No. 31. Following Directions

REQUIRED MATERIALS

None.

ROOM SETUP

A large, open space where children can freely move around.

GAME SYNOPSIS

Dodging in Personal Space involves dividing children up into two groups by counting *1, 2, 1, 2*, and so forth. The *1*s and *2*s go to opposite sides of the room. The group facilitator then gives the signal for each group to simultaneously move (e.g., walk, dance, hop) from one end of the space to the other. The goal is for each team to get to the opposite side without bumping into any other children.

STEPS FOR IMPLEMENTING *DODGING IN PERSONAL SPACE*

1. Divide children into two teams, designated by either number 1 or number 2. Tell children they are going to play a game called *Dodging in Personal Space* to learn about personal space.
2. Tell children that if they are selected as a number 1, they should go to the left end of the space. If they are selected as a number 2, they should go to the right end of the space.
3. Before the game begins, make sure all children know their number and which way they are going. On the group facilitator's command, the children will try to move (e.g., walk, dance, hop) from one end of the space to the other without bumping into any other children. The goal for each child is to stay in her or his personal space.
4. Step 3 can be repeated several times using different movements (i.e., walk, dance, hop) each time. The group facilitator calls out the movement the children are to perform before each round of the game.
5. Group process: Tell the children that the game is now over. Have them sit in their chairs or on the floor facing the front of the room and tell them it is time to discuss the game.

1. Ask the children what they needed to do to play the game.
2. Ask the children how it felt when they were moving across the room trying to maintain their personal space. Was it difficult to do?
3. Ask the children how they felt if they bumped into someone or entered another's personal space while they were playing the game.
4. Ask the children if they feel they have a better understanding of personal space than they did before playing the game.

2 GROUP PLAY INTERVENTION: *The Space Spin*

OVERVIEW — *The Space Spin* teaches children how to respect personal space. Children and the group facilitator stretch out their arms and turn in place to help children understand the boundaries of personal space.

GROUP PLAY INTERVENTION SKILLS TAUGHT — Primary: Respect for Personal Space, Following Directions
Secondary: Paying Attention, Self-Control

SKILL DIFFICULTY — Beginner

PREREQUISITE SKILLS — Children should be able to follow simple verbal instructions and have basic self-control and attention skills.

SUGGESTED GROUP SKILL SEQUENCES TO PRACTICE BEFORE GROUP PLAY INTERVENTION — No. 14. Respect for Others' Personal Space
No. 16. Self-Control
No. 31. Following Directions

REQUIRED MATERIALS — None.

ROOM SETUP — A large, open space where children can freely move around.

GAME SYNOPSIS — *The Space Spin* game involves children stretching out both arms and turning slowly in a complete circle in place. The group facilitator lets the children know that this area is their personal space. The facilitator models the same behavior by stretching out her arms and demonstrating her personal space. Once the facilitator has demonstrated what personal space looks like to the children, the facilitator puts her arms down at her sides and selects a child to walk slowly toward her. The child is to stop just before he thinks he has reached the edge of the group facilitator's personal space. When the child stops, the facilitator stretches her arms out again and slowly turns in place. If the group facilitator bumps the child an arm, the child has to try again to correctly judge the personal space of the facilitator.

STEPS FOR IMPLEMENTING *THE SPACE SPIN*

1. Tell children they are going to play a game called *The Space Spin* in which they learn about personal space and following directions.
2. The group facilitator introduces the idea of personal space to children in two ways. First, instruct children to stretch out their arms on both sides and turn slowly in a complete circle in place. The group facilitator explains that this circle area is each child's personal space.
3. Next, the group facilitator stretches out her arms on both sides and turns slowly in a complete circle in place to demonstrate her personal space. This helps the children visualize what the personal space looks like.

4. Next, the group facilitator selects a child from the group. The facilitator puts her arms down at her sides and asks the child to slowly walk toward her. The child should be instructed to stop just before he thinks he has reached the edge of the facilitator's personal space.
5. When the child stops where he believes the edge of the personal space is located, the group facilitator raises her arms and slowly turns in place. If the facilitator bumps the child with her arm, the facilitator says, "You have invaded my personal space and are tossed from the galaxy!"
6. Instruct the child that he or she can try again.
7. Repeat Steps 4 through 6 until each child has taken a turn and has succeeded at stopping at the edge of the facilitator's personal space.
8. Group process: Tell the children that the game is now over. Have them sit in their chairs or on the floor facing the front of the room and tell them it is time to discuss the game.

GROUP PROCESS QUESTIONS

1. Ask the children what they needed to do to play the game.
2. Ask the children how they felt when they had their arms stretched out and were turning slowly in place. Did they feel the limits of their personal space around them?
3. Ask the children how they felt when they saw the group facilitator demonstrate her personal space. After seeing the group facilitator demonstrate where the limits of her personal space were, did they feel they had a good idea of the boundaries of others' personal space?
4. Ask the children how they felt when they were approaching the group facilitator and trying to judge the edge of her personal space.

3 GROUP PLAY INTERVENTION: *Musical Shapes*

OVERVIEW

Musical Shapes is a game about personal space and cooperation that involves children performing a locomotor skill (e.g., skip, gallop, jog slowly, jump, slide) in a general space when music is turned on. After the music stops, children must work together in pairs to form the shape that the group facilitator says aloud.

GROUP PLAY INTERVENTION SKILLS TAUGHT

Primary: Respect for Personal Space, Cooperation
Secondary: Paying Attention, Following Directions

SKILL DIFFICULTY

Beginner

PREREQUISITE SKILLS

Children should be able to follow simple verbal instructions and have basic self-control and attention skills.

SUGGESTED GROUP SKILL SEQUENCES TO PRACTICE BEFORE GROUP PLAY INTERVENTION

No. 14. Respect for Others' Personal Space
No. 35. Cooperation
No. 30. Solving a Problem as a Group
No. 13. Respecting Others

REQUIRED MATERIALS

CD player and a CD of lively music.

ROOM SETUP

A large, open space where children can move around freely.

GAME SYNOPSIS

Musical Shapes involves teaching children to respect personal space and how to safely move around in a general space. When the music is turned on, instruct children to perform a locomotor skill throughout the general space (e.g., skip, gallop, jog slowly, jump, slide). After the music stops, the group facilitator calls out a shape, and each group of two must work together to make the shape with their arms and legs.

STEPS FOR IMPLEMENTING MUSICAL SHAPES

1. Tell children they are going to play a game called *Musical Shapes* in which they learn about personal space and cooperation. The cues for moving safely in general space are reviewed with the children before the game begins:
   a) Keep your eyes up.
   b) Slow down or speed up to avoid crashing into others or entering their personal space.
2. Instruct children to find a good space to begin the game in.
3. Next, instruct children to listen for a locomotor skill to be called out when the music begins playing. Possible locomotor skills could be skip, gallop, jog slowly, jump, or slide. Running is not recommended. Emphasize the importance of the cues to the children as they play this part of the game.
4. To start the game, the music should be turned on and a locomotor skill should be called out. Children should begin to act out the locomotor skill until the music stops.

5. Once the music stops, the group facilitator calls out a shape (e.g., wide, opposite of wide, crooked, opposite of big, opposite of crooked, number *4*, number *8*, lower case *i*, lower case *a*). A group of two children must get together and make the shape with their arms and legs. Both children must be part of the shape.

6. Repeat Steps 4 through 5, and each time a group facilitator should call out a different locomotor skill to be performed and a different shape for the children to make. Tell children that a different group of two must get together each time a new shape is called out.

7. Group process: Tell the children that the game is now over. Have them sit in their chairs or on the floor facing the front of the room and tell them it is time to discuss the game.

GROUP PROCESS QUESTIONS

1. Ask the children what they needed to do to play the game.

2. Ask the children how they felt when they were moving about the room.

3. Ask the children what strategies they used to avoid entering the personal space of others while they were moving about the room. Did they slow down or speed up to avoid crashing into someone else?

4. Ask the children how they felt when they were in groups of two making the shapes. Emphasize the importance of working together as a group to complete a task.

4 GROUP PLAY INTERVENTION: *Personal Space Bubbles*

OVERVIEW *Personal Space Bubbles* teaches children about the boundaries of personal space.

GROUP PLAY INTERVENTION SKILLS TAUGHT Primary: Respect for Personal Space, Following Directions
Secondary: Cooperation, Paying Attention, Self-Control

SKILL DIFFICULTY Beginner–Intermediate

PREREQUISITE SKILLS Children should be able to follow simple verbal instructions and have basic self-control and attention skills.

SUGGESTED GROUP SKILL SEQUENCES TO PRACTICE BEFORE GROUP PLAY INTERVENTION No. 14. Respect for Others' Personal Space
No. 16. Self-Control
No. 13. Respecting Others
No. 31. Following Directions

REQUIRED MATERIALS Hula hoops.

ROOM SETUP A large, open space where children can freely move around.

GAME SYNOPSIS *Personal Space Bubbles* involves a group of children moving slowly around the room while holding a hula hoop around their waist. This game does not require children to know how to use a hula hoop. If a child accidentally bumps into another child's hula hoop during the game, their bubble "pops" and they are out for a predetermined period of time. The child must place his or her hula hoop on the floor and sit inside it until the group facilitator reactivates his or her bubble. After children have become skilled at the game, a challenge can be introduced by making the space smaller, which will make it harder to avoid bumping into someone. Children also have the option of working together as a team to try to avoid receiving points for bumping into someone else on the other team.

STEPS FOR IMPLEMENTING PERSONAL SPACE BUBBLES
1. Tell children they are going to play a game called *Personal Space Bubbles* to learn about personal space and following directions.
2. Give the children hula hoops and instruct them to begin moving around the room slowly with their hula hoops around their waists. Children do not need to know how to hula hoop.
3. Next, instruct children to try to avoid bumping into anyone else's hula hoop or personal space as they move around the room.
4. If a child bumps another child's hula hoop, his or her bubble "pops" and he or she must place the hula hoop on the ground and sit inside it for a period of time predetermined by the group facilitator.
5. As children become more skilled at moving around the room without bumping into each other, the space can be made smaller as an additional challenge.

The children can also work as teams and try to avoid receiving points for bumping into someone on the other team. If a child from Team *A* bumps into a child from Team *B,* Team *A* receives a point. The goal is to receive the lowest number of points.

6. Group process: Tell the children that the game is now over. Have them sit in their chairs or on the floor facing the front of the room and tell them it is time to discuss the game.

GROUP PROCESS QUESTIONS

1. Ask the children what they needed to do to play the game. Emphasize that they needed to respect the personal space of the other children in order to be successful at this game.
2. Ask the children how they felt when they were moving slowly around the room without bumping into anyone else's bubble.
3. Ask the children how they felt when they bumped into another child and popped his or her bubble. How did it feel when he or she had to stop playing and sit inside the hula hoop?

5 GROUP PLAY INTERVENTION: *Personal Space Circle*

OVERVIEW

Personal Space Circle is about personal space and following directions. The game involves children sitting inside a personal space circle made out of rope or a long cord. The group facilitator adjusts the size of the circle (smaller or larger) to illustrate how personal space can vary based on the relationship a child shares with another person.

GROUP PLAY INTERVENTION SKILLS TAUGHT

Primary: Respect for Personal Space, Following Directions
Secondary: Paying Attention

SKILL DIFFICULTY

Beginner

PREREQUISITE SKILLS

Children should be able to follow simple verbal instructions and have basic self-control and attention skills.

SUGGESTED GROUP SKILL SEQUENCES TO PRACTICE BEFORE GROUP PLAY INTERVENTION

No. 14. Respect for Others' Personal Space
No. 32. Paying Attention
No. 31. Following Directions

REQUIRED MATERIALS

Rope or chord (approximately 20 ft long).

ROOM SETUP

A medium-size open space large enough for the children. The rope or chord is placed on the floor in a circle shape. The ends of the rope should overlap, so the circle is not the largest it could be. The children sit in a circle around the rope.

GAME SYNOPSIS

Personal Space Circle involves teaching children the boundaries of personal space based on the relationship they have with another person. A rope or chord is placed on the floor in the shape of a circle with the children sitting around the rope circle. A child is selected to sit in the center of the circle. The group facilitator explains that personal space is smaller for people we are very close to (i.e., Mom, Dad, brothers, sisters). The circle can be made a little larger for friends and teachers or even larger for people we don't know. The group facilitator can change the size of the circle and ask the children what type of relationship might be appropriate for this personal space size.

STEPS FOR IMPLEMENTING PERSONAL SPACE CIRCLE

1. Tell children they are going to play a game called *Personal Space Circle* to learn about personal space and following directions. The group facilitator should explain that the boundaries of personal space change based on the relationship they have with another person. For example, personal space is smaller with a parent than it would be with a teacher at school.
2. The group facilitator selects one child to sit inside the rope or chord circle. The facilitator explains that personal space is smaller for people we are very close to (i.e., Mom, Dad, brothers, sisters). The facilitator cites the current circle size as an example of personal space for people we are very close to.

3. The child in the center is given the opportunity to select the next child to sit in the center of the circle.
4. The circle is made a little larger, and the group facilitator can ask the children a question such as, "Who do you think would be a good person to have this size personal space for?" The facilitator explains that the current size personal space would be appropriate for friends and teachers.
5. Repeat Step 3. The group facilitator should make the circle even bigger and ask the children a question such as, "Who do you think would be a good person to have this size personal space for?" The facilitator should then explain that the current size personal space would be appropriate for people we don't know, such as strangers.
6. The group facilitator can change the size of the circle additional times and ask the children what type of relationship they think might be appropriate for that personal space size.
7. Group process: Tell the children that the game is now over. Have them sit in their chairs or on the floor facing the front of the room and tell them it is time to discuss the game.

GROUP PROCESS QUESTIONS

1. Ask the children what they needed to do to play the game.
2. Ask the children how they felt when it was their turn to sit inside the personal space circle.
3. Ask the children how they felt when they were on the outside of the personal space circle.
4. Ask the children what strategies they used to remember which people the personal space circle might be appropriate for. Emphasize that personal space is smallest for the people we are closest to, such as Mom and Dad. Also emphasize that the less we know someone, the bigger the personal space should be.
5. Ask the children if they felt more comfortable knowing how much personal space is appropriate for different people after playing the game.

6 GROUP PLAY INTERVENTION: *Hula Hoops*

OVERVIEW
Hula Hoops involves children learning about personal space by using hula hoops at the closest possible distance without letting their hula hoop touch another person's hula hoop.

GROUP PLAY INTERVENTION SKILLS TAUGHT
Primary: Respect for Personal Space, Self-Control, Cooperation
Secondary: Problem Solving, Paying Attention, Following Directions

SKILL DIFFICULTY
Beginner–Intermediate

PREREQUISITE SKILLS
Children should be able to hula hoop. Children should also be able to follow simple verbal instructions and have basic self-control and attention skills.

SUGGESTED GROUP SKILL SEQUENCES TO PRACTICE BEFORE GROUP PLAY INTERVENTION
No. 14. Respect for Others' Personal Space
No. 29. Solving Everyday Problems
No. 13. Respecting Others

REQUIRED MATERIALS
Hula hoops. An open space that is large enough for the children to move about freely.

ROOM SETUP
Children sit on the floor or in chairs while they are given the instructions and a demonstration of the game. Then the children are broken up into groups of two or three, and are asked to stand up.

GAME SYNOPSIS
Children are broken up into groups of two or three. The first group is instructed to start using their hula hoops and to get as close as possible to their group members without touching another's hula hoop. The goal of the game is for the children in their group to get as close to one another's hula hoops without touching them.

STEPS FOR IMPLEMENTING HULA HOOPS
1. Tell children they are going to play a game to learn about personal space using hula hoops.
2. The group facilitator should give children a demonstration on how to use a hula hoop.
3. The group facilitator breaks up the children into groups of two or three.
4. Instruct the children in each group to begin using the hula hoops at the same time. They should try to stay as close as possible to each other without letting their hula hoops touch each other.
5. Each child must decide how much room she or he will need on all sides of her- or himself so that the hula hoop does not bang into anyone else's hula hoop. Each child must try to keep the hula hoop around his or her body without letting it fall to the ground. If a child's hula hoop does fall to the ground, she or he should be encouraged to pick it up and try again.

6. Repeat Steps 4 and 5 until all children have had the chance to use their hula hoops.
7. Group process: Tell the children that the game is now over. Have them sit in their chairs or on the floor facing the front of the room and tell them it is time to discuss the game.

GROUP PROCESS QUESTIONS

1. Ask the children what they needed to do to keep their hula hoops from touching anyone else's hula hoop. Emphasize the importance of respecting other people's personal space.
2. Ask the children what they needed to do to keep their hula hoops moving around their waists and from falling to the ground. Emphasize that they succeeded with the hula hoop by following directions and paying attention to the task.
3. Ask the children how they felt when they were able to keep their hula hoops from falling and from touching anyone else's hula hoop.
4. Ask the children how they felt when they were not able to keep from touching anyone else's hula hoop and when they were not able to keep their hula hoops from falling to the ground.
5. Ask the children how it felt when they needed to cooperate with others in the group to keep their hula hoops from touching and falling.

7

GROUP PLAY INTERVENTION:
Mother/Father, May I?

OVERVIEW

Mother/Father, May I? is about personal space and following directions. It involves one child acting as the mother or father and the rest of the children following her or his directions to move around the room.

GROUP PLAY INTERVENTION SKILLS TAUGHT

Primary: Respect for Personal Space, Following Directions
Secondary: Paying Attention, Self-Control

SKILL DIFFICULTY

Intermediate

PREREQUISITE SKILLS

Children should be able to follow simple verbal instructions and have basic self-control and attention skills.

SUGGESTED GROUP SKILL SEQUENCES TO PRACTICE BEFORE GROUP PLAY INTERVENTION

No. 14. Respect for Others' Personal Space
No. 31. Following Directions
No. 16. Self-Control
No. 39. Being Assertive
No. 40. Saying No
No. 41. Accepting No

REQUIRED MATERIALS

A large, open space in which children can freely move around.

ROOM SETUP

The child who is taking a turn as Mother or Father stands facing away from the other children in the group. The other children form a line behind her or him.

GAME SYNOPSIS

Mother/Father, May I? involves one child facing away from the rest of the group and taking a turn as Mother or Father. She or he chooses a child at random and announces a direction that child should move. The child must respond with "Mother or Father, may I?" Mom or Dad then says *yes* or *no*. If the child forgets to ask, she or he goes back to the starting line and begins again. The first child to come within the correct personal space distance of Mother or Father earns a turn to be Mother or Father next.

STEPS FOR IMPLEMENTING *MOTHER/FATHER, MAY I?*

1. Tell children they are going to play a game called *Mother/Father, May I?* to learn about personal space and following directions.
2. Select one child to begin the game as Mother or Father. Instruct this child to stand facing away from the group. Tell the rest of the children to form a line (approximately 8 ft) in front of the child selected to be Mother or Father so that the chosen child can move easily towards Mother or Father and the group can watch the game unfold.
3. Instruct Mother or Father to choose a child from the group at random and announce a direction that child should move and what type of movement he or she should make. For example, forward or backward; giant, regular, or baby

steps. Mother or Father should also instruct the child on how many steps he or she should take.

4. The child should then respond with "Mother or Father, may I?"

5. Instruct Mother or Father to state *yes* or *no*, at which point the child can move. If the child forgets to ask "Mother or Father, may I?" she or he must go back to the starting line and begin again.

6. Repeat Steps 4 and 5 until one child comes within the correct personal space distance (approximately 1 ft) of Mother or Father. This child should now get to take a turn as Mother or Father.

7. Continue playing the game until all members of the group have taken a turn at being Mother or Father. If a child is the first to come within the correct personal space distance of Mother or Father and she or he has already had a turn to be Mother or Father, she or he should return to the starting line and begin again.

8. Group process: Tell the children that the game is now over. Have them sit in their chairs or on the floor facing the front of the room and tell them it is time to discuss the game.

GROUP PROCESS
QUESTIONS

1. Ask the children what they needed to do to play the game.
2. Ask the children how they felt when it was their turn to be Mother or Father.
3. Ask the children how they felt when they did not follow directions and had to go back to the starting line.
4. Ask the children what strategies they used to remember to ask "Mother or Father, may I?" before moving.

8 GROUP PLAY INTERVENTION: *Bouncing Balls*

OVERVIEW

Bouncing Balls teaches children about self-control and respect for personal space.

GROUP PLAY INTERVENTION SKILLS TAUGHT

Primary: Respect for Personal Space, Self-Control
Secondary: Following Directions, Paying Attention, Gross Motor Skills

SKILL DIFFICULTY

Intermediate–Advanced

PREREQUISITE SKILLS

Children should be able to follow simple verbal instructions and have basic self-control and attention skills.

SUGGESTED GROUP SKILL SEQUENCES TO PRACTICE BEFORE GROUP PLAY INTERVENTION

No. 14. Respect for Others' Personal Space
No. 28. Setting Goals and Obtaining Them
No. 31. Following Directions
No. 37. Being a Good Sport

REQUIRED MATERIALS

Playground balls, cones (or other obstacles), and a CD player.

ROOM SETUP

A large, open space where children can freely move around. Cones should be set up as an obstacle course for children to bounce their balls through.

GAME SYNOPSIS

Bouncing Balls involves children bouncing a playground ball within the boundaries of their personal space. The group facilitator should model appropriate personal space to the children before the game begins. After the children are skilled at bouncing balls in a controlled manner, they are instructed to begin bouncing their balls through an obstacle course (e.g., cones). They are instructed to keep track of how many obstacles they were able to bounce their ball through without losing control of their ball or bouncing it into someone else's personal space.

As the children become more skilled at moving through the obstacle course, the course design can be changed or the space between the obstacles made smaller as an additional challenge. The children can also work as teams and combine the points they receive for making it around an obstacle without allowing the ball to enter another player's personal space.

STEPS FOR IMPLEMENTING BOUNCING BALLS

1. Tell children they are going to play a game called *Bouncing Balls* to learn about personal space and self-control. The group facilitator should model appropriate personal space to the children before the game begins.
2. Give the children playground balls and instruct them to stand 3 to 5 ft apart. Tell children to begin bouncing their balls in their personal space.
3. After the children have become skilled at bouncing the balls in their personal space, instruct them to bounce their balls through an obstacle course of cones without losing control of their balls or allowing them to bounce into someone else's personal space. A group facilitator can also play music at different speeds

during the game to alter the speed that the children bounce their balls through the obstacle course.

4. Children can keep track of how well they are maintaining their self-control and respect for others' personal space by counting to themselves how many obstacles they were able to bounce their ball through. Children can also work as teams and combine the points they receive for making it around an obstacle without allowing the ball to enter another player's personal space.

5. Group process: Tell the children that the game is now over. Have them sit in their chairs or on the floor facing the front of the room and tell them it is time to discuss the game.

GROUP PROCESS QUESTIONS

1. Ask the children what they needed to do to play the game. Emphasize how self-control allowed them to respect the boundaries of others' personal space successfully. Also, emphasize that taking a deep breath, slowing down, and being conscious of one's actions can help a child respect others' personal space.

2. Ask the children how they felt when they were bouncing their balls in their personal space.

3. Ask the children how they felt when they were bouncing their balls through the obstacle course. How did they feel when the pace of the music was slower? How did they feel when the pace of the music got faster?

9 GROUP PLAY INTERVENTION: *Personal Space Guessing*

OVERVIEW   *Personal Space Guessing* teaches children about the different types of personal space they will encounter in social situations.

GROUP PLAY INTERVENTION SKILLS TAUGHT   Primary: Respect for Personal Space, Differentiate Levels of Personal Space
Secondary: Paying Attention, Following Directions

SKILL DIFFICULTY   Intermediate–Advanced

PREREQUISITE SKILLS   Children should be able to follow simple verbal instructions and have basic self-control and attention skills.

SUGGESTED GROUP SKILL SEQUENCES TO PRACTICE BEFORE GROUP PLAY INTERVENTION   No. 14. Respect for Others' Personal Space
No. 9. Learning About Others
No. 32. Paying Attention

REQUIRED MATERIALS   Cards depicting levels of personal space (e.g., public, social, personal, intimate).

ROOM SETUP   A large, open space where children can freely move around. The children can either be sitting in a group on the floor or in chairs, with the cards in a designated spot off to the side.

GAME SYNOPSIS   *Personal Space Guessing* involves partners selecting one card from the stack of possible personal space scenarios and role playing an example of the type of personal space on the card. Before starting the game, the group facilitator should demonstrate the types of personal space (e.g., public, social, personal, intimate). She or he should also facilitate a discussion with the children in the role-play scenario and the group. For example, if the children selected a card for *public space,* the facilitator could ask them to describe a public space situation and what people would be included in that situation. If the children are having difficulty, the facilitator can ask the group to provide suggestions.

STEPS FOR IMPLEMENTING PERSONAL SPACE GUESSING

1. Tell children they are going to play a game called *Personal Space Guessing* to learn about personal space and that the amount of appropriate personal space can vary depending on the relationship they have with the person involved. A group facilitator should provide examples of each type of personal space, how much personal space between people is appropriate, and what people would be involved with each type of personal space before the game begins:
   a) *public space:* 5 to 6 ft apart, strangers
   b) *social space:* 1 to 3 ft apart, teachers or friends
   c) *personal space:* less than 1 ft apart, close friends or extended family members
   d) *intimate space:* little or no space, Mom, Dad, brothers, sisters

2. Select two children to work together as partners to start the game. Instruct the two children to select one of the personal space cards. The children should show the card they have selected to the group facilitator and the group.
3. Next, a group facilitator should facilitate a discussion with the partners about the type of personal space that is represented on the card. For example, if the children selected a card for public space, the group facilitator could ask the following sample questions:
    a) Could you describe a public space situation?
    b) Who would be appropriate to involve in this type of personal space?
    c) How far apart do you think the people should be from each other?
    d) How do you plan to role play your type of personal space?
4. The group facilitator can open up the discussion to the group so the level of participation is increased for all children. The group facilitator should also ask questions to children who are quiet and not raising their hands.
5. Next, ask the partners to role play the type of personal space they have selected.
6. Repeat Steps 2 through 5 until all children in the group have a turn to role play a personal space scenario.
7. Group process: Tell the children that the game is now over. Have them sit in their chairs or on the floor facing the front of the room and tell them it is time to discuss the game.

GROUP PROCESS QUESTIONS

1. Ask the children what they needed to do to play the game.
2. Ask the children how it felt to role play their type of personal space.
3. Ask the children for examples of who would be involved in a personal space, social space, and so forth.
4. Ask the children how far apart they think people should be from each other in a personal space, intimate space, and so forth.
5. Ask the children whether they have a better understanding of personal space than they did before playing the game. Do they understand how the appropriate amount of personal space differs based on the relationship with the other person?

Teaching Module 8

Effective Planning and Time Management

1 GROUP PLAY INTERVENTION: *How Long Does It Take?*

OVERVIEW

How Long Does It Take? teaches time management skills by having children predict or estimate how long it takes to complete various activities.

GROUP PLAY INTERVENTION SKILLS TAUGHT

Primary: Time Management
Secondary: Following Directions

SKILL DIFFICULTY

Beginner

PREREQUISITE SKILLS

Children should be able to follow simple verbal instructions and have basic self-control and attention skills.

SUGGESTED GROUP SKILL SEQUENCES TO PRACTICE BEFORE GROUP PLAY INTERVENTION

No. 28. Setting Goals and Obtaining Them
No. 29. Solving Everyday Problems
No. 31. Following Directions

REQUIRED MATERIALS

Activity cards.

ROOM SETUP

An open space for the children and facilitator to sit in a circle on the floor.

GAME SYNOPSIS

Activity cards are prepared ahead of time by the group facilitator. The cards contain questions about how long it would take to do certain tasks or activities. The children select an activity card and predict or estimate how much time they think it will take to perform the task.

STEPS FOR IMPLEMENTING *HOW LONG DOES IT TAKE?*

1. Tell children they are going to play a game called *How Long Does It Take?* that involves estimating how long it takes to complete a task.
2. Direct the first child to select an activity card and read it aloud. A facilitator can help the child read the card if he or she has difficulty reading it. Examples of tasks or activities written on the cards are
   a) How long does it take to walk from your classroom to the school office?
   b) How long does it take you to get dressed?
   c) How long does it take to do your homework each night?
   d) How long do you sleep for at night?
   e) How long does it take to drive from your house to school?
3. Repeat Step 2 until each child has had a turn to select an activity card and predict or estimate how long it takes to complete the task on the card.
4. Group process: Tell the children that the game is now over. Have them sit in their chairs or on the floor facing the front of the room and tell them it is time to discuss the game.

GROUP PROCESS
QUESTIONS

1. Ask the children what they needed to do to play the game.
2. Ask the children how they determined how long a task would take.
3. Ask the children how they felt after the game was over.

2   GROUP PLAY INTERVENTION: *Clothing Routine*

OVERVIEW *Clothing Routine* is a game in which children race to get their clothes on. The children are taught time management skills.

GROUP PLAY INTERVENTION SKILLS TAUGHT Primary: Time Management
Secondary: Following Directions

SKILL DIFFICULTY Beginner

PREREQUISITE SKILLS Children should be able to follow simple verbal instructions and have basic self-control and attention skills.

SUGGESTED GROUP SKILL SEQUENCES TO PRACTICE BEFORE GROUP PLAY INTERVENTION No. 29. Solving Everyday Problems
No. 31. Following Directions

REQUIRED MATERIALS Hat, stopwatch or timer, coat, shirt or sweatshirt, sweatpants, gloves, and scarf. Children should also be wearing sneakers with laces.

ROOM SETUP An open space that is large enough for children to move around in.

GAME SYNOPSIS *Clothing Routine* teaches children planning and time management skills. Parents are asked to bring in a variety of clothing for their child (i.e., hat, coat, shirt or sweatshirt, sweatpants, gloves, scarf, sneakers with laces). Children place their pile of clothes in front of them and are timed to see how long it takes them to put on all the clothes in the pile over the clothes they are already wearing. Next, the children are timed again to see if they can beat their old time, in addition to racing against the other kids to see who can put on their extra clothes the fastest.

STEPS FOR IMPLEMENTING *CLOTHING ROUTINE*

1. Tell children they are going to play a game called *Clothing Routine* with the clothing their parents brought for them (i.e., hat, coat, shirt or sweatshirt, sweatpants, gloves, scarf, sneakers with laces).
2. Ask the children to place their clothing items in a pile in front of them.
3. Tell children they will be timed to see how long it takes them to put on all the clothing over their current clothing. (This time will be used as a baseline time for the second race.) A group facilitator should begin the race by counting down from 10.
4. Once a child has finished putting on his or her clothes, a group facilitator should record the child's time. When all the children have completed the race, instruct them to remove their clothing items and put them back in a pile.
5. Next, instruct the children to race again. They should race against themselves and each other during the second race to complete the game.

6. If there is enough time after the two races, all of the clothing can be placed in a pile and children have to race to get back into their own clothing.

7. Group process: Tell the children that the game is now over. Have them sit in their chairs or on the floor facing the front of the room and tell them it is time to discuss the game.

GROUP PROCESS QUESTIONS

1. Ask the children what they needed to do to play the game.

2. Ask the children how they felt when they were putting on the clothing during the first race. How did they feel during the second race?

3. Ask the children how they felt after the game was over.

3

GROUP PLAY INTERVENTION:
Morning Routine

OVERVIEW	*Morning Routine* is a game in which children are taught time management, organizational, and planning skills.
GROUP PLAY INTERVENTION SKILLS TAUGHT	Primary: Time Management, Organization, Planning Secondary: Following Directions, Teamwork, Cooperation
SKILL DIFFICULTY	Beginner–Intermediate
PREREQUISITE SKILLS	Children should be able to follow simple verbal instructions and have basic self-control and attention skills.
SUGGESTED GROUP SKILL SEQUENCES TO PRACTICE BEFORE GROUP PLAY INTERVENTION	No. 28. Setting Goals and Obtaining Them No. 29. Solving Everyday Problems No. 35. Cooperation No. 30. Solving a Problem as a Group No. 38. Being Patient
REQUIRED MATERIALS	Hat, coat, shirt or sweatshirt, sweatpants, gloves, scarf; children should be wearing sneakers with laces; breakfast props (bowl, spoon); tooth brushing props (toothpaste, toothbrush); and school books.
ROOM SETUP	An open space that is large enough for children to move around in.
GAME SYNOPSIS	Children are separated into teams and work together to complete a morning routine. Children get dressed, eat breakfast (sit at the table for 15 seconds), brush their teeth (5 seconds), get their books together, and touch the door. After the first child completes the routine, he or she tags another member of the team to go next. The team that finishes first wins. Team members can encourage and assist the child performing the morning routine.

STEPS FOR IMPLEMENTING *MORNING ROUTINE*	1. Tell children they are going to play a game called *Morning Routine* related to time management and organization involving their daily morning routine.
	2. The children are separated into teams. The number of teams will depend on the total number of children that participate. Teams of three to five children is recommended. One member at a time from each team will be timed and must complete the following morning routine tasks:
	  a) Get dressed.
	  b) Eat breakfast (sit at the table for 15 seconds).
	  c) Brush teeth (5 seconds).
	  d) Get books together.
	  e) Touch the door.
	  f) Tag one of the members of team.

3. A group facilitator should time each child on how long it takes him or her to complete the (pretend) morning routine (e.g., getting ready in the morning). The children can complete the tasks in any order they prefer. The team members can encourage and assist the child performing the morning routine.

4. After each child finishes his or her morning routine, he or she should tag the next person on the team to take a turn.

5. Repeat Steps 2 through 4 until each child on the team has taken a turn. Although this is a race, winning and losing is not emphasized.

6. Group process: Tell the children that the game is now over. Have them sit in their chairs or on the floor facing the front of the room and tell them it is time to discuss the game.

GROUP PROCESS QUESTIONS

1. Ask the children what they needed to do to play the game.

2. Ask the children how they felt when they were being timed while completing the morning routine.

3. Ask the children how they felt when their teammates were encouraging and helping them complete the morning routine. Emphasize that cooperation and teamwork within the group can help manage time better and complete the task.

4. Ask the children how they felt after the game was over.

4 GROUP PLAY INTERVENTION: *My Day*

OVERVIEW

My Day teaches time management, planning, and organizational skills by having children plan out a typical day in their life.

GROUP PLAY INTERVENTION SKILLS TAUGHT

Primary: Time Management, Planning, Organization
Secondary: Following Directions

SKILL DIFFICULTY

Beginner–Intermediate

PREREQUISITE SKILLS

Children should be able to follow simple verbal instructions and have basic self-control and attention skills. They should also have basic reading and writing skills (the group facilitator can do the reading and writing for younger children).

SUGGESTED GROUP SKILL SEQUENCES TO PRACTICE BEFORE GROUP PLAY INTERVENTION

No. 31. Following Directions
No. 29. Solving Everyday Problems
No. 28. Setting Goals and Obtaining Them

REQUIRED MATERIALS

Poster board and marker.

ROOM SETUP

An open space for children to sit on the floor or at tables.

GAME SYNOPSIS

My Day has children plan out a typical day in their lives. Each child contributes an activity that occurs during his or her day and estimates how much time the activity will take. The day is planned by the group and is written on the poster board.

STEPS FOR IMPLEMENTING *MY DAY*

1. Tell children they are going to play a game called *My Day* that involves planning and organizing their day.
2. A group facilitator should select a child and ask, "What is an activity that you do each day?" The group facilitator can provide examples such as eating breakfast or dinner, getting ready for school, doing homework, and walking the dog. Once the child determines an activity that he or she does each day, he or she writes it on the poster board (the group facilitator can do the writing if needed). The group facilitator guides the children through their daily activities by creating a sensible timeline.
3. Repeat Step 2 until each child has a turn to select an activity and write it on the poster board.
4. Once each child has had a turn to describe an activity that takes place during his or her day, how long it takes to complete the activity, and where it fits into the daily schedule, the group can look over the day they have planned and organized.
5. Group process: Tell the children that the game is now over. Have them sit in their chairs or on the floor facing the front of the room and tell them it is time to discuss the game.

1. Ask the children what they needed to do to play the game.
2. Ask the children how they determined which activity they thought would take place next during the course of the day.
3. Ask the children how they determined how long a task would take.
4. Ask the children how they felt after the game was over.

5 GROUP PLAY INTERVENTION: *Scavenger Hunt*

OVERVIEW   *Scavenger Hunt* teaches planning, organization, and time management skills.

GROUP PLAY INTERVENTION SKILLS TAUGHT   Primary: Planning, Organization, Time Management
Secondary: Following Directions, Teamwork, Cooperation

SKILL DIFFICULTY   Beginner–Intermediate

PREREQUISITE SKILLS   Children should be able to follow simple verbal instructions and have basic self-control and attention skills. They should also have some basic reading skills (group facilitator can read for younger children).

SUGGESTED GROUP SKILL SEQUENCES TO PRACTICE BEFORE GROUP PLAY INTERVENTION   No. 34. Working Independently
No. 31. Following Directions
No. 1. Communicating With Others
No. 42. Asking For Help

REQUIRED MATERIALS   Scavenger hunt form, items listed on the scavenger hunt form, and writing instruments.

ROOM SETUP   A large open space for children to perform the scavenger hunt in.

GAME SYNOPSIS   *Scavenger Hunt* teaches children planning, organizational, and time management skills. Each child is given the scavenger hunt form containing a list of items that they need to find. Some will be tangible items, and some will be informational. Tell children that they need to find the items or information and write where or what they are. After 15 minutes have elapsed or a child has finished, the game is over.

STEPS FOR IMPLEMENTING *SCAVENGER HUNT*

1. Tell children they are going to play a game that involves going on a scavenger hunt. Each child is given a scavenger hunt form containing a list of items they need to find during the scavenger hunt. The task list might include the following:
   a) Write down where or what the following items are
      - You can use me to write, but you can't erase with me. Find me . . .
      - You can use me to become less angry. Find me . . .
      - You can use me when you are bored. Find me . . .
      - You can use me when you are hungry. Find me . . .
      - You can use me when you are sad. Find me . . .
      - You can use me to make someone else feel less sad. Find me . . .
      - You can read me. Find me . . .
      - I can roll. Find me . . .
      - I am sticky. Find me . . .
      - I sometimes smell bad. Find me . . .
      - You can sit on me. Find me . . .
      - You can stand on me, but I can't stand on you. Find me . . .

b) Write down answers to these questions:
- Find out how many kids like baseball.
- Find out how many kids like video games.
- Find out how old all the group facilitators are.
- Find out how old another child in the group is.
- Find out who in the group has pets and what kind of animals they are.
- Find out who in the group has brothers or sisters.
- Find out someone in the group's favorite TV show.
- Find out what someone in the group's favorite subject in school is.
- Find out what someone in the group's favorite color is.
- Find out what someone in the group's favorite food is.

2. Next, tell children they need to search for the items or information, find them, and write down where or what they are. They should not have any items in their possession at the end of the scavenger hunt.

3. Instruct children that they have 15 minutes to find the items or information on the list. A group facilitator should begin the 15-minute period and the children should begin searching for the items or information.

4. After a child has finished or 15 minutes have elapsed, tell children the game is over.

5. A group facilitator should assess which children have a completed scavenger hunt list and which do not.

6. If there are children who have not found all the items or information on the list, a group facilitator can break the children into pairs (or small groups if there are an uneven number of children). The pairs or groups should consist of at least one child who has found all the items and one child who needs help to complete the rest of his or her list. The child who has found all the items or information on the list can help his "buddy" find the missing items or information.

7. Group process: Tell the children that the game is now over. Have them sit in their chairs or on the floor facing the front of the room and tell them it is time to discuss the game.

GROUP PROCESS QUESTIONS

1. Ask the children what they needed to do to play the game.
2. Ask the children how they organized their scavenger hunt list to find the items. What planning was involved in organizing their list? How did they plan and manage their time during the 15-minute scavenger hunt? Emphasize how planning, organizing their list items, and managing their time well helped make it easier to find the items.
3. Ask the children how they felt while they were searching for the items or information on their list.
4. Ask the children how they felt when their buddy helped them find items missing from their list. Ask the buddies how it felt to help friends find the items they were missing. Emphasize the value of teamwork, cooperation, and helping others to all the children.
5. Ask the children how they felt when the scavenger hunt was over.

6

GROUP PLAY INTERVENTION:
Let's Plan a Trip!

OVERVIEW

Let's Plan a Trip! is a game in which children pretend to take an imaginary trip anywhere in the world.

GROUP PLAY INTERVENTION SKILLS TAUGHT

Primary: Planning, Organization
Secondary: Following Directions, Paying Attention

SKILL DIFFICULTY

Intermediate–Advanced

PREREQUISITE SKILLS

Children should be able to follow simple verbal instructions and have basic self-control and attention skills. Children should also be familiar with characteristics of different places.

SUGGESTED GROUP SKILL SEQUENCES TO PRACTICE BEFORE GROUP PLAY INTERVENTION

No. 31. Following Directions
No. 32. Paying Attention
No. 35. Cooperation

REQUIRED MATERIALS

Paper, writing instruments, recipe ingredients for the meal, supplies to make decorations, and books about the location to which the children decide to take a trip.

ROOM SETUP

The children should be seated at tables. As they move through the planning stages of this game, they will need to move around the room to set up decorations or snacks.

GAME SYNOPSIS

Let's Plan a Trip! is a game in which children make a list of all the places they would like to visit. After it has been decided where they will go, they create a list of ideas that would help them experience what it would be like to be there (i.e., plan a meal using foods from that place, make decorations that will make it feel as though children are there, use books to come up with ideas). After the children have come up with a list, a group facilitator can help to plan and organize which things they do. This game can be flexibly designed for a broad range of children with different ability levels. This game also requires more than one session to execute, since there are several steps in the planning and organization of the trip.

STEPS FOR IMPLEMENTING *LET'S PLAN A TRIP!*

1. Tell children they are going to play a game called *Let's Plan a Trip!* about taking an imaginary trip anywhere in the world. Instruct them to brainstorm location ideas. A group facilitator can help the children plan and organize their destination by keeping a list of their ideas.
2. A group facilitator can also make suggestions to get started. Trip ideas could include the following:
   a) Victorian England to have a tea party;

b) A safari in Africa (a tape with animal sounds can be played, children can pack their lunches in a backpack and pretend they are on a trail, and they can use stuffed animals to add to the jungle scenery); or

c) Egypt to experience the tombs and pyramids!

3. After the group has selected a destination, they should make another list of possible activities they will do to make it feel as though they are really there! Allow the group to use books or the Internet to help them find out more information about the destination they have chosen and to help choose their activities. Possible activities could include the following:

a) Planning a meal from the location.

b) Making and hanging decorations that help children imagine they there.

c) Playing music that helps children feel as though they are there.

A group facilitator can guide the children in organizing their own lists.

4. Next, guide the children in selecting two to three activities from the list to create the atmosphere of their destination.

5. Over the next few sessions, a group facilitator should help the children complete the various activities that relate to their destination.

6. Group process: Tell the children that the game is now over. Have them sit in their chairs or on the floor facing the front of the room and tell them it is time to discuss the game.

GROUP PROCESS QUESTIONS

1. Ask the children what they needed to do to play the game. How did they plan ahead and organize the trip so it felt like they were at that destination?

2. Ask the children how they felt while they were pretending to be in the place they selected. How did they feel about the effort they put into planning and organizing the trip? Emphasize that the trip might not have been as fun if they had not planned and organized so well.

3. Ask the children how they felt after the game was over.

7 GROUP PLAY INTERVENTION: *Program the Robot*

OVERVIEW

Program the Robot teaches children planning, organization, and time management skills. Small groups of children are given a list of tasks to program their robot (a child) to do within a specific time frame.

GROUP PLAY INTERVENTION SKILLS TAUGHT

Primary: Planning, Organization, Time Management
Secondary: Following Directions, Cooperation

SKILL DIFFICULTY

Intermediate–Advanced

PREREQUISITE SKILLS

Children should be able to follow simple verbal instructions and have basic self-control and attention skills. They should be able to read.

SUGGESTED GROUP SKILL SEQUENCES TO PRACTICE BEFORE GROUP PLAY INTERVENTION

No. 35. Cooperation
No. 30. Solving a Problem as a Group
No. 31. Following Directions

REQUIRED MATERIALS

Paper and a writing instrument.

ROOM SETUP

An open space that is large enough for children to move around in.

GAME SYNOPSIS

Program the Robot is a game in which children are broken down into small groups (five children in each group), and told they are going to play a game about programming their robot. The group facilitator selects one child from the small group to play the role of the robot. The other members are the programmers. The programmers are given a list of eight tasks (four tasks can be used for younger children) they must guide their robot to do within 5 minutes in order to program him or her. Each of the four programmers is assigned two of the eight tasks (one of the four tasks for younger children). The programmers must work together to organize and plan which group members will be assigned to which tasks.

STEPS FOR IMPLEMENTING *PROGRAM THE ROBOT*

1. Tell children they are going to play a game that requires them to program a robot (children in the group). Break the children down into small groups of five.
2. Assign one of the five group members to play the role of robot. The rest of the group members should be the programmers.
3. The programmers are given a list of eight tasks to program their robot with within a 5-minute time period (the number of programmers and tasks on the list can be adjusted according to the number of children in the group). Tasks on the list could include the following:
    a) Turning the lights on or off in the room.
    b) Walking around a piece of furniture.
    c) Turning to the right 90 degrees.

d) Taking 10 steps forward or backward.

e) Locating a book (e.g., *Green Eggs and Ham* by Dr. Seuss) in the room and placing it on the table.

4. Each programmer is responsible for programming the robot with two of the eight tasks. The programmers must work together to plan and organize who will be assigned which tasks and the order in which the tasks will be completed. Children must plan, organize, and execute the programming of the robot within a 5-minute time period.

5. After each programmer has his or her two tasks, the first programmer guides the robot through the task (i.e., take ten steps backward). A group facilitator should begin timing the children at this point. The programmers check off the task on the list after it is completed.

6. Repeat Step 5 until all eight tasks have been completed and the robot has been fully programmed. A group facilitator should record how long it took the children to complete the tasks. If the children do not program the robot within the 5-minute time period, they can try again without the time limit. They must still use planning and organizational skills to program the robot but without the pressure of a time limit.

7. Group process: Tell the children that the game is now over. Have them sit in their chairs or on the floor facing the front of the room and tell them it is time to discuss the game.

GROUP PROCESS QUESTIONS

1. Ask the children what they needed to do to play the game. What did they need to do when they were the programmers? What did they need to do when they were the robot?

2. Ask the children how they felt when they were the programmers. Emphasize how organizing the list of tasks and planning the order made it easier to get the programming done.

3. Ask the children how they felt when they were the robot.

4. Ask the children how they felt after the game was over.

8

GROUP PLAY INTERVENTION:
The Restaurant

OVERVIEW

The Restaurant is a game in which children work together to take orders and serve customers a meal in a pretend restaurant. The children are taught cooperation, planning, organizational, and time management skills.

GROUP PLAY INTERVENTION SKILLS TAUGHT

Primary: Time Management, Planning, Organization, Cooperation
Secondary: Following Directions

SKILL DIFFICULTY

Intermediate–Advanced

PREREQUISITE SKILLS

Children should be able to follow simple verbal instructions and have basic self-control and attention skills. Children should also have basic reading and writing skills (group facilitator can read for younger children).

SUGGESTED GROUP SKILL SEQUENCES TO PRACTICE BEFORE GROUP PLAY INTERVENTION

No. 30. Solving a Problem as a Group
No. 35. Cooperation
No. 2. Using Nice Talk
No. 5. Joining in a Conversation

REQUIRED MATERIALS

Notepad, stopwatch or timer, writing utensil (for taking meal orders), plates, cups, napkins, utensils, menus, a tablecloth, and menu items (real or pretend food items).

ROOM SETUP

An open space that is large enough for children to move around in. The customers in the restaurant should be seated at a table. The tablecloth, utensils, cups, napkins, and menus should already be in place at the table, and the plates should be set aside for use by the cooks.

GAME SYNOPSIS

The Restaurant is a game in which each child in the group is assigned a role (i.e., customer, host or hostess, waiter or waitress, cook). The children are in charge of running the restaurant and must work together to serve a meal to the customers in a given time period (e.g., 3–5 minutes, depending on how many customers there are).

STEPS FOR IMPLEMENTING *THE RESTAURANT*

1. Tell children they are going to play a game that involves running their own restaurant. They are told they need to work together as a team to plan, prepare, and serve a meal in the given time period (based on the group facilitators' preference and children's need for assistance/practice). Tell children they will be timed to see how long it takes them to serve the meal to the customers.
2. Assign each child a role in the restaurant (i.e., customer, host or hostess, waiter or waitress, cook).
3. Tell the customers they should walk into the restaurant and ask to be seated. The hostess should then seat the customers at the table. All utensils, cups, napkins, and menus should already be in place. Repeat this step until all customers are seated.

4. Next, instruct the customers to read the menus on the table and decide what food items they would like to order.

5. Then, instruct the waiter or waitress to write down the customers' names and corresponding orders on a notepad. At this point, the group facilitator should begin timing the children. After all the customers' orders are placed, tell the waiter or waitress to take the orders to the cooks in the kitchen. The waiter or waitress should assist the cooks by reading the items on the notepad.

6. Instruct the cooks to prepare the real or pretend food for the customers by placing the appropriate food items on the plates.

7. Next, the waiter or waitress should serve the meals to the correct customers. Once all the customers have their meals, the group facilitator should record the time it took to complete the ordering process.

8. Allow the customers to eat (or pretend to eat) their meals. Announce the time it took to complete the process.

9. Repeat Steps 2 through 8 until all the children have had a chance to perform a different role. Each time the game is repeated, encourage the children to meet the required time period if they have not done so yet, or to beat their previous time.

10. Group process: Tell the children that the game is now over. Have them sit in their chairs or on the floor facing the front of the room and tell them it is time to discuss the game.

GROUP PROCESS QUESTIONS

1. Ask the children what they needed to do to play the game.

2. Ask the children how they felt when they were performing their assigned roles. What did they need to do to successfully get the meal served to the customers in the assigned time period? Emphasize that the cooperation, planning, organization, and time management skills they used made it possible to get the meal served.

3. Ask the children how they felt after the game was over.

IV
CONCLUSION

FINAL COMMENTS AND FUTURE DIRECTIONS

This volume offered practitioners the first generation of innovative, well-designed group play interventions, grounded in cognitive–behavioral principles, that promote prosocial skills in elementary school children. In this book, positive instructional and behavioral management strategies are key ingredients for teaching and reinforcing group play skill sequences (Part II) and group play interventions (Part III).

It is suggested that the second generation of group play intervention models broaden the scope and focus of programming. The scope of new play interventions should incorporate targeted play interventions for children 2 to 5 years of age and 12 to 18 years of age. This volume was designed for children 5 to 12 years old. New models should continue to adopt integrative, empirically supported training approaches that include targeted developmentally appropriate skills and activities, focused teaching and learning opportunities, and behavioral and cognitive–behavioral techniques. Likewise, broadening the type of intervention agents (e.g., nurses, peers, siblings, parents, foster care parents, coaches) and service delivery settings (e.g., sport teams, clubs, summer camp, home, residential treatment center, hospital) used would be beneficial.

It would also be useful to expand the focus of group play interventions in the context of children, families, and school systems. For children, group play interventions could be designed to target (i.e., improve) symptom concerns (e.g., aggression, bullying, noncompliance, anxiety, depression), difficulties related to moderate to acute psychosocial stressors (e.g., death, chronically ill family members, separation or divorce, sexual or physical abuse, natural disasters, substance-dependent parents), and adaptive behaviors and competencies (e.g., self-control, eye contact, self-expression, creativity). For the family, new models could focus on enhancing family cohesion, resiliency, communication, coping, relationships, flexibility, and adaptability. For the school, new models could focus on increasing schoolwide or classroom problem solving, rule following, safety, and sense of belonging or affiliation.

When developing new group play intervention models, it is imperative to answer four questions. First, *who* will implement the group intervention (e.g., a teacher, nurse, psychologist, social worker, parent, older peer)? This decision should be made carefully, as it will affect the transfer, maintenance, and generalizability of gains to the targeted and nontargeted settings. Second, *what* group play interventions will be implemented? Third, *when* will the group play interventions be introduced into the treatment process? Interventions should be carefully timed so they occur at appropriate developmental points in children's lives. Fourth, *where* will the group play interventions be delivered? Interventions can be implemented in a number of settings (e.g., home, sports setting, camp, school, clinic, hospital). Each setting can uniquely influence the transfer and maintenance of gains.

It is essential that future play intervention models are well-conceived in relation to comprehensive outcome assessment approaches. Future group play interventions should include measures that are (a) targeted to the specific goals of the group training; (b) clinically practical (brief) for repeatedly administered during the group training process; (c) sensitive to change during the group training process; (d) highly reliable, possessing strong stability (consistency) over time; and (e) valid (construct relevant) to the group training process and outcomes. Finally, practitioners may wish to adopt a multidimensional outcome assessment approach for new models. For example, outcome assessment can be tailored to assess (a) group behavioral goals that are reinforced throughout each group training session, (b) individual child behavioral goals, (c) children's perceptions of the group process (see the example child feedback form http://pubs.apa.org/books/supp/reddy), (d) adult group facilitators' perceptions of the group process, (e) adult group facilitators' adherence to the group training agenda and key steps of the selected group play skill sequences and group play interventions, and (f) caregivers' report of the generalizability of training gains to other settings. Thus, the success of future group play intervention models rests on the thoughtful integration of intervention components and outcome assessment.

In sum, it is hoped that this book represents a timely, clinically relevant, and comprehensive presentation of group play intervention training that serves as a springboard for future group intervention development and research. Deep appreciation is expressed to all of the children, parents, teachers, and graduate students who provided invaluable feedback on the implementation and usefulness of the training described.

Appendix A: Example Group Play Intervention Session
(Approximately 60-Minute Session)

- Welcome the children to the group.
- Therapists introduce themselves.
- Use name tags for children and group therapists.
- Describe to the children the group agenda (structure).
- Review group goals:
  1. Follow directions.
  2. Keep my hands and feet to myself.
  3. Use my words to express my thoughts and feelings.
- Discuss how stickers are awarded: One sticker for each goal.
- If three stickers are earned, an extra sticker is awarded to take home.
- Discuss the use of bathroom passes.
- Discuss the use of *time out* passes—it is *good* to take time out when one does not feel in control. Role play time out for the children. Do this spontaneously in the middle of the group.
- Show the group the Group Complaint Book and how to use it.
- Briefly review the games to be played in the group!
- Positive Motivational System—in front of the group, review each child's efforts toward each of the three group goals. Give one sticker award for each group goal accomplished (allow 10 minutes).
- This activity involves two therapists.
  Therapist 1: Calls each child up to receive his or her stars (one to three stars) and places them on group star chart. Make sure each child follows the process. The group claps at the end for each child.
  Therapist 2: Helps each child choose stickers to place into the sticker book, one at a time.
- Prepare for parent pickup.

TEACHING MODULE: *ASKING FOR HELP* AND *HELPING OTHERS*

Purpose

The purpose of this module is to teach children ways to: (a) identify situations in which they require help, (b) obtain appropriate help, (c) identify situations when others need help, and (d) help others.

Accessing help and helping others are two powerful protective factors (strengths) related to academic and social success in children (Ryan & Patrick, 2001).

Five teaching methods are recommended:

1. Group play skill sequences—provides structured play activities that promote specific prosocial skills.
2. Modeling—the adult facilitator demonstrates specific behaviors and skills.
3. Role playing—provides guided opportunities to practice and rehearse appropriate interpersonal behaviors.

4. Performance feedback (coaching, corrective feedback, praise)—adult facilitators frequently praise and provide children with feedback on how well they modeled the skills and behavior that were demonstrated. Facilitators also assist children in correcting any mistakes that are made.

5. Group play interventions—allow children to use the skills and behaviors in a fun, practical, real-world context that enhances and promotes skill utilization and generalization.

Suggested Group Play Skill Sequences

1. Asking for Help (No. 42)
2. Helping Others (No. 43)

Required Materials for Group Play Skill Sequences

Easel with large poster board, dry erase board, or blackboard.

Room Setup for Group Play Skill Sequences

Boards should be set up in front of the room with group play skill sequences written on them. Children should sit facing the boards.

Group Play Skill Sequence: Asking for Help

1. *Decide* what the problem is and if you need help; for example, "I am having a problem with my math homework."
2. *Decide* who to ask; for example, "I will ask my mom."
3. *Choose* what to say; for example, "Mom, can you help me with my math homework?"
4. *Wait* until you get the other person's attention and say, "Excuse me."
5. *Tell* the person what you need in a friendly way; for example, "Mom, can you please help me with my math homework?"

Other Examples

- You cannot reach something that you need or want (e.g., book, video game, snack).
- Someone hit you and you do not know what to do.
- You received a bad grade on a test and need help to do better next time.

Group Play Skill Sequence: Helping Others

1. *Decide* what the problem is.
2. *Decide* if someone needs your help; for example, a friend tells you that he is "mad at Jeff (another classmate) for cheating during a basketball game."
3. *Ask* your friend if you can help him or her: "Can I help?"
4. If your friend says yes, *offer* help: "You can tell Jeff that you will not play with him if he does not follow the rules. If he still cheats, we can play basketball together instead."

Other Examples

- A mother is having trouble carrying in the groceries.
- A friend was teased by another classmate during recess.
- Your sister is having difficulties playing a video game.

Steps for Implementing Group Play Skill Sequences

1. Write each skill sequence on a large poster board so each step is listed numerically. Underline the action words listed in this book for each skill sequence.
2. Group play skill sequences should be introduced as a game to the group. It is important that group facilitators introduce and reinforce the group play skill sequences in a playful manner. For example, before performing a group skill sequence, have the children pretend it is a movie set. Explain that the observing children are *directors,* and the children and group facilitators who are role playing the skill sequence are *actors.* Tell the children that when the actors indicate that they are ready, the directors should put their arms apart in the air and count, "1, 2, 3, Action!" The directors close their arms and hands on the word *action.* This will be a signal to the children and group facilitator actors to begin role playing the skill sequence.
3. Explain that the game requires each member to follow directions, take turns, and clap for each other. The game also requires each member to listen and remain quiet when group members are *acting.*
4. Initially, group facilitators should act out the group play skill sequence to the children. Next, with encouragement and feedback from a group facilitator, one or two child volunteers are invited to demonstrate the group skill sequence to the group. After several demonstrations of the skill sequence, facilitators may wish to split the group up into smaller groups so all children have an opportunity to practice and correctly demonstrate the skill sequence.
5. After the skill sequences for *Asking for Help* and *Helping Others* have been successfully practiced, the following group play intervention can be introduced and implemented. Group play interventions offer fun, real-world contexts for children to learn targeted prosocial skills and generalize their skills to other settings.

GROUP PLAY INTERVENTION: *ISLANDS*

Overview

The *Islands* game places children in an imaginary, dangerous situation. This game requires children to ask for help, help others, share, cooperate, control their hands and feet (i.e., self-control), and manage stress effectively.

Group Play Intervention Skills Taught

Primary: Asking for Help, Helping Others
Secondary: Following Directions, Self-Control, Stress Management

Skill Difficulty

Basic

Prerequisite Skills

Prior to playing this game children should possess basic abilities to follow simple directions and keep their bodies in control with redirection or reminders.

Suggested Group Sequences to Practice Before Group Play Intervention

- No. 42. Asking for Help
- No. 43. Asking corners for Help
- No. 16. Self-Control

Required Materials

Bath towels (three or four) and a radio, tape, or CD player.

Room Setup

Towels are placed on the floor of the room and evenly spaced out. There should be ample room for children to comfortably move in between the towels. A radio should be set up near a group facilitator so that the group facilitator can easily turn the radio's volume *slowly* up and down. The radio should not be abruptly shut off, like in the game of musical chairs because this will induce unnecessary anxiety and impulsivity in the children. An age-appropriate radio station, CD, or tape with dance music should be identified before the game is started. As the game progresses, towels are gradually folded and later removed.

Game Synopsis

Islands is an interactive game in which children are told to pretend that they live on islands, which are represented by towels. Imaginary crocodiles share the islands and water with the children. The group facilitator instructs the children about how to live peacefully with the crocodiles and how to avoid being bitten or eaten. While the music is playing, the crocodiles go to sleep on the islands, allowing the children to swim freely in the water. However, when the music stops, the crocodiles wake up, go into the water, and become aggressive. As a result, the children should swim around the islands while the music is playing. After the music stops, they should go onto the islands. However, if a child is found to be in the water for more than a couple of seconds after the music stops, they must ask one of the other children for help getting onto an island. As the game progresses, the tide comes in and the islands get smaller (towels are folded and are eventually removed), thereby increasing the number of children asking for help.

Steps for Implementing Islands

1. Introduce *Islands* to the children in a positive and playful manner. Tell children that they are about to play a special game that involves following directions, asking for help, helping others, controlling their hands and feet, and managing their stress.

2. Read the story of the *Islands* to the children.

   You are islanders who live on a beautiful group of islands, and the water around the islands is warm and blue. You like to swim every day, but there is one problem. There are crocodiles that travel together and also live in the water and on the islands. When the wind blows over the water and through the trees, a musical sound starts. The music causes the crocodiles to go onto the islands and fall asleep, leaving the waters peaceful. But when *the music stops,* the crocodiles wake up [make a yawning gesture and sound], go into the water, and look for food. When the music is playing, you should swim around in the water by walking, floating, or dancing slowly around the islands. Make sure that when the music is playing you are not on an island, because you do not want to disturb the peaceful crocodiles. When the music stops you must leave the water and climb onto an island. If you are not on an island right away, you need to ask someone on an island for help. One of the other islanders will help you onto an island to safety. If you are on an island and someone asks you for help, you should put out your arm and help them onto the island. When the tide comes in, the water covers some of the beaches on the islands and you need to share the islands more with your friends or find another island to stay on. Sharing islands and helping others will keep you safe and happy.

3. Before the game starts, instruct children that they need to
   a) keep their arms in control—do not hit or push others;
   b) keep their feet in control—walk, not run, and stand and avoid bumping into objects and other group members;
   c) listen for the music to start or stop;
   d) Not run or jump onto islands.
4. Have everyone repeat the directions (out loud) before beginning the game.
5. Start playing the music. While the music is playing, encourage the children to walk slowly, (pretend) swim, and dance around the islands without stepping on them. Group facilitators should encourage the children to keep moving around all the islands and avoid stepping on or touching the islands. After approximately a minute, *slowly* turn the music down. After a few seconds, tell the children to "freeze". Remind children who are not on an island that they should ask someone on an island for help. The children on an island who are asked for help should extend one of their arms to help others onto the island. If some children jumped onto an island after they were told to "freeze", tell those children to step off the island and ask others for help onto one. The children asking for help should do so loud enough for the entire group to hear them.
7. Continue to repeat Step 6. After a couple of times, fold the towels, signifying that the tide is coming in. After a couple of additional times, fold the towels again to make the islands even smaller. Then remove one towel at a time until only a single towel is left. All the children should have at least one opportunity to ask others for help during the game.
8. Group process: Tell the children that the game is now over. Have them sit in their chairs or the floor facing the front of the room and tell them it is time to discuss the game.

Group Process Questions

1. Ask the children what they needed to do to play the game. Emphasize the importance of asking for help and helping others.
2. Ask the children how they felt when the music was playing.
3. Ask the children how they felt when the music was becoming lower and lower.
4. Ask the children how they felt when the music was off.
5. Ask the children when they needed help from others.
6. Ask the children how they felt when they needed help.
7. Ask the children how they felt when others helped them.
8. Ask the children how they felt when they helped others.

Appendix B: Recommended Web Resources for Play Therapy

American Psychological Association:

APA Division 7 Developmental Psychology
http://www.apa.org/about/division/div7.html

APA Division 12 Clinical Psychology
http://www.apa.org/about/division/div12.html

APA Division 16 School Psychology
http://www.apa.org/about/division/div16.html

APA Division 27 Society for Community Research and Action
http://www.apa.org/about/division/div27.html

APA Division 37 Society for Child and Family Policy and Practice
http://www.apa.org/about/division/div37.html

APA Division 43 Society for Family Psychology
http://www.apa.org/about/division/div43.html

APA Division 49 Group Psychotherapy
http://www.apa.org/about/division/div49.html

APA Division 53 Society of Clinical Child and Adolescent Psychology
http://www.apa.org/about/division/div53.html

APA Division 54 Society of Pediatric Psychology
http://www.apa.org/about/division/div54.html

Association for Behavioral and Cognitive Therapies
http://www.abct.org/Home/

Association for Play Therapy
http://www.a4pt.org/

Association for Specialists in Group Work
http://www.asgw.org/

Center for Play Therapy—University of North Texas
http://cpt.unt.edu/

Children's Group Therapy Association
http://www.cgta.net/conference/index.html

Family Enhancement and Play Therapy Center
http://www.play-therapy.com/

Mental Health America
http://www.nmha.org/

National Association of School Psychologists
http://www.nasponline.org/

National Institute of Mental Health
http://www.nimh.nih.gov/index.shtml

Office of the Surgeon General
http://www.surgeongeneral.gov/index.html

Play Therapy Corner
http://www.playtherapycorner.com/home.html

Play Therapy International
http://www.playtherapy.org/

U.S. Department of Health and Human Services
SAMHSA (Substance Abuse and Mental Health Services Administration)
http://mentalhealth.samhsa.gov/

REFERENCES

Abramowitz, C. V. (1976). The effectiveness of group psychotherapy with children. *Archives of General Psychiatry, 33,* 320–326.

Achenbach, T. M., & Rescorla, L. A. (2001). *Manual of the Achenbach System of Empirically Based Assessment—Child Behavior Checklist, Teacher Report Form, and Youth Report.* Burlington: University of Vermont, Research Center for Children, Youth, and Families.

Ackerman, B. P., & Izard, C. E. (2004). Emotion cognition in children and adolescents: Introduction to the special issues. *Journal of Experimental Child Psychology, 89,* 271–275. doi:10.1016/j.jecp.2004.08.003

Alpert-Gillis, L. J., Pedro-Carroll, J. L., & Cowen, E. L. (1989). The children of divorce intervention program: Development, implementation, and evaluation of a program for young urban children. *Journal of Consulting and Clinical Psychology, 57,* 583–589. doi:10.1037/0022-006X.57.5.583

American Psychiatric Association. (2000). *Diagnostic and statistical manual of mental disorders* (4th ed., text rev.). Washington, DC: Author.

Amerikaner, M., & Summerlin, M. L. (1982). Group counseling with learning disabled children: Effects of social skills and relaxation training on self-concept and classroom behavior. *Journal of Learning Disabilities, 15,* 340–343. doi:10.1177/002221948201500607

Anastopoulos, A. D., Shelton, T. L., DuPaul, G. J., & Geuvremont, D. C. (1993). Parent training for attention-deficit/hyperactivity disorder: Its impact on parent functioning. *Journal of Abnormal Child Psychology, 21,* 581–596. doi:10.1007/BF00916320

Anastopoulos, A. D., Smith, J. A., & Wein, E. E. (1998). Counseling and training parents. In R. A. Barkley (Ed.), *Attention-deficit/hyperactivity disorder: A handbook for diagnosis and treatment* (pp. 373–393). New York, NY: Guilford Press.

Andrews, J., Swank, P., Foorman, B., & Fletcher, J. (1995). Effects of educating parents about attention-deficit/hyperactivity disorder on the subsequent behavior of their ADHD children. *ADHD Report, 3*(4), 12–13.

Arean, P. A., Gum, A., McCulloch, C. E., Bostrom, A., Gallagher-Thompson, D., & Thompson, L. (2005). Treatment of depression in low-income older adults. *Psychology and Aging, 20,* 601–609. doi:10.1037/0882-7974.20.4.601

Asher, S. R., Parker, J. G., & Walker, D. L. (1996). Distinguishing friendship from acceptance: Implications for intervention and assessment. In W. M. Bukowski, A. F. Newcomb, & W. W. Hartup (Eds.), *The company they keep: Friendships in childhood and adolescence* (pp. 366–405). New York, NY: Cambridge University Press.

Association for Play Therapy. (2001, June). Play therapy. *Association for Play Therapy Newsletter, 20,* 20.

Baer, R. A., & Nietzel, M. T. (1991). Cognitive and behavioral treatment of impulsivity in children: A meta-analytic review of the outcome literature. *Journal of Clinical Child Psychology, 20,* 400–412. doi:10.1207/s15374424jccp2004_9

Baggerly, J., & Parker, M. (2005). Child-centered group play therapy with African-American boys at the elementary school level. *Journal of Counseling & Development, 83,* 387–396.

Bandura, A. (1993). Perceived self-efficacy in cognitive development and functioning. *Educational Psychologist, 28,* 117–148. doi:10.1207/s15326985ep2802_3

Bar-Haim, Y., Aviezer, O., Berson, Y., & Sagi, A. (2002). Attachment in infancy and personal space regulation in early adolescence. *Attachment & Human Development, 4*(1), 68–83. doi:10.1080/14616730210123111

Barkley, R. A. (1990). Attention-deficit disorders: History, definition, and diagnosis. In M. Lewis & S. M. Miller (Eds.), *Handbook of developmental psychopathology* (pp. 65–75). New York, NY: Plenum Press.

Barkley, R. A. (1997). *ADHD and the nature of self-control.* New York, NY: Guilford Press.

Barkley, R. A. (1998). Attention-deficit/hyperactivity disorder. In E. J. Marsh & R. A. Barkley (Eds.), *Treatment of childhood disorders* (2nd ed., pp. 55–110). New York, NY: Guilford Press.

Barrett, P. M. (2000). Treatment of childhood anxiety: Developmental aspects. *Clinical Psychology Review, 20,* 479–494. doi:10.1016/S0272-7358(99)00038-0

Bay-Hinitz, A. K., & Wilson, G. R. (2005). A cooperative games intervention for aggressive preschool children. In L. A. Reddy, T. M. Files-Hall, & C. E. Schaefer (Eds.), *Empirically based play interventions for children* (pp. 215–239). Washington, DC: American Psychological Association. doi:10.1037/11086-011

Beeferman, D., & Orvaschel, H. (1994). Group psychotherapy for depressed adolescents: A critical review. *International Journal of Group Psychotherapy, 44,* 463–475.

Bennett, D., Power, T. J., Rostain, A. L., & Carr, D. E. (1996). Parent acceptability and feasibility of ADHD interventions: Assessment, correlates, and predictive validity. *Journal of Pediatric Psychology, 21,* 643–657. doi:10.1093/jpepsy/21.5.643

Berner, M. L., Fee, V. E., & Turner, A. D. (2001). A multicomponent social skills training program for preadolescent girls with few friends. *Child & Family Behavior Therapy, 23,* 1–18. doi:10.1300/J019v23n02_01

Bertera, E. M. (2007). The role of positive and negative social exchanges between adolescents, their peers and family as predictors of suicide ideation. *Child & Adolescent Social Work Journal, 24,* 523–538. doi:10.1007/s10560-007-0104-y

Bettmann, J. E. (2006). Using attachment theory to understand the treatment of adult depression. *Clinical Social Work Journal, 34,* 531–542. doi:10.1007/s10615-005-0033-1

Beyer, B. (1997, October). *Effective therapy groups.* Paper presented at the 14th Annual Association for Play Therapy International Conference, Orlando, FL.

Bloom, B. S. (1974). Time and learning. *American Psychologist, 29*, 682–688. doi:10.1037/h0037632

Boivin, M., Hymel, S., & Bukowski, W. M. (1995). The roles of social withdrawal, peer rejection, and victimization by peers in predicting loneliness and depressed mood in childhood. *Development and Psychopathology, 7*, 765–785. doi:10.1017/S0954579400006830

Bornstein, M. H. (1989). Between caretakers and their young: Two modes of interaction and their consequences for cognitive growth. In M. H. Bornstein & J. S. Bruner (Eds.), *Interaction in human development* (pp. 197–214). Hillsdale, NJ: Erlbaum.

Bornstein, M. H., & O'Reilly, A. (1993). *New directions for child development: The role of play in the development of thought.* San Francisco, CA: Jossey-Bass

Bowlby, J. (1980). *Attachment and loss: Vol. 3. Loss.* New York, NY: Basic Books.

Bradley, S. (2000). *Affect regulation and the development of psychopathology.* New York, NY: Guilford Press.

Bratton, S., & Landreth, G. (1995). Filial therapy with single parents: Effects on parental acceptance, empathy, and stress. *International Journal of Play Therapy, 4*(1), 61–80. doi:10.1037/h0089142

Bratton, S., Ray, D., Rhine, T., & Jones, L. (2005). The efficacy of play therapy with children: A meta-analytic review. *Professional Psychology: Research and Practice, 36*, 376–390. doi:10.1037/0735-7028.36.4.376

Brent, D. A., Poling, K., McKain, B., & Baugher, M. (1993). A psychoeducational program for families of affectively ill children and adolescents. *Journal of the American Academy of Child & Adolescent Psychiatry, 32*, 770–774. doi:10.1097/00004583-199307000-00010

Brestan, E. V., & Eyberg, S. M. (1998). Effective psychosocial treatments of conduct-disordered children and adolescents: 29 years, 82 studies, and 5,272 kids. *Journal of Clinical Child Psychology, 27*, 180–189. doi:10.1207/s15374424jccp2702_5

Bridges, L. J., & Grolnick, W. S. (1995). The development of emotional self-regulation in infancy and early childhood. In N. Eisenberg (Ed.), *Review of personality and psychology* (pp. 185–211). Newbury Park, CA: Sage.

Briesmeister, J. M., & Schaefer, C. E. (1998). *Handbook of parent training: Parents as co-therapists for children's behavior problems.* New York, NY: Wiley.

Brotman, L. M., Dawson-McClure, S., Gouley, K. K., McGuire, K., Burraston, B., & Bank, L. (2005). Older siblings benefit from a family-based preventive intervention for preschoolers at risk for conduct problems. *Journal of Family Psychology, 19*, 581–591. doi:10.1037/0893-3200.19.4.581

Brownell, C. A., Ramani, G. B., & Zerwas, S. (2006). Becoming a social partner with peers: Cooperation and social understanding in one- and two-year-olds. *Child Development, 77*, 803–821.

Buettel, M. (2006). Exploring current knowledge on Asperger syndrome and best practices for school-based interventions. *School Psychology Quarterly, 21*, 349–357. doi:10.1521/scpq.2006.21.3.349

Bunker, L. K. (1991). The role of play and motor skill development in building children's self-confidence and self-esteem. [Special Issue: Sport and physical education]. *The Elementary School Journal, 91*, 467–471. doi:10.1086/461669

Butler, S. F., & Fontenelle, S. F. (1995). Cognitive–behavioral group therapy: Application with adolescents who are cognitively impaired and sexually act out. *Journal for Specialists in Group Work, 20*, 121–127. doi:10.1080/01933929508411335

Campbell, C. A., & Bowman, R. P. (1993). The "fresh start" support club: Small group counseling for academically retained children. *Elementary School Guidance and Counseling, 27*, 172–185.

Campbell, J., Lamb, M., & Hwang, C. (2000). Early child-care experiences and children's social competence between 1 and one half and 15 years of age. *Applied Developmental Science, 4*, 166–175. doi:10.1207/S1532480XADS0403_5

Carroll, J. B. (1963). A model of school learning. *Teachers College Record, 64*, 723–733.

Cheney, D., & Barringer, C. (1995). Teacher competence, student diversity, and staff training for the inclusion of middle school students with emotional and behavioral disorders. *Journal of Emotional and Behavioral Disorders, 3*, 174–182. doi:10.1177/106342669500300307

Chermak, G. D., Somers, E. K., & Seikel, J. A. (1998). Behavioral signs of central auditory processing disorder and attention-deficit/hyperactivity disorder. *Journal of the American Academy of Audiology, 9*, 78–84.

Chermak, G. D., Tucker, E., & Seikel, J. A. (2002). Behavioral characteristics of auditory processing disorder and attention-deficit hyperactivity disorder: predominantly inattentive type. *Journal of the American Academy of Audiology, 13*, 332–338.

Christner, R. W., Stewart, J. L., & Freeman, A. (2007). *Cognitive–behavior group therapy with children and adolescents.* New York, NY: Routledge.

Christophersen, E. R., & Mortweet, S. L. (2003). *Parenting that works: Building skills that last a lifetime.* Washington, DC: American Psychological Association.

Clarke, G. N., Rohde, P., Lewinsohn, P. M., Hops, H., & Seeley, J. R. (1999). Cognitive–behavioral treatment of adolescent depression: Efficacy of acute group treatment and booster sessions. *Journal of the American Academy of Child & Adolescent Psychiatry, 38*, 272–279. doi:10.1097/00004583-199903000-00014

Cole, P. M. (1986). Children's spontaneous control of facial expression. *Child Development, 57*, 1309–1321. doi:10.2307/1130411

Colombo, J., & Cheatham, C. L. (2006). The emergence and basis of endogenous attention in infancy and early childhood. In R. Kail (Ed.), *Advances in child development and behavior* (Vol. 34, pp. 283–310). Oxford, England: Academic Press.

Comer, J. P., Haynes, N. M., Joyner, E. T., & Ben-Avie, M. (1996). *Rallying the whole village: The Comer process for reforming education.* New York, NY: Teachers College Press.

Compas, B. E., Connor-Smith, J. K., Saltzman, H., Thomsen, A. H., & Wadsworth, M. E. (2001). Coping with stress during childhood and adolescence: Problems, progress, and potential in theory and research. *Psychological Bulletin, 127*, 87–127. doi:10.1037/0033-2909.127.1.87

Connell, S., Sanders, M. R., & Markie-Dadds, C. (1997). Self-directed behavioral family intervention for parents of oppositional children in rural and remote areas. *Behavior Modification, 21*, 379–408. doi:10.1177/01454455970214001

Corkum, P., Rimer, P., & Schachar, R. (1999). Parental knowledge of ADHD and opinions of treatment options: Impact on enrollment and adherence to a 12-month treatment trial. *Canadian Journal of Psychiatry, 44*, 1043–1048.

Costas, M., & Landreth, G. (1999). Filial therapy with nonoffending parents of children who have been sexually abused. *International Journal of Play Therapy, 8*(1), 43–66. doi:10.1037/h0089427

Cousins, L. S., & Weiss, G. (1993). Parent training and social skills training for children with attention-deficit/hyperactivity disorder: How can they be combined for greater effectiveness? *Canadian Journal of Psychiatry, 38*, 449–457.

Crosbie-Burnett, M., & Newcomer, L. L. (1990). Group counseling children of divorce: The effects of multimodal intervention. *Journal of Divorce, 13*(3), 69–78.

Dagley, J. C., Gazda, G. M., Eppinger, S. J., & Stewart, E. A. (1994). Group psychotherapy research with children, preadolescents, and adolescents. In A. Fuhriman & G. M. Burlingame (Eds.), *Handbook of group psychotherapy* (pp. 340–369). New York, NY: Wiley.

Daniel, S. S., Walsh, A. K., Goldston, D. B., Arnold, E. M., Reboussin, B. A., & Wood, F. B. (2006). Suicidality, school dropout, and reading problems among adolescents. *Journal of Learning Disabilities, 39,* 504–514. doi:10.1177/00222194060390060301

Dawson, G., Osterling, J., Meltzoff, A. N., & Kuhl, P. (2000). Case study of the development of an infant with autism from birth to 2 years of age. *Journal of Applied Developmental Psychology, 21,* 299–313. doi:10.1016/S0193-3973(99)00042-8

Deblinger, E., Stauffer, L. B., & Steer, R. A. (2001). Comparative efficacies of supportive and cognitive therapies for young children who have been sexually abused and their nonoffending mothers. *Child Maltreatment, 6,* 332–343. doi:10.1177/1077559501006004006

Denham, S. A. (1998). *Emotional development in young children.* New York, NY: Guilford Press.

Dennis, T. (2006). Emotion self-regulation in preschoolers: The interplay of child approach reactivity, parenting, and control capacities. *Developmental Psychology, 42,* 84–97. doi:10.1037/0012-1649.42.1.84

Drewes, A. A. (2009). *Blending play therapy with cognitive–behavioral therapy: Evidence-based and other effective treatments and techniques.* New York, NY: Wiley.

Drewes, A. A., & Schaefer, C. (Eds.). (2009). *School based play therapy* (2nd ed.). New York, NY: Wiley.

Duchnowski, A. J., & Friedman, R. M. (1990). Children's mental health: Challenge for the nineties. *Journal of Mental Health Administration, 17,* 3–12. doi:10.1007/BF02518575

Duhamel, F., & Talbot, L. R. (2004). A constructivist evaluation of family systems nursing interventions with families experiencing cardiovascular and cerebrovascular illness. *Journal of Family Nursing, 10,* 12–32. doi:10.1177/1074840703260906

Duman, S., & Margolin, G. (2007). Parents' aggressive influences and children's aggressive problem solutions with peers. *Journal of Clinical Child and Adolescent Psychology, 36*(1), 42–55. doi:10.1207/s15374424jccp3601_5

Dunn, J., Cutting, A. L., & Fisher, N. (2002). Old friends, new friends: Predictors of children's perspective on their friends at school. *Child Development, 73,* 621–635.

DuPaul, G. J., & Stoner, G. (2003). *ADHD in the schools: Assessment and intervention strategies* (2nd ed.). New York, NY: Guilford Press.

Edelson, J. L., & Rose, S. D. (1981). Investigations into the efficacy of short-term group social skills training for socially isolated children. *Child Behavior Therapy, 3,* 1–16.

Edwards, M. E. (2002). Attachment, mastery, and interdependence: A model of parenting processes. *Family Process, 41,* 389–404. doi:10.1111/j.1545-5300.2002.41308.x

Eisenberg, N., & Fabes, R. A. (1998). Prosocial development. In W. Damon (Series Ed.) & N. Eisenberg (Ed.), *Handbook of child psychology: Vol. 3. Social, emotional, and personality development* (5th ed., pp. 701–778). New York, NY: Wiley.

Eyberg, S. M. (2003). Parent–child interaction therapy. In T. H. Ollendick & C. S. Schroeder (Eds.), *Encyclopedia of clinical child and pediatric psychology* (pp. 446–447). New York, NY: Plenum Press.

Falconer, M. K., Haskett, M. E., McDaniels, L., Dirkes, T., & Siegel, E. C. (2008). Evaluation of support groups for child abuse prevention: Outcomes of four state evaluations. *Social Work With Groups, 31,* 165–182. doi:10.1080/01609510801960890

Ferland, F. (1997). *Play, children with physical disabilities, and occupational therapy.* Ottowa, Canada: The University of Ottawa Press.

Fine, S., Forth, A., Gilbert, M., & Haley, G. (1991). Group therapy for adolescent depressive disorder: A comparison of social skills and therapeutic support. *Journal of the American Academy of Child & Adolescent Psychiatry, 30,* 79–85. doi:10.1097/00004583-199101000-00012

Fine, S., Gilbert, M., Schmidt, L., Haley, G., Maxwell, A., & Forth, P. (1989). Short-term group therapy with depressed adolescent outpatients. *Canadian Journal of Psychiatry, 34,* 97–102.

Fine, S. E., Izard, C. E., Mostow, A. J., Trentacosta, C. J., & Ackerman, B. P. (2003). First grade emotion knowledge as a predictor of fifth grade self-reported internalizing behaviors in children from economically disadvantaged families. *Development and Psychopathology, 15,* 331–342. doi:10.1017/S095457940300018X

Fischer, M. (1990). Parenting stress and the child with attention-deficit/hyperactivity disorder. *Journal of Clinical Child Psychology, 19,* 337–346. doi:10.1207/s15374424jccp1904_5

Fombonne, E. (2005). Epidemiology of autistic disorder and other developmental disorders. *The Journal of Clinical Psychiatry, 66*(10), 3–8.

Foulkes, S. H., & Anthony, E. J. (1957). *Group psychotherapy: The psychoanalytic approach.* Oxford, England: Penguin Books.

Frederickson, N. L., & Furnham, A. F. (2004). Peer-assessed behavioral characteristics and sociometric rejection: Differences between pupils who have moderate learning difficulties and their mainstream peers. *British Journal of Educational Psychology, 74,* 391–410. doi:10.1348/0007099041552305

Frei, J. R., & Shaver, P. R. (2002). Respect in close relationships: Prototype definition, self-report assessment, and initial correlates. *Personal Relationships, 9,* 121–139. doi:10.1111/1475-6811.00008

Fuhriman, A., & Burlingame, G. M. (1994). Measuring small group process: A methodological application of chaos theory. *Small Group Research, 25,* 502–519. doi:10.1177/1046496494254005

Garaigordobil, M., & Echebarria, A. (1995). Assessment of peer-helping program on children's development. *Journal of Research in Childhood Education, 10,* 63–69. doi:10.1080/02568549509594688

Garton, A. F., & Pratt, C. (2001). Peer assistance in children's problem solving. *British Journal of Developmental Psychology, 19,* 307–318. doi:10.1348/026151001166092

Gay, K. (2003). *Circle of Parents: Advice to communities on supporting today's parents.* Program Advisory Series, Issue 2. Raleigh, NC: Prevent Child Abuse.

Gazda, G. M., & Larsen, M. J. (1968). A comprehensive appraisal of group and multiple counseling research. *Journal of Research and Development in Education, 1*(2), 57–132.

Gest, S. M., & Gest, J. M. (2005). Reading tutoring for students at academic and behavioral risk: Effects on time-on-task in the classroom. *Education & Treatment of Children, 28*(1), 25–47.

Gifford-Smith M., & Brownell, C. (2003). Childhood peer relationships: Social acceptance, friendships & peer networks. *Journal of School Psychology, 41,* 235–284.

Ginsburg, G. S., & Schlossberg, M. C. (2002). Family-based treatment of childhood anxiety disorders. *International Review of Psychiatry, 14,* 143–154. doi:10.1080/09540260220132662

Gonzalez, L. O., & Sellers, E. W. (2002). The effects of a stress-management program on self-concept, locus of control, and the acquisition of coping skills in school-age children diagnosed with attention-deficit/hyperactivity disorder. *Journal of Child and Adolescent Psychiatric Nursing, 15*(1), 5–15. doi:10.1111/j.1744-6171.2002.tb00318.x

Goodvin, R., Carlo, G., & Torquati, J. (2006). The role of child emotionality and maternal negative emotion expression in children's coping strategy use. *Social Development, 15,* 591–611. doi:10.1111/j.1467-9507.2006.00359.x

Greco, L. A., & Morris, T. L. (2001). Treating childhood shyness and related behavior: Empirically evaluated approaches to promote positive social interactions. *Clinical Child and Family Psychology Review, 4,* 299–318. doi:10.1023/A:1013543320648

Green, V. A., Cillessen, A. H., Reichis, R., Patterson, M. M., & Hughes, J. M. (2008). Social problem solving and strategy use in young children. *The Journal of Genetic Psychology, 169*(1), 92–112. doi:10.3200/GNTP.169.1.92-112

Greenwood, C. R., Walker, D., Carta, J., & Higgins, S. (2006). Developing a general outcome measure of growth in cognitive abilities of children 1 to 4 years old: The early problem-solving indicator. *School Psychology Review, 35,* 535–551.

Greig, A., Minnis, H., Millward, R., Sinclair, C., Kennedy, E., Towlson, K., . . . Hill, J. (2008). Relationships and learning: A review and investigation of narrative coherence in look-after children in primary school. *Educational Psychology in Practice, 24*(1), 13–27. doi:10.1080/02667360701841189

Gresham, F. M. (2000). Assessment of social skills in students with emotional and behavioral disorders. *Assessment for Effective Intervention, 26*(1), 51–58. doi:10.1177/073724770002600107

Guerney, B. (1964). Filial therapy: Description and rationale. *Journal of Consulting Psychology, 28,* 304–310. doi:10.1037/h0041340

Hale, J. B., & Fiorello, C. A. (2004). *School neuropsychology: A practitioner's handbook.* New York, NY: Guilford Press.

Hale, J. B., Fiorello, C. A., & Brown, L. (2005). Determining medication treatment effects using teacher ratings and classroom observations of children with ADHD: Does neuropsychological impairment matter? *Educational and Child Psychology, 22,* 39–61.

Hale, J. B., & Rubenstein, J. (2006). *Reconceptualizing nonverbal learning disabilities for academic and behavioral intervention efficacy.* Workshop presented to the West Chester Association of School Psychologists, West Chester, PA.

Hall, T., & Reddy, L. A. (2005). Present status and future directions for play interventions for children. In L. A. Reddy, T. M. Hall, & C. Schaefer (Eds.), *Empirically based play interventions for children* (pp. 267–279). Washington, DC: American Psychological Association.

Hand, L. (1996). *Comparison of selected developmentally oriented low organized games and traditional games on the behavior of students with emotional disturbance.* (Unpublished master's thesis). Temple University, Philadelphia, PA.

Hart, B., & Risley, T. R. (1995). *Meaningful differences in the everyday experience of young American children.* Baltimore, MD: Brookes.

Hoag, M. J., & Burlingame, G. M. (1997). Evaluating the effectiveness of child and adolescent group treatment: A meta-analytic review. *Journal of Clinical Child Psychology, 26,* 234–246. doi:10.1207/s15374424jccp2603_2

Holtman, M., Bolte, S., & Poustka, F. (2005). ADHD, Asperger syndrome, and high-functioning autism. *Journal of the American Academy of Child & Adolescent Psychiatry, 44*, 1101. doi:10.1097/01.chi.0000177322.57931.2a

Horner, T. M. (1983). On the formation of personal space and self-boundary structures in early human development: The case of infant stranger reactivity. *Developmental Review, 3*, 148–177. doi:10.1016/0273-2297(83)90028-X

Howes, C. (2000). Socioemotional classroom climate in child care, child–teacher relationships and children's second grade peer relations. *Social Development, 9*, 191–204. doi:10.1111/1467-9507.00119

Howes, C., & James, J. (2002). Children's social development within the context of childcare and early childhood education. In P. K. Smith & C. H. Hart (Eds.), *Blackwell handbook of social development* (pp. 137–155). Malden, MA: Blackwell.

Howes, C., & Matheson, C. (1992). Sequences in the development of competent play with peers: Social and social pretend play. *Developmental Psychology, 28*, 961–974. doi:10.1037/0012-1649.28.5.961

Howes, C., & Phillipsen, L. (1998). Continuity in children's relations with peers. *Social Development, 7*, 340–349. doi:10.1111/1467-9507.00071

Humphreys, L., Forehand, R., McMahon, R., & Roberts, M. (1978). Parent behavioral training to modify child noncompliance: Effects on untreated siblings. *Journal of Behavior Therapy and Experimental Psychiatry, 9*, 235–238. doi:10.1016/0005-7916(78)90034-4

Hunter, S. C., Boyle, J. M., & Warden, D. (2004). Help seeking amongst child and adolescent victims of peer-aggression and bullying: The influence of school-stage, gender, victimization, appraisal, and emotion. *British Journal of Educational Psychology, 74*, 375–390. doi:10.1348/0007099041552378

Ingalls, S., & Goldstein, G. (1999). Learning disabilities. In S. Goldstein & C. R. Reynolds (Eds.), *Handbook of neurodevelopmental and genetic disorders in children* (pp. 101–153). New York, NY: Guilford Press.

Izard, C. E., Fine, S., Schultz, D., Mostow, A., Ackerman, B. P., & Youngstrom, E. A. (2001). Emotion knowledge as a predictor of social behavior and academic competence in children at risk. *Psychological Science, 12*, 18–23. doi:10.1111/1467-9280.00304

Janssen, R. M., & Janssen, J. J. (1996). *Growing up in ancient Egypt*. London, England: Rubicon Press.

Jellesma, F. C., Reiffe, C., & Terwogt, M. M. (2008). My peers, my friend, and I: Peer interactions and somatic complaints in boys and girls. *Social Science & Medicine, 66*, 2195–2205. doi:10.1016/j.socscimed.2008.01.029

Johnson, M. L. (1988). Use of play group therapy in promoting social skills. *Issues in Mental Health Nursing, 9*(1), 105–112. doi:10.3109/01612848809140913

Kaduson, H., Cangelosi, D., & Schaefer, C. E. (1997). *The playing cure: Individualized play therapy for specific childhood problems*. Northvale, NJ: Jason Aronson.

Kaminski, J. W., Valle, L. A., Filene, J. H., & Boyle, C. L. (2008). A meta-analytic review of components associated with parent training program effectiveness. *Journal of Abnormal Child Psychology, 36*, 567–589. doi:10.1007/s10802-007-9201-9

Karpov, Y. V. (2003). Internalization of children's problem solving and individual differences in learning. *Cognitive Development, 18*, 377–398. doi:10.1016/S0885-2014(03)00042-X

Katz, J., & Tillery, K. (2004). Central auditory processing. In L. Verhoeven & H. van Balkom (Eds.), *Classification of developmental language disorders: Theoretical issues and clinical implications* (pp. 191–208). Mahwah, NJ: Erlbaum.

Kazdin, A. E., & Wassell, G. (2000). Therapeutic changes in children, parents, and families resulting from treatment of children with conduct problems. *Journal of the American Academy of Child & Adolescent Psychiatry, 39,* 414–420. doi:10.1097/00004583-200004000-00009

Kellogg, R. T. (1994). *The psychology of writing.* New York, NY: Oxford University Press.

Kendall, P. C., Chansky, T. E., Kane, M. T., Kim, R. S., Kortlander, E., Ronan, K. R., . . . Siqueland, L. (1992). *Anxiety disorders in youth: Cognitive–behavioral interventions.* Boston, MA: Allyn & Bacon.

Kendall, P. C., Chu, B. C., Pimentel, S. S., & Choudhury, M. (2000). Treating anxiety disorders in youth. In P. C. Kendall (Ed.), *Child and adolescent therapy: Cognitive–behavioral procedures* (pp. 235–287). New York, NY: Guilford Press.

Klin, A., Volkmar, F., & Sparrow, S. (2000). *Asperger syndrome.* New York, NY: Guilford Press.

Kochenderfer-Ladd, B., & Pelletier, M. (2008). Teachers' views and beliefs about bullying: Influences on classroom management strategies and students' coping with peer victimization. *Journal of School Psychology, 46,* 431–453. doi:10.1016/j.jsp.2007.07.005

Kopp, C. B. (1982). Antecedents of self-regulation: A developmental perspective. *Developmental Psychology, 18,* 199–214. doi:10.1037/0012-1649.18.2.199

Koszycki, D., Benger, M., Shlik, J., & Bradwejn, J. (2007). Randomized trial of a meditation-based stress reduction program and cognitive–behavior therapy in generalized social anxiety disorder. *Behaviour Research and Therapy, 45,* 2518–2526. doi:10.1016/j.brat.2007.04.011

Kranowitz, C. S. (2005). *Preschool SENSE (SENsory Scan for Educations): A tool for OT's in schools.* Las Vegas, NV: Sensory Resources.

Kronenberger, W. G., & Meyer, R. G. (2001). *The child clinician's handbook* (2nd ed.). Boston, MA: Allyn & Bacon.

Kutash, K., Duchnowski, A. J., Sumi, W. C., Rudo, Z., & Harris, K. M. (2002). A school, family, and community collaborative program for children who have emotional disturbances. *Journal of Emotional and Behavioral Disorders, 10,* 99–107. doi:10.1177/10634266020100020401

Ladd, G. W., Buhs, E. S., & Troop, W. (2002). Children's interpersonal skills and relationships in school settings. In P. K. Smith & C. H. Hart (Eds.), *Blackwell handbook of childhood social development* (pp. 394–415). Malden, MA: Blackwell.

La Greca, A. M., & Santogrossi, D. A. (1980). Social skills training with elementary school students: A behavioral group approach. *Journal of Consulting and Clinical Psychology, 48,* 220–227. doi:10.1037/0022-006X.48.2.220

Lakin, B. L., Brambila, A. D., & Sigda, K. B. (2004). Parental involvement as a factor in the readmission to a residential treatment center. *Residential Treatment for Children & Youth, 22*(2), 37–52. doi:10.1300/J007v22n02_03

Landreth, G. L. (2002). *The art of the relationship* (2nd ed.). New York, NY: Brunner-Routledge.

Landreth, G. L., Sweeney, D. S., Ray, D. C., Homeyer, L. E., & Glover, G. J. (2005). *Play therapy interventions with children's problems: Case studies with DSM-IV-TR diagnosis* (2nd ed.). Lanham, MD: Jason Aronson.

Lasky, S. (2000). The cultural and emotional politics of teacher–parent interactions. *Teaching and Teacher Education, 16,* 843–860. doi:10.1016/S0742-051X(00)00030-5

Lauth, G. W., Heubeck, B. G., & Mackowiak, K. (2006). Observation of children with attention-deficit/hyperactivity (ADHD) problems in three natural classroom contexts. *British Journal of Educational Psychology, 76,* 385–404. doi:10.1348/000709905X43797

LeBlanc, M., & Ritchie, M. (1999). Predictors of play therapy outcomes. *International Journal of Play Therapy, 8*(2), 19–34. doi:10.1037/h0089429

Lebo, D. (1953). The present status of research on nondirective play therapy. *Journal of Consulting Psychology, 17,* 177–183. doi:10.1037/h0063570

Leflot, G., van Lier, P. A. C., Onghena, P., & Colpin, H. (2010). The role of teacher behavior management in the development of disruptive behaviors: An intervention study with the good behavior game. *Journal of Abnormal Child Psychology, 38,* 869–882. doi:10.1007/s10802-010-9411-4

Lim, K. M., Khoo, A., & Wong, M. Y. (2007). Relationship of delinquent behaviors to pro-social orientations of adolescents. *North American Journal of Psychology, 9,* 183–188.

Linden, W., Hogan, B. E., Rutledge, T., Chawla, A., Lenz, J. W., & Leung, D. (2003). There is more to anger coping than "in" or "out." *Emotion, 3,* 12–29. doi:10.1037/1528-3542.3.1.12

Liss, M., Fein, D., Allen, D., Dunn, M., Feinstein, C., Morris, R., . . . Rapin, I. (2001). Executive functioning in high-functioning children with autism. *Journal of Child Psychology and Psychiatry, 42,* 261–270. doi:10.1111/1469-7610.00717

Livanis, A., Solomon, E. R., & Ingram, D. H. (2007). Guided social stories: Group treatments of adolescents with Asperger's disorder in the schools. In R. W. Christner, J. L. Stewart, & A. Freeman (Eds.), *Handbook of cognitive–behavior group therapy with children and adolescents* (pp. 408–427). New York, NY: Routledge.

Loeb, K. L., Wilson, G., Gilbert, J. S., & Labouvie, E. (2000). Guided and unguided self-help for binge eating. *Behavior Research and Therapy, 38,* 259–272. doi:10.1016/S0005-7967(99)00041-8

Lowenfeld, M. (1939). The world pictures of children: A method of recording and studying them. *British Journal of Medical Psychology, 18,* 65–101.

Lyneham, H. J., & Rapee, R. M. (2006). Evaluation of therapist-supported parent-implemented CBT for anxiety disorders in rural children. *Behavior Research and Therapy, 44,* 1287–1300. doi:10.1016/j.brat.2005.09.009

Lyytinen, P., Poikkeus, A.-M., & Laakso, M.-L. (1997). Language and symbolic play in toddlers. *International Journal of Behavioral Development, 21,* 289–302. doi:10.1080/016502597384875

Mains, J. A., & Scogin, F. R. (2003). The effectiveness of self-administered treatments: A practice-friendly review of the research. *Journal of Clinical Psychology, 59,* 237–246. doi:10.1002/jclp.10145

Maroni, B., Gnisci, A., & Pontecorvo, C. (2008). Turn-taking in classroom interactions: Overlapping, interruptions and pauses in primary school. *European Journal of Psychology of Education, 23*(1), 59–76. doi:10.1007/BF03173140

Marsh, L.C. (1931). Group treatment of the psychoses by psychological equivalent of revival. *Mental Hygiene in New York,* 328–349.

Mastrangelo, S. (2009). Play and the child with Autism spectrum disorder: From possibilities to practice. *International Journal of Play Therapy, 18*(1), 13–30. doi:10.1037/a0013810

Mayes, S. D., Calhoun, S. L., & Crowell, E. W. (2000). Learning disabilities and ADD. *Journal of Learning Disabilities, 33,* 417–424. doi:10.1177/002221940003300502

McConnell, S. R. (2002). Interventions to facilitate social interaction for young children with autism: Review of available research and recommendations for educational intervention and future research. *Journal of Autism and Developmental Disorders, 32,* 351–372. doi:10.1023/A:1020537805154

McCune, L. (1995). A normative study of representational play in the transition to language. *Developmental Psychology, 31,* 198–206. doi:10.1037/0012-1649.31.2.198

McGain, B., & McKinzey, R. K. (1995). The efficacy of group treatment in sexually abused girls. *Child Abuse & Neglect, 19,* 1157–1169. doi:10.1016/0145-2134(95)00076-K

McKendree-Smith, N. L., Floyd, M., & Scogin, F. R. (2003). Self-administered treatments for depression: A review. *Journal of Clinical Psychology, 59,* 275–288. doi:10.1002/jclp.10129

McMahon, R. J., & Forehand, R. L. (2003). *Helping the noncompliant child: Family-based treatment for oppositional behavior* (2nd ed.). New York, NY: Guilford Press.

McNaughton, D., Hamlin, D., McCarthy, J., Head-Reeves, D., & Schreiner, M. (2008). Learning to listen: Teaching an active listening strategy to preservice education professionals. *Topics in Early Childhood Special Education, 27,* 223–231. doi:10.1177/0271121407311241

Meister, H., von Wedel, H., & Walger, M. (2004). Psychometric evaluation of children with suspected auditory processing disorders (APDs) using a parent-answered survey. *International Journal of Audiology, 43,* 431–437. doi:10.1080/14992020400050054

Mendlowitz, S. L., Manassis, K., Bradley, S., Scapillato, D., Miezitis, S., & Shaw, B. F. (1999). Cognitive–behavioral group treatments in childhood anxiety disorders: The role of parental involvement. *Journal of the American Academy of Child & Adolescent Psychiatry, 38*(10), 1223–1229. doi:10.1097/00004583-199910000-00010

Miers, A. C., Rieffe, C., Terwogt, M. M., Cowan, R., & Linden, W. (2007). The relation between anger coping strategies, anger mood and somatic complaints in children and adolescents. *Journal of Abnormal Child Psychology, 35,* 653–664. doi:10.1007/s10802-007-9120-9

Moreno, J. L. (1932). *Application of the group method to classification.* New York, NY: National Committee on Prisons and Prison Labor.

Mortberg, E., Karlsson, A., Fyring, C., & Sundin, O. (2006). Intensive cognitive–behavioral group treatment (CBGT) of social phobia: A randomized controlled study. *Journal of Anxiety Disorders, 20,* 646–660. doi:10.1016/j.janxdis.2005.07.005

National Institute of Child Health and Human Development Early Child Care Research Network. (2008a). Mothers' and fathers' support for child autonomy and early school achievement. *Developmental Psychology, 44,* 895–907. doi:10.1037/0012-1649.44.4.895

National Institute of Child Health and Human Development Early Child Care Research Network. (2008b). Social competence with peers in third grade: Associations with earlier peer experiences in childcare. *Social Development, 17,* 419–453. doi:10.1111/j.1467-9507.2007.00446.x

National Institute of Mental Health. (2000). *Autism spectrum disorders (pervasive developmental disorders)* (NIH Publication No. 01-4960). Washington, DC: Government Printing Office.

National Institute of Neurological Disorders and Stroke. *NINDS pervasive developmental disorders information page.* Retrieved from http://www.ninds.nih.gov/disorders/pdd/pdd.htm

National Resource Center on AD/HD. *Symptoms and diagnostic criteria.* Retrieved from http://www.help4adhd.org/en/treatment/guides/dsm

Newman, R. S. (2008). Adaptive and nonadaptive help seeking with peer harassment: An integrative perspective of coping and self-regulation. *Educational Psychologist, 43*(1), 1–15.

Newman, M. G., Erickson, T., Preworski, A., & Dzus, E. (2003). Self-help and minimal-contact therapies for anxiety disorders: Is human contact necessary for therapeutic efficacy? *Journal of Clinical Psychology, 59,* 251–274. doi:10.1002/jclp.10128

Nixon, R., Sweeney, L., Erickson, D. B., & Touyz, S. W. (2003). Parent–child interaction therapy: A comparison of standard and abbreviated treatments for oppositional defiant preschoolers. *Journal of Consulting and Clinical Psychology, 71,* 251–260. doi:10.1037/0022-006X.71.2.251

Noser, K., & Bickman, L. (2000). Quality indicators of children's mental health services: Do they predict improved client outcomes? *Journal of Emotional and Behavioral Disorders, 8,* 9–18. doi:10.1177/106342660000800102

Orlick, T. (1988). Enhancing cooperative skills in games and life. In F. L. Smoll, R. Magill, & M. Ash (Eds.), *Children in sport* (pp. 149–159). Champaign, IL: Human Kinetics.

Papolos, J., & Papolos, D. F. (2004). Why Jonny and Jenny can't write: Disorders of written expression and children with Bipolar disorder. *Bipolar Child Newsletter, 17.* Retrieved from http://www.bipolarchild.com/Newsletters/0406.html

Parten, M. B. (1932). Social participation among preschool children. *The Journal of Abnormal and Social Psychology, 27,* 243–269. doi:10.1037/h0074524

Paul, R. (2008). Auditory processing disorder. *Journal of Autism and Developmental Disorders, 38,* 208–209. doi:10.1007/s10803-007-0437-6

Pedro-Carroll, J. L. (2005). Fostering resilience in the aftermath of divorce: The role of evidence-based programs for children. *Family Court Review, 43*(1), 52–64. doi:10.1111/j.1744-1617.2005.00007.x

Pedro-Carroll, J. L., & Jones, S. H. (2005). A preventive play intervention to foster children's resilience in the aftermath of divorce. In L. A. Reddy (Ed.), *Empirically based play interventions for children* (pp. 51–75). Washington, DC: American Psychological Association. doi:10.1037/11086-004

Pellegrini, A. D., & Smith, P. K. (1998). Physical activity play: The nature and function of a neglected aspect of play. *Child Development, 69,* 577–598.

Penner-Williams, J., Smith, T. E. C., & Gartin, B. C. (2009). Written language expression: Assessment instruments and teacher tools. *Assessment for Effective Intervention, 34,* 162–169. doi:10.1177/1534508408318805

Phillips, R. (1985). Whistling in the dark? A review of play therapy research. *Psychotherapy: Theory, Research, & Practice, 22,* 752–760. doi:10.1037/h0085565

Piaget, J. (1962). *Play, dreams, and imitation in childhood.* New York, NY: Norton.

Pierce, K. (2010). Developmental disorders of learning, communication and motor skills. In M. K. Dulcan (Ed.), *Dulcan's textbook of child and adolescent psychiatry* (pp. 191–203). Arlington, VA: American Psychiatric Publishing.

Piker, R. A., & Rex, L. A. (2008). Influences of teacher–child social interactions on English language development in a head start classroom. *Early Childhood Education Journal, 36,* 187–193. doi:10.1007/s10643-008-0267-y

Pintrich, P. R., & Schunk, D. H. (2002). *Motivation in education: Theory, research, and applications* (2nd ed.). Upper Saddle River, NJ: Pearson Education.

President's New Freedom Commission on Mental Health. (2003). *Achieving the promise: Transforming mental health care in America.* Rockville, MD.

Prior, M. (Ed.). (2003). *Learning and behavior problems in Asperger syndrome.* New York, NY: Guilford Press.

Rao, P. A., Beidel, D. C., & Murray, M. J. (2008). Social skills interventions for children with Asperger's syndrome or high-functioning autism: A review and recommendations. *Journal of Autism and Developmental Disorders, 38,* 353–361. doi:10.1007/s10803-007-0402-4

Rapee, R. M., Abbott, M. J., & Lyneham, H. J. (2005). *Bibliotherapy in the treatment of child anxiety disorders.* Manuscript in preparation.

Rapee, R. M., Abbott, M. J., & Lyneham, H. J. (2006). Bibliotherapy for children with anxiety disorders using written materials for parents: A randomized controlled study. *Journal of Consulting and Clinical Psychology, 74,* 436–444. doi:10.1037/0022-006X.74.3.436

Ray, D., Bratton, S., Rhine, T., & Jones, L. (2001). The effectiveness of play therapy: Responding to the critics. *International Journal of Play Therapy, 10*(1), 85–108. doi:10.1037/h0089444

Reade, S., Hunter, H., & McMillan, I. (1999). Just playing . . . is it time wasted? *British Journal of Occupational Therapy, 62,* 157–162.

Reddy, L. A. (2010). Group play interventions for children with attention-deficit/hyperactivity disorder. In A. A. Drewes & C. Schaefer (Eds.), *School-based play therapy* (2nd ed., pp. 307–329). New York, NY: Wiley.

Reddy, L. A., Atamanoff, T., Hauch, Y., Braunstein, D., Springer, C., & Kranzler, R. (2004). Psychosocial group prevention and intervention programs for children and adolescents. In B. Leventhal & P. Zimmerman (Eds.), *Child and adolescent psychiatric clinics of North America: Residential Treatment* (pp. 363–380). Philadelphia, PA: Saunders/Elsevier Science. doi:10.1016/S1056-4993(03)00123-8

Reddy, L. A., & De Thomas, C. (2006). Assessment of attention-deficit/hyperactivity disorder with children. In S. R. Smith & L. Handler (Eds.), *The clinical assessment of children and adolescents: A practitioner's guide* (pp. 365–387). Mahwah, NJ: Erlbaum.

Reddy, L. A., Files-Hall, T. M., & Schaefer, C. E. (Eds.). (2005). *Empirically based play interventions for children.* Washington, DC: American Psychological Association. doi:10.1037/11086-000

Reddy, L. A., & Goldstein, A. P. (2001). Aggressive replacement training: A multimodal intervention for aggressive children. In S. I. Pfeiffer & L. A. Reddy (Eds.), *Innovative mental health prevention programs for children* (pp. 47–62). New York, NY: Haworth Press.

Reddy, L. A., & Hale, J. (2007). Inattentiveness. In A. R. Eisen (Ed.), *Treating childhood behavioral and emotional problems: A step-by-step evidence-based approach* (pp. 156–211). New York, NY: Guilford Press.

Reddy, L. A., & Newman, E. (2009). School-based programs for children with emotional disturbance: Obstacles to program design and implementation and guidelines for school practitioners. *Journal of Applied School Psychology, 25,* 169–186.

Reddy, L. A., Newman, E., DeThomas, C., & Chun, V. (2009). Effectiveness of school-based prevention and intervention programs for children and adolescent with emotional disturbance: A meta-analysis. *Journal of School Psychology, 47,* 77–99. doi:10.1016/j.jsp.2008.11.001

Reddy, L. A., & Savin, H. A. (2000). Designing and conducting outcome studies. In H. A. Savin & S. S. Kiesling (Eds.), *Accountable systems of behavioral health care* (pp. 132–158). San Francisco, CA: Jossey-Bass.

Reddy, L. A., Spencer, P., Hall, T. M., & Rubel, E. (2001). Use of developmentally appropriate games in a child group training program for young children with attention-deficit/hyperactivity disorder. In A. A. Drewes, L. J. Carey, & C. E. Schaefer (Eds.), *School-based play therapy* (pp. 256–274). New York, NY: Wiley.

Reddy, L. A., Springer, C., Files-Hall, T. M., Benisz, E. S., Hauch, Y., Braunstein, D., & Atamanoff, T. (2005). Childhood ADHD multimodal program: An empirically-supported intervention for young children with ADHD. In L. A. Reddy, T. M. Files-Hall, & C. E. Schaefer (Eds.), *Empirically based play interventions for children* (pp. 145–167). Washington, DC: American Psychological Association. doi:10.1037/11086-009

Reddy, L. A., Weissman, A., & Hale, J. B. (in press). Integration of neuropsychological assessment and intervention for children with ADHD. In L. A. Reddy, A. Weissman, & J. B. Hale (Eds.), *Neuropsychological assessment and intervention for emotional and behavior disordered youth: An integrated step-by-step evidence-based approach.* Washington, DC: American Psychological Association.

Reed, M., Black, T., & Eastman, J. (1978). A new look at perceptual-motor therapy. *Academic Therapy, 14,* 55–65.

Reeker, J., Ensing, D., & Elliott, R. (1997). A meta-analytic investigation of group treatment outcomes for sexually abused children. *Child Abuse & Neglect, 21,* 669–680. doi:10.1016/S0145-2134(97)00024-0

Reijntjes, A., Stegge, H., & Terwogt, M. M. (2006). Children's coping with peer rejection: The role of depressive symptoms, social competence, and gender. *Infant and Child Development, 15,* 89–107. doi:10.1002/icd.435

Riccio, C. A., Hynd, G. W., Cohen, M. J., Hall, J., & Molt, L. (1994). Comorbidity of central auditory processing disorder and attention-deficit/hyperactivity disorder. *Journal of the American Academy of Child & Adolescent Psychiatry, 33,* 849–857. doi:10.1097/00004583-199407000-00011

Richards, M. M., Bowers, M. J., Lazicki, T., Krall, D., & Jacobs, A. K. (2008). Caregiver involvement in the intensive mental health program: Influence on changes in child functioning. *Journal of Child and Family Studies, 17,* 241–252. doi:10.1007/s10826-007-9163-0

Rief, S. F. (2005). *How to reach and teach children with ADD/ADHD: Practical techniques, strategies, and interventions* (2nd ed.). San Francisco, CA: Jossey-Bass.

Rogers, S. J. (2005). Play interventions for young children with autism spectrum disorders. In L. A. Reddy, T. M. Files-Hall, & C. E. Schaefer (Eds.), *Empirically based play interventions for children* (pp. 215–239). Washington, DC: American Psychological Association. doi:10.1037/11086-014

Rostain, A. L., Power, T. J., & Atkins, M. S. (1993). Assessing parents' willingness to pursue treatment for children with attention-deficit/hyperactivity disorder. *Journal of the American Academy of Child & Adolescent Psychiatry, 32,* 175–181. doi:10.1097/00004583-199301000-00025

Rourke, B. P. (1994). Neuropsychological assessment of children with learning disabilities. In G. R. Lyon (Ed.), *Frames of reference for the assessment of learning disabilities* (pp. 475–514). Baltimore, MD: Brookes.

Ruitenbeek, H. M. (1969). *Group therapy today: Styles, methods, and techniques.* Oxford, England: Atherton.

Ryan, A. M., & Patrick, H. (2001). The classroom social environment and changes in adolescents' motivation and engagement during middle school. *American Educational Research Journal, 38,* 437–460. doi:10.3102/00028312038002437

Saarni, C. (1984). An observational study of children's attempts to monitor their expressive behavior. *Child Development, 55,* 1504–1513. doi:10.2307/1130020

Saarni, C. (1999). *The development of emotional competence.* New York, NY: Guilford Press.

Salvador, A. (2005). Coping with competitive situations in humans. *Neuroscience and Biobehavioral Reviews, 29,* 195–205. doi:10.1016/j.neubiorev.2004.07.004

Sanders, M. R., Markie-Dadds, C., Tully, L. A., & Boron, W. (2000). The triple P—Positive Parenting Program: A comparison of enhanced, standard, and self-directed behavioral family intervention for parents of children with early onset conduct problem. *Journal of Consulting and Clinical Psychology, 68,* 624–640. doi:10.1037/0022-006X.68.4.624

Sansosti, F. J., & Powell-Smith, K. A. (2006). Using social stories to improve the social behavior of children with Asperger's syndrome. *Journal of Positive Behavior Interventions, 13*(2), 43–57.

Savin-Williams, R. C., & Berndt, T. J. (1990). Friendship and peer relations. In S. S. Feldman & G. R. Elliott (Eds.), *At the threshold: The developing adolescent* (pp. 277–307). Cambridge, MA: Harvard University Press.

Schaefer, C. E. (1993). *The therapeutic powers of play.* Northvale, NJ: Jason Aronson.

Schneider, L. B. (1989). *The effect of selected low organized games on the self-esteem of kindergartners.* Unpublished manuscript, Leonard Gorgon Institute for Human Development Through Play, Temple University, Philadelphia, PA.

Schultz, D., Izard, C. E., Ackerman, B. P., & Youngstrom, E. A. (2001). Emotion knowledge in economically disadvantaged children: Self-regulatory antecedents and relations to social difficulties and withdrawal. *Development and Psychopathology, 13,* 53–68. doi:10.1017/S0954579401001043

Sebanc, A. M., Pierce, S. L., Cheatham, C. L., & Gunnar, M. R. (2003). Gendered social worlds in preschool: Dominance, peer acceptance and assertive social skills in boys' and girls' peer groups. *Social Development, 12*(1), 91–106. doi:10.1111/1467-9507.00223

Selman, R. (1980). *The growth of interpersonal understanding.* New York, NY: Academic Press

Sharp, E., Caldwell, L. L., Graham, J., & Ridenour, T. (2006). Individual motivation and parental influence on adolescents' experiences of interest in the free time context: A longitudinal examination. *Journal of Youth and Adolescence, 35,* 340–353.

Shelley-Tremblay, J., O'Brien, N., & Langhinrichsen-Rohling, J. (2007). Reading disability in adjudicated youth: Prevalence rates, current models, traditional and innovative treatments. *Aggression and Violent Behavior, 12,* 376–392. doi:10.1016/j.avb.2006.07.003

Shen, Y. J. (2002). Short-term group play therapy with Chinese earthquake victims: Effects of anxiety, depression, and adjustment. *International Journal of Play Therapy, 11*(1), 43–63. doi:10.1037/h0088856

Shipman, K. L., & Zeman, J. (2001). Socialization of children's emotion regulation in mother–child dyads: A developmental psychopathology perspective. *Development and Psychopathology, 13,* 317–336.

Shoda, Y., Mischel, W., & Peake, P. K. (1990). Predicting adolescent cognitive and self-regulatory competencies from preschool delay of ratification: Identifying diagnostic conditions. *Developmental Psychology, 26,* 978–986. doi:10.1037/0012-1649.26.6.978

Shulman, S., & Margalit, M. (1985). Suicidal behavior at school: A systemic perspective. *Journal of Adolescence, 8,* 263–269. doi:10.1016/S0140-1971(85)80058-0

Siebes, R. C., Wijnroks, L., Ketelaar, M., Van Schie, P. E., Gorter, J. W., & Vermeer, A. (2007). Parent participation in pediatric rehabilitation treatment centers in the

Netherlands: A parent's viewpoint. *Child: Care, Health and Development, 33,* 196–205. doi:10.1111/j.1365-2214.2006.00636.x

Siepher, B., & Kandaras, C. (1985). *Group therapy with children and adolescents.* New York, NY: Human Sciences Press.

Simonoff, E., Pickles, A., Charman, T., Chandler, S., Loucas, T., & Baird, G. (2008). Psychiatric disorders in children with autism spectrum disorders: prevalence, comorbidity, and associated factors in a population derived sample. *Journal of the American Academy of Child & Adolescent Psychiatry, 47,* 921–929. doi:10.1097/CHI.0b013e318179964f

Skinner, E. A., Edge, K., Altman, J., & Sherwood, H. (2003). Searching for the structure of coping: A review and critique of category systems classifying ways of coping. *Psychological Bulletin, 129,* 216–269. doi:10.1037/0033-2909.129.2.216

Slowik, M., Willson, S. W., Loh, E., & Noronha, S. (2004). Service innovations: Developing a parent/care support group in an in-patient adolescent setting. *Psychiatric Bulletin, 28*(5), 177–179. doi:10.1192/pb.28.5.177

Smith, N., & Landreth, G. (2003). Intensive filial therapy with child witnesses of domestic violence: A comparison with individual and sibling group play therapy. *International Journal of Play Therapy, 12,* 67–88. doi:10.1037/h0088872

Smith, D. M., & Landreth, G. (2004). Filial therapy with teachers of deaf and hard of hearing preschool children. *International Journal of Play Therapy, 13,* 13–33. doi:10.1037/h0088883

Sommerville, J. A., & Hammond, A. J. (2007). Treating another's actions as one's own: Children's memory of and learning from joint activity. *Developmental Psychology, 43,* 1003–1018. doi:10.1037/0012-1649.43.4.1003

Soucy, M. D. (1997). An empirical response to the issue of full inclusion for students with autism. *Exceptionality Education Canada, 7,* 19–39.

Springer, C., & Reddy, L. A. (2010). Measuring parental treatment adherence in a multimodal treatment program for children with ADHD: A preliminary investigation. *Child and Family Behavior Therapy, 32,* 272–279.

Stinchfield, R., Owen, P. L., & Winters, K. C. (1994). Group therapy for substance abuse: A review of the empirical research. In A. Fuhriman & G. M. Burlingame (Eds.), *Handbook of group psychotherapy* (pp. 458–488). New York, NY: Wiley.

Storch, E. A., Masia-Warner, C., & Brassard, M. R. (2003). The relationship of peer victimization to social anxiety and loneliness in adolescence. *Child Study Journal, 33,* 1–18.

Sugai, G., & Horner, R. H. (2002). The evolution of discipline practices: School-wide positive behavior supports. *Child & Family Behavior Therapy, 24,* 23–50. doi:10.1300/J019v24n01_03

Suveg, C., Roblek, T. L., Robin, J., Krain, A., Aschenbrand, S., & Ginsburg, G. S. (2006). Parental involvement when conducting cognitive–behavioral therapy for children with anxiety disorders. *Journal of Cognitive Psychotherapy, 20,* 287–299. doi:10.1891/jcop.20.3.287

Suveg, C., & Zeman, J. (2004). Emotion regulation in children with anxiety disorders. *Journal of Clinical Child and Adolescent Psychology, 33,* 750–759. doi:10.1207/s15374424jccp3304_10

Sweeney, D. S. (1997). *Counseling children through the world of play.* Wheaton, IL: Tyndale House.

Sweeney, D. S., & Homeyer, L. E. (1999). *The handbook of group play therapy: How to do it, how it works, whom it's best for.* San Francisco, CA: Jossey-Bass.

Szente, J. (2007). Empowering young children for success in school and in life. *Early Childhood Education Journal, 34,* 449–453.

Tamis-LeMonda, C. S., & Bornstein, M. H. (1994). Specificity in mother–toddler language play relations across the second year. *Developmental Psychology, 30,* 283–292. doi:10.1037/0012-1649.30.2.283

Tannock, R., & Brown, T. E. (2000). Attention deficit disorders with learning disorders in children and adolescents. In T. E. Brown (Ed.), *Attention deficit disorders and comorbidities in children, adolescents, and adults* (pp. 125–170). Washington, DC: American Psychiatric Publishing.

Thompson, R. A. (1994). Emotion regulation: A theme in search of definition. In N. Fox (Ed.), Emotion regulation: Behavioral and biological considerations. *Society for Research in Child Development Monographs, 59* (Serial No. 240), 25–52.

Timler, G. R., Olswang, L. B., & Coggins, T. E. (2005). Social communication interventions for preschoolers: Targeting peer interactions during peer group entry and cooperative play. *Seminars in Speech and Language, 26*(3), 170–180. doi:10.1055/s-2005-917122

Torbert, M., & Schneider, L. (1993). *Follow me too.* Menlo Park, CA: Addison-Wesley.

U.S. Department of Education, Institute of Education Sciences, National Center for Education Statistics. (2003). *Statistics of public elementary and secondary school systems, 2003 (data 1989–90 through 2001–02).* Retrieved from http://nces.ed.gov/programs/digest/d03/tables/dt052.asp

U.S. Department of Education, Office of Special Education and Rehabilitative Services. (2003). *24th annual report to Congress on the implementation of the Individuals with Disabilities Education Act (data 1976–77 through 2001–02).* Retrieved from http://nces.ed.gov/programs/digest/d03/tables/dt052.asp

U.S. Department of Health and Human Services, Substance Abuse and Mental Health Services Administration, Center for Mental Health Services, National Institutes of Health and Mental Health. (2000). *Mental health: A report of the Surgeon General.* Rockville, MD.

Valeski, T. N., & Stipek, D. J. (2001). Young children's feelings about school. *Child Development, 72,* 1198–1213.

Vandell, D. L., & Hembree, S. E. (1994). Peer social status and friendship: Independent contributors to children's social and academic adjustment. *Journal of Developmental Psychology, 40,* 461–477.

Visser, S. N., & Lesesne, C. A. (2005). Mental health in the United States: Prevalence of diagnosis and medication treatment for attention-deficit/hyperactivity disorder—United States, 2003. *Morbidity and Mortality Weekly Report, 54,* 842–847

Volker, M. A., & Lopata, C. (2008). Autism: A review of biological bases, assessment, and intervention. *School Psychology Quarterly, 23,* 258–270. doi:10.1037/1045-3830.23.2.258

Waugh, T. A., & Kjos, D. L. (1992). Parental involvement and the effectiveness of an adolescent day treatment program. *Journal of Youth and Adolescence, 21,* 487–497. doi:10.1007/BF01537899

Webster-Stratton, C. (2000). *The incredible years training series bulletin.* Washington, DC: U.S. Department of Justice, Office of Juvenile Justice and Delinquency Prevention.

Whitehurst, G. J., Fischel, J. E., Lonigan, C. J., Valdez-Menchaca, M. C., DeBaryshe, B. D., & Caulfield, M. B. (1988). Verbal interaction in families of normal and expressive-language-delayed children. *Developmental Psychology, 24,* 690–699.

Wiener, J., & Schneider, B. H. (2002). A multisource exploration of the friendship patterns of children with and without learning disabilities. *Journal of Abnormal Child Psychology, 30,* 127–141. doi:10.1023/A:1014701215315

Wills, T. A., Ainette, M. G., Mendoza, D., Gibbons, F. X., & Brody, G. H. (2007). Self-control, symptomatology, and substance use precursors: Test of a theoretical model in a community sample of 9-year-old children. *Psychology of Addictive Behaviors, 21,* 205–215.

Wilson, B. J. (2003). The role of attentional processes in children's prosocial behavior with peers: Attention shifting and emotion. *Development and Psychopathology, 15,* 313–329.

Wimpory, D. C., Hobson, R. P., Williams, M. G., & Nash, S. (2000). Are infants with autism socially engaged? A study of recent retrospective parental reports. *Journal of Autism and Developmental Disorders, 30,* 525–536. doi:10.1023/A:1005683209438

Wood, A., Trainor, G., Rothwell, J., Moore, A., & Harrington, R. (2001). Randomized trial of group therapy for repeated deliberate self-harm adolescents. *Journal of the American Academy of Child & Adolescent Psychiatry, 40,* 1246–1253. doi:10.1097/00004583-200111000-00003

Yalom, I. D. (2005). *The theory and practice of group psychotherapy.* New York, NY: Basic Books.

Yu, G., Zhang, Y., & Yan, R. (2005). Loneliness, peer acceptance, and family functioning of Chinese children with learning disabilities: Characteristics of relationships. *Psychology in the Schools, 42,* 325–331. doi:10.1002/pits.20083

Zeman, J., Shipman, K., & Suveg, C. (2002). Anger and sadness regulation: Predictions to internalizing and externalizing symptoms in children. *Journal of Clinical Child and Adolescent Psychology, 31,* 393–398.

INDEX

ABOUT THE AUTHOR

Linda A. Reddy, PhD, is an associate professor of psychology at Rutgers University, where she also serves as director of the Child ADHD and ADHD-Related Disorders Clinic. Dr. Reddy received a PhD in school psychology and MA in educational psychology (measurement) from the University of Arizona and a BA in psychology from Boston University. She has published over 60 manuscripts and book chapters in the areas of attention-deficit/hyperactivity disorder (ADHD) and related disorders, group play interventions, school and family interventions, and test development/validation. She developed the Child ADHD Multimodal Program for children with ADHD. Dr. Reddy is a Fellow of the American Psychological Association (APA) and serves on the editorial board of over 10 journals. She is the lead editor of *Empirically Based Play Interventions for Children* (2005), *Neuropsychological Assessment and Intervention for Emotional and Behavior Disordered Youth: An Integrated Step-by-Step Evidence-Based Approach* (in press), and the second edition of *Empirically Based Play Interventions for Children.* She coedited (with Steven I. Pfeiffer) *Innovative Mental Health Interventions for Children: Programs That Work* and *Inclusion Practice in Special Education: Research, Theory, and Application.* Dr. Reddy serves on the APA Inter-Divisional Task Force on Child and Adolescent Mental Health and the APA Task Force on Violence Against Teachers, and on the Translation of Science to School Practice Work Group. She is the recipient of several research and service awards and has received over $2 million in funding for her research. She received the 2009 Research Article of the Year Award for the *Journal of School Psychology*—Society for the Study of School Psychology. Dr. Reddy is a licensed psychologist in New Jersey who has extensive clinical experience working with families; schools; and children with emotional, behavioral, and neurocognitive difficulties.

DATE DUE

JUL 22 2014 ILL* 062.85483 OLD	
GAYLORD	PRINTED IN U.S.A.